THE JOURNEY OF A BOOK

Bartholomew the Englishman and the Properties of Things

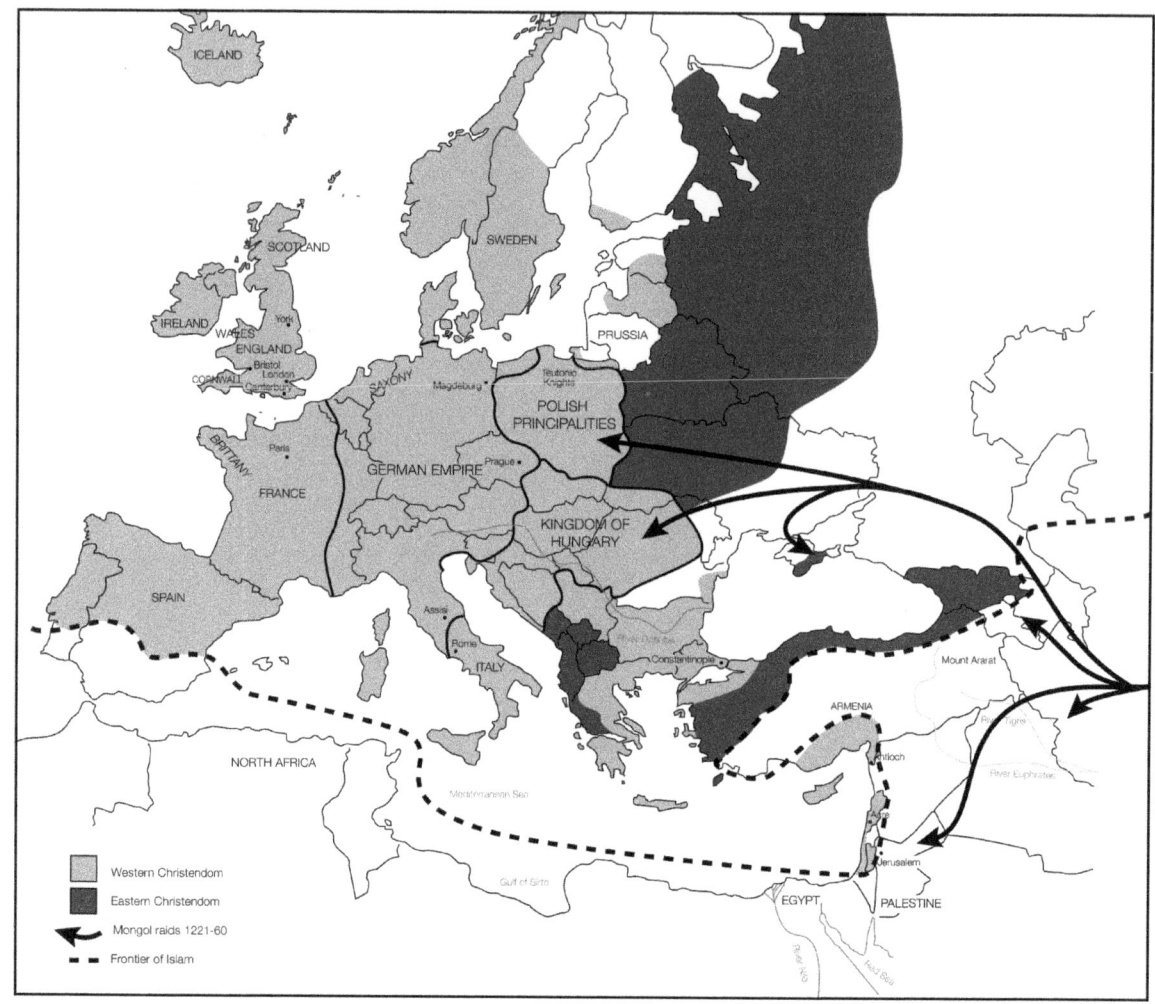

Map of Europe in c.1230, showing locations significant within *The Journey of a Book*. Approx. indications of the frontiers of Christendom (western and eastern) and Islam, and of the Mongol advance, are based on McEvedy, Colin. *The New Penguin Atlas of Medieval History*. London: Penguin Books, 1992, pp.73, 77.

THE JOURNEY OF A BOOK

Bartholomew the Englishman and the Properties of Things

Elizabeth Keen

E PRESS

Published by ANU E Press
The Australian National University
Canberra ACT 0200, Australia
Email: anuepress@anu.edu.au
This title is also available online at: http://epress.anu.edu.au/journey_citation.html

---

National Library of Australia
Cataloguing-in-Publication entry

Keen, Elizabeth Joy.
    Journey of a book : Bartholomew the Englishman and the
    Properties of things.

    ISBN 9781921313066 (pbk.).
    ISBN 9781921313073 (web).

    1. Bartholomaeus Anglicus, 13th cent. De proprietatibus
    rerum. 2. Encyclopedias and dictionaries - Early works to
    1600 - History and criticism. 3. Philosophy of nature -
    Early works to 1800. I. Title.

All rights reserved. No part of this publication may be reproduced, stored in a retrieval system or transmitted in any form or by any means, electronic, mechanical, photocopying or otherwise, without the prior permission of the publisher.

Cover design by ANU E Press
Cover image: *Cambridge University Library Gg. 6. 42. f. 5. St. Francis and Companion* used by permission of the Syndics of Cambridge University Library.

This edition © 2007 ANU E Press

Table of Contents

List of Figures	vii
Abbreviations	ix
Acknowledgements	xi
Chapter 1. Introduction	1
Chapter 2. Literary approaches	15
Chapter 3. 'Properties' as a guide to salvation	29
Chapter 4. The world and the journey	57
Chapter 5. 'Properties', salvation and social order in late-medieval England	77
Chapter 6. An authoritative source	103
Chapter 7. Navigating tides of change: Bartholomew and the English	127
Chapter 8. Conclusion	161
Appendix A. British Library Manuscript Arundel 123, the contents of the codex.	167
Appendix B. Abridgement of 'Properties' in Bodleian Library Manuscript Laud Miscellany 682.	169
References	171

List of Figures

Figure 1: Map of thirteenth-century Christendom showing places significant in the making, transmission and English reception of *De proprietatibus rerum*. ii

Figure 2: The 19 Books of *De proprietatibus rerum*. 7

Figure 3: The Psalter Map, British Library Additional Ms 28681, f.9 recto. Circa 1260. 67

Figure 4: The Psalter Map, British Library Additional Ms 28681, f.9 verso. Circa 1260. 68

Figure 5: Map of the world on the title page of Book 8, *Bartholomeus De Proprietatibus Rerum*. Printed by Wynkyn de Worde, 1495. 120

Figure 6: Title-page woodcut for Book 19, *Bartholomeus De Proprietatibus Rerum*. Printed by Wynkyn de Worde, 1495. 121

Figure 7: Title-page and part of Table of Contents, *Bartholomeus De Proprietatibus Rerum*. Printed by Thomas Berthelet, 1535. Copy BL 456.a.1 formerly owned by Joseph Banks. 152

Abbreviations

AV	The Bible, Authorised Version
BA	Bartholomaeus Anglicus (Bartholomew the Englishman)
BL	British Library
BNF	Bibliothèque nationale de France
BVM	The Blessed Virgin Mary
BuB	*Batman uppon Bartholome*, Bateman [sic], Stephen, London: Thomas and Lucretia East, 1582
DrP	*De rerum Proprietatibus*, Angelicus, Bartholomaeus, Frankfurt: 1601
LM	*Liber de moralitatibus corporum celestium, elementorum, avium, piscium, animalium, arborum sive plantarum et lapidum preciosorum.* BNF lat. 3332 and other mss
ODCC	*The Oxford Dictionary of the Christian Church*, Cross, F. L., ed., London: Oxford University Press, 1974
ODNB	*Oxford Dictionary of National Biography*, Oxford University Press, 2004
OED	*Oxford English Dictionary*
'Properties'	*De proprietatibus rerum*
Properties	*On the Properties of Things. John Trevisa's Translation of Bartholomeus Anglicus, De Proprietatibus Rerum*, Seymour, M. C., ed., 3 vols. Oxford: The Clarendon Press, 1975–88
Propriétés	*Le Livre des Propriétés des Choses,* Corbechon, Jean, 1372
STC	Short Title Catalogue of the British Library

Acknowledgements

Many people have made this project possible and supported it along the way. I am grateful to those in the History Department of The Australian National University who provided resources and guidance during my doctoral study of Bartholomew: Doug Craig and Anne Curthoys, Bob Barnes, Bill Craven, Stephanie Tarbin, and, above all, John Tillotson, whom I thank for his patient support, encouragement and friendship from the beginning of the project. I thank Alisdair Greig and the staff of the ANU School of Social Studies for my accommodation as a Visiting Fellow from 2003 to 2007. Dr Bruce Moore and the ANU Publication Subsidies Committee have kindly helped to finance production of the book. The scope of my topic has led me to trespass at times into others' fields and I thank Merridee Bailey, Anke Bernau, Tania Colwell, Julie Hotchin, Val Spear and Janet Hadley Williams for their generosity in reading drafts and sharing insights. Thank you to Kathy Hagon and Pam Kelloway for their constant encouragement. I thank the staff of the Bibliothèque nationale in Paris; the University of London Library, the British Library, the Wellcome History of Medicine Library and the Warburg Institute Library; the Bodleian Library, Balliol College Library and Corpus Christi College, Oxford; Cambridge University Library, and Bristol City Library for all their help. I am grateful to the British Library and to Cambridge University Library for permission to reproduce images from their manuscript collections. ANU E Press have been a pleasure to work with, as has John Owen, whom I thank for his judicious editing. Thanks to Yasmine Musharbash for her assistance with material in German and to Geoff Hinchcliffe for technical help. Particular thanks go to my family, especially Ian.

Chapter 1. Introduction

As I gather, Bartholomaeus Glanville took his name from the most noble family of the earls of Suffolk. As a youth he faithfully observed the Franciscan way of life. When older he frequented the Vale of Isis, Paris, and even, if the surmise is correct, Rome herself. A wise man, he spent the first parts of his studies acquiring skill in philosophy and, equally, theology: in the former, so that he might investigate more precisely the causes of material things; in the latter, so that he might, so to speak, illumine his mind with a divine radiance. Aristotle, Plato and Pliny were his companions in that situation; distinguished by his mastery of them, he elegantly composed and put forth the book of *Properties of Things*: which the hand of time constantly tended, so that its fame has justly grown to greatness.[1]

Historians have been interested in the *De proprietatibus rerum* of Bartholomew the Englishman since the sixteenth century, when John Leland (d.1552) included the compiler in his catalogue of esteemed English writers and planted the notion of Bartholomew's Glanville origins. Successive ages and literary cultures have found their own uses for the work and its compiler and their own reasons to investigate him and the image of creation that he helped to perpetuate. The present age is no exception — Bartholomew's identity, career, philosophy and achievement have all been examined and re-assessed since Leland's time. It is not the intention here to enter into the debate about Bartholomew's identity but, rather, to draw conclusions about the ways in which later cultures perceived and represented him. We do have sufficient evidence to be able to introduce him as a not-too-shadowy figure, and to follow traces of some of the *personae* he acquired over time. These traces, in the form of written responses and attitudes to him and his work, invite the historian's scrutiny as testimony to changes in medieval people's ideas about things and their properties. The work becomes a point of reference by which we can judge adherences to, or departures from, orthodox medieval representations of the world and society.

Who was Bartholomew the Englishman?

Bartholomew is known today from his single large compilation of knowledge referred to throughout the Middle Ages as *De proprietatibus rerum*, 'On the properties of things'. There have been debates about his nationality and background: when he lived; whether he was an Englishman, Frenchman or Burgundian, or in the English 'nation' at Paris; whether he was educated at Oxford or Chartres. In the nineteenth century Léopold Delisle questioned the accepted notion, illustrated above, that Bartholomew was a fourteenth-century member of the Glanville family of Suffolk and identified him as a French compiler of the thirteenth century. Michael Seymour has suggested that Johannes Anglicus and Bartholomaeus Anglicus, both of whom were sent to Magdeburg, may have been members of the *natio anglicana* in Paris after studying at Oxford. Seymour tentatively identifies him with Bartholomew of Prague, minister provincial of newly-converted Bohemia in 1255–56.[2] Gerald Se Boyar argues that he was educated at Chartres. It is generally agreed, however, that Bartholomew completed 'Properties' in Saxony in about 1240, that he was extremely well read, but that he might not have had with him in Magdeburg all the books he draws on — in other words, he cites from memory.[3]

For a contemporary account of him we must rely on a few mentions by early Franciscan writers. Giordano of Giano (professed c.1217 and a member of the second mission to Germany in 1221) supplies the few contemporary glimpses we have of Bartholomew's career. According to Giordano, brother Bartholomaeus Anglicus was one of two friars then in France sent to organise the new Franciscan province of Saxonia; he himself arranged to conduct them thither in 1231. According to the Franciscan chronicler Thomas of Eccleston, writing in the following century, the Englishman Haymo of Faversham and 'three other professors' were admitted to the Order at St Denys in Paris in about 1223.[4] One of these others may have been Bartholomew. He became the sixth minister provincial of Saxonia in 1262 and held the office for almost 10 years. The date of his death may have been 1272, since another brother was elected in his place at the provincial chapter held at Magdeburg that year.[5] A younger Franciscan, Salimbene of Parma, looking back from the vantage point of the 1280s, recalls that Bartholomew had gained a reputation over the years as a great master of the Scriptures in Paris and refers to 'his book on the properties of things, which volume is divided into nineteen separate books'.[6]

Evidence suggests that Magdeburg had been a site of violent conversion to Christianity.[7] According to Giordano, the Franciscans had settled at Magdeburg as recently as 1223, and his account indicates that in the middle years of the century the church was still involved in efforts to extend its control eastwards. It also reveals that at that time Saxony still had a reputation (if only from a Parisian perspective) as a dangerous frontier of Christendom.[8] Bartholomew may have compiled 'Properties' to provide instruction, spiritual and practical guidance, and moral encouragement to recruits in the *studium*, since he tells us that his compilation brings together simply the words of wise and holy men for simple and humble brethren who might not otherwise have access to them.[9] This was a conventional statement of a compiler's intent, but Bartholomew's clear language style and accessible imagery do seem to take into account the comprehension levels of educated and less-educated students; while he himself was clearly a scholar, his language and content appear to cater for a spectrum of readers from the scholarly to the earthy.[10]

The early membership of the Order was made up of laymen and laywomen, but clerics began to fill its offices during Francis' lifetime. As Lawrence Landini shows, coercive popes, able ministers and sympathetic bishops were all factors in the Order's growth and social integration but also in its inexorable clericalisation.[11] The date of the completion of 'Properties' coincided with events of great significance for the Order, as Juris Lidaka points out, because the dismissal of Elias as Minister General in 1239 turned recruitment policy away from laity and towards those with a clerical education.[12] This hastened the clericalisation process but worsened controversy over the possession of books and other material goods. After difficult years of division, papal support resumed under Nicholas III, who issued the Bull *Exiit qui seminat* in 1279, formalising the right of Friars Minor to have the use not only of food, clothes and office books but also 'necessary material for the pursuit of wisdom'.[13]

Bartholomew's work is often referred to as the most popular medieval encyclopaedia, and grouped with other large-scale compilations of the late twelfth to thirteenth centuries, in particular *De naturis rerum* of Alexander Neckam (1156–1217); *De natura rerum* of Thomas de Cantimpré (1201–80); *Speculum naturale* of Vincent de Beauvais (1187–1264); and the interpretations of Aristotle of Albert the Great (1193–1280).[14] These compilers were close contemporaries who all produced their major works in the 1230s to 1250s. They did not necessarily come into contact with each other, and they differ in the degree to which each incorporates the liberal arts curriculum, in the empiricism or otherwise of their approaches to nature, and in the way they organise their material. The works have in common that their compilers were clerics and mendicant scholars who drew upon the writings of the church fathers and of the classical philosophers, their commentators and translators. While the group as a whole has in the past been described as innovative, it has now been convincingly identified with a much earlier-established genre of medieval *compilatio*, or 'world book', following early-medieval models such as Isidore of Seville's *Etymologiae* and Honorius of Autun's *Imago mundi*. Bartholomew is the only Franciscan compiler among them whose work is accessible to English-speaking readers.[15] 'Properties' can then be considered as one of a peer-group of compilations of knowledge made in the twelfth and thirteenth centuries that arose from the church's immediate need but that gained lasting prestige during the Middle Ages. The works of Bartholomew's near contemporaries Neckam, de Cantimpré, Albert the Great and Vincent de Beauvais also have histories of reception during the later Middle Ages but, while their traces can be found in the work of later writers (for example, Ranulph Higden made much use of Vincent's *Speculum maius* in his fourteenth-century universal history *Polychronicon*, and Geoffrey Chaucer also evidently knew Vincent's work), they were not translated into English or printed in England.[16]

Michael Twomey, discussing how one might approach a reception history of medieval encyclopaedias, has proposed three phases in the history of the genre: the earliest phase from the seventh century, when encyclopaedias were used as pedagogical aids in the schools, both setting and ownership being institutional and the user a teacher; a later phase when encyclopaedias were used as raw material for sermons and the chief users were preachers; and the still-later period when the encyclopaedia might be part of a private library, a possession with monetary value figuring in inheritances and bequests. In this phase production might be by professional scribe, possibly in the vernacular, and users might be educated laymen together with regular and secular clergy. The reception history of Bartholomew's work exemplifies and firms these suggested phases. Twomey concludes that 'Properties' became 'the pearl of great price' for book owners and for writers in later-medieval England: 'For literary authors, both religious and secular, Bartholomaeus' encyclopaedia is far and away the encyclopaedia of choice — at least, as far as current research suggests — with Vincent's *Speculum* a distant second.'[17] Moreover it continues after 1500, into the era of print and Protestantism. Twomey warns, however, that, although there might be evidence to identify individuals and intellectual communities who owned and used the book, the motives of users are extremely difficult to reconstruct and any reception history must necessarily be tentative. While individual use and ownership can only occasionally be substantiated within the life story of 'Properties', the hope is that we may learn from such a long span of use something about the successive cultures that found it significant.

Evidence for the travels and longevity of 'Properties'

First, a note on nomenclature used in this book: since we have no definitive version of the Latin text of *De proprietatibus rerum* and no copy extant from Bartholomew's time, I have chosen to use an abbreviated name, 'Properties', for his work. This is intended to distinguish what we might call the notional compilation, known to us only through a variable array of manuscript material, from the concrete and complete versions of it that are available between hard covers. A printed edition of the Latin text produced in Germany in 1601 is available in facsimile edition and I abbreviate this to 'DrP' in citations.[18] The Oxford critical edition of John Trevisa's English-dialect translation completed in 1398, *On the Properties of Things*, is abbreviated to *Properties*.[19]

Bartholomew's compilation is extant in about 100 Latin manuscripts and fragments; a complete manuscript runs to about 400 folios. The layout, running headings, *tabula* and marginalia of the earliest extant manuscripts of 'Properties' testify that scribes were reproducing the work in scholarly format by the end of the thirteenth century, consistent with the view that it was promoted as a handy reference work for preachers.[20] Lidaka concludes that Bartholomew compiled 'Properties' as a useful manual for the evangelising German friars in the 1230s: 'As a general introduction, *De proprietatibus rerum* aided those who needed help in finding material: this made it useful for libraries and for the less advanced, but it would not be of much value to the well educated.' He adduces evidence for its reception in the thirteenth century that 'places it squarely at such a lower level of readership'.[21] Nevertheless, research into the ownership of 'Properties' manuscripts suggests that the work's readership soon came to extend beyond the boundaries of the Franciscan Order, and that the text was used by scholars of other Orders who required moralised compendia of knowledge as an aid to sermon writing and biblical exegesis. In 1297 the Dominican Master General Boccasini (later Pope Benedict XI) may have given the book to a Dominican convent, and Pope John XXII may have bought a copy in 1329.[22] Charles Samaran suggests that the copy owned by the Avignon Cardinal Pierre de Prés was the one acknowledged by his protégé, the Benedictine Pierre Bersuire, to be a main source for his *Reductorium morale* of c.1343.[23]

A vernacular translation of 'Properties' appeared in 1309 when Vivaldo Belcalzar made an abridged version in the dialect of Mantua for his lay patron, Guido Buonalcosi. Later manuscripts and printed editions testify that 'Properties' was subsequently translated into several European languages, including English, during the fourteenth century, and that translation and original were copied, adapted and mined for material over the next two centuries. It was printed in Germany and France as soon as presses were active in the 1470s. In 1398 John Trevisa completed the English translation, *On the Properties of Things*, for his patron Lord Thomas Berkeley IV (d.1417). Of this version, Seymour lists eight manuscripts and three fragments extant in England, the United States and Japan, dating from the early to the late fifteenth century. In 1495 Wynkyn de Worde made the first printed edition of the English version, followed by the editions of Thomas Berthelet in 1535, and Stephen Batman in 1582.[24] There are in existence, therefore, incunables and early printed editions of the work, in both the Latin and the vernacular versions, dating from the 1470s to about 1600.[25] After the early 1600s it ceased to be reprinted but remained of interest to antiquarians and to modern historians.

The Franciscan Order was an international mendicant brotherhood whose members travelled widely to study, preach and evangelise. The wide distribution of Bartholomew's work reflects its rapid spread across Europe and across social milieux. Of the Latin text, Seymour lists nearly 100 manuscripts of English, French, German and Italian provenance, now found in collections in western and eastern Europe and the United States, dating from the late-thirteenth to the sixteenth centuries. From the fourteenth century, vernacular versions — Italian, French, English, Provençal, Spanish and Dutch — add to this number.[26] As a result 'Properties' was absorbed into separate continental cultures and has other reception histories, and other bodies of literature, beyond the scope of this book.

Tracing the journey

It will be seen that the materials present a wide array of possible avenues for the scholar to explore: in the manuscript and printed material available across countries and continents; through the work's association with the growth-years of an international religious order; and in the range of questions raised by existing studies. It is also hard to separate the functions of the continental and English translations made at a time when France and England were closely engaged through war and also through a shared chivalric culture. Here, a cross-section of available manuscripts and printed materials, testifying to the work's status and function at key points in that story, form a longitudinal sample of the compilation's English reception. These key points are: the time of its composition in the 1240s; of its translation into English in the 1390s and of subsequent manuscript production; and the era of change accompanying the Protestant Reformation and the growth of printing, from the 1490s to the 1580s. Such focal points allow us to examine how far it can be of use to the historian in defining the mental horizons of past readers; and to ask whether, as an account of the significance of things that fed into later-medieval and early-modern literature, it might help us to understand those cultures better. Different medieval readerships produced changes in content, dissemination and modes of production: for how long could 'Properties' remain valid as a library substitute, repository of knowledge and guide to salvation? During the English Reformation, why did this Catholic work find favour with sponsors and censors at a time of so much controversy about the English church and its doctrine? What continuities emerge to account for its survival?

The present book includes a survey of the modern literature on Bartholomew and his work, and outlines changes that have taken place in historians' assessments of the character and worth of 'Properties'. New light is still being thrown on the medieval literary *compilatio*, and on the place of Bartholomew within it. Chapter 2 points to significant recent and ongoing projects and locates the present study with reference to them. The aim has been to bring together English-language scholarship on and surrounding the subject, but some of the most significant work at the time of writing is being carried out in Belgium, Germany and France, and is gratefully acknowledged.

Figure 2: The 19 Books of *De proprietatibus rerum*. [27]

Book 1	De Deo	On God and the names of God
Book 2	De proprietatibus angelorum	On angels, good and bad
Book 3	De anima	On the soul and reason
Book 4	De humani corporis	On the bodily humours
Book 5	De hominis corpore	On the parts of the body
Book 6	De etate hominis	On daily life
Book 7	De infirmitatibus	On diseases and poisons
Book 8	De mundo	On earth and the heavenly bodies
Book 9	De temporibus	On time and motion
Book 10	De materia et forma	On matter, form and fire
Book 11	De aere	On the air and weather
Book 12	De avibus	On birds
Book 13	De aqua	On water and fishes
Book 14	De terra	On the earth and its surface
Book 15	De regionibus et provinciis	On regions and places
Book 16	De lapidibus et metallis	On rocks, gems and minerals
Book 17	De herbis et plantis	On plants and trees
Book 18	De animalibus	On land animals
Book 19	De accidentibus	On colours, smells and tastes, substances, measurements, numbers and music

The context of the early years of the Franciscan Order provides the starting-point for the story of 'Properties' and its journey through time. Chapter 3 sets the reader in the world of the book at a mundane level of household, vineyard and rural domain. It explores the notion that the reader may access Bartholomew's work through more than one mode of interpretation, and not only by starting at the beginning. The first level of organisation apparent to the reader is the text's ordered sequence of 19 Books, comprising headed chapters on topics from the esoteric to the mundane (see Figure 2). At this level, the headings and sequence of the 19 Books and their chapters signal the linear ordering of the compilation and reflect the hierarchy of the universe from God down to the humblest of earthly things. However, at another level Bartholomew creates a web-like structure, accessible at many points, based on relationships between people and objects through their biblical, symbolic and affective associations. Many of the topics are earthy and practical, and (it is argued) could be dipped-into and cross-referenced for subjects on which to reflect or prepare a sermon. This exploration is preparatory to an examination in Chapter 4 of ways in which the text could have functioned for thirteenth-century readers, especially the new Orders of friars, as world-book and library substitute in both spiritual and practical senses. These chapters explore the possibility that, while the work can be read sequentially or even piecemeal, an underlying complexity of content, connotation and levels of discourse amplifies the range of meaning available to contemplative readers. Bartholomew was writing for members of an innovative and controversial Order while being answerable to the highest authorities of the established church. It is arguable that the church's campaign to teach and train orthodox preachers affects the way Bartholomew presents, to recruits of varying levels of education, Francis' unconventional teaching on the properties of the created world, and prepares them for a form of religious life that pushes at the boundaries of accepted clerical practice.

The marginal glosses

At this point mention must be made of a manuscript feature that is used in this study to support the notion of underlying meaning. At some stage in the thirteenth century a reader recorded interpretations of the column text in the margins of a manuscript. The earliest glossed Latin manuscripts have been dated close to the time of Bartholomew's death in about 1270. These interpretations were accepted and copied (with some anomalies) along with the rest of the work, forming an integral part of it for readers and copiers of thirteenth-century manuscripts.[28] The marginal commentary constitutes an essential aspect of the early reception of the work, dating as it might from the lifetime of the author, but even if the glosses are contemporary with Bartholomew we cannot, of course, infer authorial intentions from them. All the glosses can do is tell us something about the work's reception by a generation of readers close to him in time.

Meyer considers that although we cannot dismiss the possibility that the glosses originated with Bartholomew, they may reflect interpretations most useful to preachers. According to Lidaka, Bartholomew 'is cited in sermons and sermon aids more often than in any other kind of work'.[29] While we do not have an accompanying gloss for the whole work (and none, for example, in Book 15), there are sufficient to support the theory that for readers of the later thirteenth century the 'hidden meanings' related to the tasks of preaching and to the correct interpretations of biblical texts. Overall, the glosses strongly suggest that 'Properties' could be and was read by some as a vocational guide for prelates and preachers, whether within or outside the Franciscan Order, who could find in the work subject matter for sermons to strengthen orthodoxy at a time when the church was combatting heresy.

The glosses are quite dense in the Books where they have survived but elswhere we have none. The vernacular translators discarded them, effectively freeing non-clerical readers from prescribed responses to the main text. Manifestations of the text or parts of it made in later centuries demonstrate very different readings. Given the nature of the glosses as a disseminated body they must, however, be taken into account as significant for at least those readers who treated them as a necessary accompaniment to the text, whether these were early readers close to Bartholomew in time or much later readers with access to Latin manuscripts preserved in libraries. This is not to suggest that the glosses show us a 'correct' reading of 'Properties', or even the one that Bartholomew expected or intended: they do show us one possible reading, meaningful in a certain time and place. It must also be acknowledged that such a work might contain a great many allusions and nuances of meaning that are no longer available to the historian. While the glosses give us clues to the sub-textual lessons that could be construed or reinforced at the time they were written, they do not make those lessons fully explicit to us today.

The focus in subsequent chapters is upon the lively presence of 'Properties' in the world of English letters during the later-Plantagenet and Tudor reigns. Chapter 5 examines changes wrought upon 'Properties' under the patronage of noble secular bibliophiles and scholars in late-medieval England. The English translation of 1398 provides a focal point for the work's reception in a particular cultural context — one in which 'Properties' retains authority while undergoing changes to its language, content and presentation. Chapter 6 uses manuscript examples to show that 'Properties' not only survives but increases its readership over the late Middle Ages, while re-writers invoke the compiler as 'master' of received knowledge about the properties of the created world. It also discusses the first English printed version of 'Properties'. Chapter 7 examines Bartholomew's status as a supposedly English writer, and the late-Elizabethan printed version made by Stephen Batman at a time when much new knowledge was becoming available from various sources. A sample of Batman's responses helps us to measure the distance — long in some respects but surprisingly short in others — between his image of the world and his conception of 'property', and those of Bartholomew.

Approach and method

An early motivation for this study was the sense that Bartholomew's work should not be described, as it has been in the past, as an early encyclopaedia — with consequent emphasis on its apparent failures of logic, objectivity and consistency.[30] A modern response to it may involve pleasure and a sense of participation in glimpses of narratives and scenes from everyday life; a panorama that a reader could enter at any point, pull apart into separate Books, or re-read many times — one tempered to the needs of readers with close links to a rural community or accustomed to monastic reading practices. Remarkably, the modern Canadian poet David Solway has found inspiration in Bartholomew; finding 'a growing sense of delight with ... the language of both the Latin original and of Trevisa's translation. ... It was the earthy and material quality of the language, its floral exuberance, rather than the encyclopaedia of often abstract subjects, which I found compelling, almost irresistible.'[31] A historian too may appreciate the vitality and narrative colour that Bartholomew infuses into a morally useful compilation of knowledge.

The approach taken here follows pointers from the work of educationists of the 1970s based upon Wolfgang Iser's theories of reading. These theories produced empirical models of the reading process and literacy acquisition that are arguably relevant to the study of medieval readers.[32] Presumably, as we do, medieval readers decoded written symbols and, as they did so, constructed meaning from them with varying degrees of competence. If we can assume that the physiological/phenomenological processes involved in reading were the same in the thirteenth-century reader as they are in us, and also that good teachers of that time knew from experience how to help students to learn and remember, then Iser's notion of 'active reading' may tend to support the idea that Bartholomew constructed 'Properties' with students' learning needs in mind.[33]

We have no information on, or concrete evidence about, the text of 'Properties' as Bartholomew first presented it for students at Magdeburg. For later readers, including ourselves, it has come mediated by the responses of many others; yet much of the existing literature on 'Properties' has focused on attempts to pin down the 'authentic' text, as an idealised abstraction or exemplar. There has been little attention paid to the individuals who commissioned, produced and read such books, then as now, in response to a desire or need specific to their own lives. Carl Reiter offers another useful approach to the responses of medieval readers who copied and amended earlier works; they can, he argues, be regarded in a sense as that work's re-writers or re-creators. What they pass on to the next reader is something new to some extent, but the work's authority remains. He invokes Iser's theory of the active nature of the reading process to support his view of manuscripts as concrete, battered objects behind which lurk actual historical readers. Whether produced in professional scriptoria or owner-produced in the home for here-and-now purposes, we can see the books they re-created as 'artifacts of the reading process' rather than, or as well as, carriers of an established text.[34] It must be acknowledged, however, that historical hindsight requires a complementary approach that does treat works as entities (for example Chaucer's *Canterbury Tales* or the Bible). Nor can it be denied that scholarly and painstaking studies of manuscript affiliations provide vital evidence about a work's transmission over time. They are a valued prerequisite for longitudinal studies such as this one.

The text of 'Properties' is long and dense, even in Trevisa's English translation, so the approach taken here is to limit detailed examinations and close readings to a sample of the Books and to examples from the work's themes as they emerge, and as the referential and multi-stranded nature of the text reveals itself. The study does not pretend to be a comprehensive explanation of the range of things and properties that Bartholomew treats: rather, it aims to highlight parts of the textual landscape and the possible relationships between them, to indicate the way the whole may have worked for its medieval readers as they roamed within the text or stopped to ruminate at particular points.

NOTES

[1] *Barptolemaeus [sic] Glannovillanus ex nobilissimo, ut ego colligo, genere Comitum Sudovolcorum eiusdem appellationis originem duxit. Adolescens professionem excolebat Franciscanum. Maturior annis factus, Isidis Vadum, Lutetiam atque adeo, si vera conjectura, Roman ipsam celebravit. Primas studiorum partes prudens philosophiae impendebat iuxta ac theologiae: illa ut naturalium rerum causas subtilius excuteret; hac ut mentem tanquam divino quodam illustraret radio. Aristoteles, Plato, et Plinius illi familiarium fuerunt loco; quorum fultus autoritate, librum de Rerum Proprietate concinnavit, et edidit: quem illa assidua terebrat aetas manu, unde & eius in justam excrevit fama magnitudinem*: Leland, John, *Commentarii de scriptoribus Britannicis, auctore Joanne Lelando Londinate*, Vol.1, Oxford: Antonius Hall, 1709, p.336. Author's paraphrase.

[2] Delisle, Léopold, "Traités divers sur les propriétés des choses", *Histoire Littéraire de la Langue Francaise* XXX (1888): 334–88, pp.352–4; Se Boyar, G. E., "Bartholomeus and his encyclopedia", *The Journal of English and Germanic Philology* XIX (1920): 168–89, pp.174, 185; Seymour M.C. and Colleagues, *Bartholomeus Anglicus and His Encyclopedia*, London: Variorum, 1992, pp.4, 10.

[3] Lidaka, Juris G., "Bartholomaeus Anglicus in the thirteenth century" in *Pre-Modern Encyclopaedic Texts. Proceedings of the Second COMERS Congress, Groningen, 1–4 July 1996*, edited by Peter Binkley, 393–406. Leiden: Brill, 1997, 393–5, p.395) argues for 1239/40 as the date of completion, on the basis of the Order's circumstances at the time and of Bartholomew's citations.

[4] Sherley-Price, Leo, *Thomas of Eccleston's The Coming of the Friars*, London, A.R.Mowbray and Co. Ltd., 1964, pp.1–10.

[5] Brooke, Rosalind B., *The Coming of the Friars*, London: George Allen and Unwin, 1975, pp.205–13; Lidaka, 1996; Seymour, 1992, pp.1–10.

[6] Baird, Joseph L, Guiseppe Baglivi and John Robert Kane, eds, *The Chronicle of Salimbene de Adam*, Binghampton, N.Y. 1986, p.73. See Figure 2.

[7] Constable, Giles, "The place of the Magdeburg Charter of 1107/08 in the history of eastern Germany and of the crusades" in *Vita Religiosa im Mittelalter: Festschrift für Kaspar Elm zum 70. Geburtstag*, edited by Franz J. Felton and Nikolas Jaspert, 283–99. Berlin: Duncker & Humbolt, 1999.

[8] The settlement was established as a *studium provinciale* under Simon of Sandwich in 1228: Seymour, 1992, pp.2–6. Teutonic knights (aided by Dominicans) did not subdue the pagan area east of Saxony (Prussia) until 1231: Freed, John B., *The Friars and German Society in the Thirteenth Century*, Cambridge, Mass: The Medieval Academy of America, 1977, pp.65–9; Matthew, Donald, *Atlas of Medieval Europe*, Oxford: Phaidon, 1983, p.191.

[9] DrP, *Praefatio*, pp.1–3, and *Epilogus*, p.1261: *Protestor autem in fine huius opusculi, quemadmodum in principio, quod in omnibus, quae secundum diversas materias in hoc tractatu continentur, parum vel nihil de meo apposui: sed simpliciter Sanctorum verba, & philosophorum dicta pariter & commenta veritate parvia sum secutus, ut simplices & parvuli, qui propter librorum infinitatem singularum rerum proprietates, de quibus tractat scriptura investigare non possunt, in promptu invenire valeant saltem superficialiter quod intendunt.*

[10] For discussions of Bartholomew's rhythmic, mnemonic prose style, see Lawler, Traugott, "On the properties of John Trevisa's major translations", *Viator* 14 (1983): 267–88, pp.283–4; Long, R. James, *On the Properties of Soul and Body: De Proprietatibus Rerum Libri III and IV*, Toronto: Institute of Medieval Studies, 1980, pp.7–8.

[11] Landini, Lawrence C., *The Causes of the Clericalization of the Order of Friars Minor 1209–1260 in the Light of Early Franciscan Sources*, Chicago: Pontificia Universitas Gregoriana, 1968, pp.42–5.

[12] Lidaka, 1997, p.395.

[13] Bull *Exiit qui seminat*, 1279; Pope Nicholas III (d.1280), a former Cardinal-Protector of the Order, may have been influenced by the teaching of the Franciscan St Bonaventure: Moorman, John, *A History of the Franciscan Order From Its Origins to the Year 1517*, Oxford: The Clarendon Press, 1968, pp.179–80.

[14] Surveys of the genre include Delisle, 1888; Collison, Robert, *Encyclopedias: Their History Throughout the Ages*, New York and London: Hafner, 1966; Michaud-Quantin, P., "Les petites encyclopédies du XIIIe siecle" in *Pensée encyclopédique au Moyen Age*, Neuchatel, 1966; Klingender, Francis, *Animals in Art and Thought to the End of the Middle Ages*, London: Routledge and Kegan Paul, 1971, pp.339–58; Meier, Christel, "Grundzüge der mittelalterlichen Enzyklopädik. Zu Inhalten, Formen und Funktionen einer problematischen Gattung" in *Litteratur und Laienbildung im Spätmittelalter und in der Reformationszeit. Symposium Wolfenbüttel 1981*, edited by Ludger Grenzmann und Karl Stackmann, 467–500. Stuttgart, 1984; Twomey, Michael W., "Appendix: Medieval Encyclopedias" in *Medieval Christian Imagery: A Guide to Interpretation*, edited by R. E. Kaske, Arthur Groos and Michael Twomey,

182–215: University of Toronto Press, 1988; Meyer, Heinz, "Zum Verhältnis von Enzyklopädik und Allegorese im Mittelalter", *Frühmittelalterliche Studien* 24 (1990): 290–313; Meier, Christel, ed, *Die Enzyklopädie im Wandel vom Hochmittelalter bis zur frühen Neuzeit*: Munich, 2002. For ongoing studies, see Cyclopes, *Encyclopédies comme images du monde et comme vecteurs d'échanges intellectuels dans l'Islam et l'Occident au Moyen Age*, Projet F. S. R. de l'Université catholique de Louvain, Belgium, 2006: <http://cyclopes.fltr.ucl.ac.be/recherches/index.htm>.

[15] French, Roger, and Andrew Cunningham, *Before Science: The Invention of the Friars' Natural Philosophy*, London: Scolar Press, 1996, pp.215–6, note the existence of a compilation by Juan Gil of Zamora, a Paris-trained Castillian Franciscan; McVaugh, Michael R., "Johannis Aegidii Zamorensis. *Historia naturalis*", edited by Avelino Domínguez García and Luis García Ballester, Salamanca: Junta de Castilla y León, 1994. *Isis* 87: 1 (1996), 158, notes that the Spaniard's unfinished compilation of 1275–95, 'the last of the great medieval encyclopedias of natural knowledge', was huge in intended scope, with pronounced emphasis on medicine and the animal world.

[16] William Caxton did print a version of Vincent de Beauvais' version of Henry of Mainz *Imago mundi*: Vincentius. *The Mirrour of the World*, London: Caxton, 1481.

[17] Twomey, Michael W., "Towards a reception history of western mediaeval encyclopaedias in England before 1500" in Binkley (ed), pp.329–62; Michael Seymour comes to the same conclusion from his study of medieval English owners of 'Properties': Seymour, M. C., "Some medieval English owners of De Proprietatibus Rerum", *The Bodleian Library Record* IX, no.3 (1974): 156–65, p.165.

[18] Angelicus, Bartholomaeus, *De rerum Proprietatibus*, Frankfurt: Minerva, 1601. At the time of writing, this is the only Latin printed edition available. An edition of the earlier Latin mss is projected; see Van den Abeele, Baudouin, H. Meyer & B. Ribémont, "Editer l'encyclopédie de Barthélemy l'Anglais: Vers une édition bilangue du De Proprietatibus Rerum" in *Cahiers de Recherches Médiévales* (13m–15m s) 6 (1999): 7–18.

[19] The critical edition of the Middle English text is available in Seymour, M. C., ed, *On the Properties of Things. John Trevisa's Translation of Bartholomeus Anglicus, De Proprietatibus Rerum*, 3 vols, Oxford: The Clarendon Press, 1975–88, Vols.i and ii, with critical apparatus in Vol.iii.

[20] Parkes, M. B., "The influence of the concepts of *ordinatio* and *compilatio* on the development of the book" in *Medieval Learning and Literature: Essays Presented to RW Hunt*, edited by J. J. G. Alexander and M. T. Gibson, 115–41: Oxford University Press, 1976.

[21] Lidaka, 1997, p.405.

[22] Se Boyar, p.185.

[23] Samaran, Charles, "Pierre Bersuire, Prieur de Saint-Eloi de Paris", *Histoire Littéraire de la France* 39 (1962): 259–450; see pp.315–6.

[24] *Bartholomeus De Proprietatibus Rerum*. Printed by Wynkyn de Worde, 1495.

STC 1536; *Bartholomeus De Proprietatibus Rerum. Londini in Aedibus Thomae Bertheleti Regii Impressoris. Cum Privilegio a Rege indulto. 1535*, STC 1537; *Batman vppon Bartholome , his booke De proprietatibus rerum, enlarged and amended by Stephen Bateman*. Printed by Thomas and Lucretia East, London, 1582, STC 1538.

[25] See Seymour, 1975–88 Vol.iii, pp.10–26; Voigt, Edmund, "Bartholomaeus Anglicus, De proprietatibus rerum: Litterarhistorisches und bibliographisches", *Englische Studien* 41 (1910): 337–59.

[26] Seymour, 1992, pp.257–61, *Index manuscriptorum*; Long, p.2. Lidaka, Juris, "John Trevisa and the English continental traditions of Bartholomaeus Anglicus", *Essays in Medieval Studies* 5 (1988): 71–92, p.82, concludes that '[t]he relationships of the Latin mss are mutable and fickle, depending on which portions of the text are read'. The question of English provenance is the subject of an unpublished PhD thesis: Clinton, S. M. M., The Latin Manuscript Tradition in England of the De Proprietatibus Rerum of Bartholomaeus Anglicus. An analysis based on Book 10, Northwestern USA, 1982.

[27] The Latin Book titles are abbreviated from those of DrP, which are more elaborate than the simple rubrics found in early mss.

[28] Meyer, 1988 and Lidaka, 1988, offer valuable discussions of the glosses, their possible origins and incidence across some of the earliest mss of 'Properties'. See Meyer, Heinz, "Zum Verhältnis von Enzyklopädik und Allegorese im Mittelalter", *Frühmittelalterliche Studien* 24 (1990), pp.290–313. See also Meyer, Heinz, "Die Enzyklopädie des Bartholomäus Anglicus: Untersuchungen zur Überlieferungs und Rezeptiongeschichte von De proprietatibus rerum", *Münstersche Mittelalter-Shriften* 77 (2000).

[29] Meyer, 1988, p.246 foll; Lidaka, 1997, p.404.

[30] See Chapter 3 below.

[31] David Solway, interview with Shane Neilson for *The Danforth Review* in Spring 2003; see Solway, David, *The Properties of Things: The Poems of Bartholomew the Englishman*, Montreal: Véhicule Press, in press: <http://www.danforthreview.com/features/interviews/solway/david_solway.htm>.

[32] Iser, Wolfgang, "Interaction between text and reader" in *The Reader in the Text: Essays on Audience and Interpretation*, edited by Susan R. Suleiman and Inge Crosman, 106-119: Princeton University Press, 1980. See also Jauss, Hans Robert, "Literary history as a challenge to literary theory" in *New Directions in Literary History*, edited by Ralph Cohen, 11–41, London: Routledge and Kegan Paul, 1974, pp.16–7.

[33] Smith, Frank, *Understanding reading: a psycholinguistic analysis of reading and learning to read*, Hillsdale, New Jersey: Lawrence Erlbaum Associates, 1986.

[34] Reiter, Eric H., "The reader as author of the user-produced manuscript: reading and rewriting popular Latin theology", *Viator* 27 (1996): 151–69, p.152.

Chapter 2. Literary approaches

There is a still-increasing quantity of evidence attesting to the long life and wide dissemination of 'Properties', in the form of manuscripts, incunables and fragments of the 19 Books, and in other medieval writings deemed to be derived from the compilation. In the past, students of 'Properties' worked in some isolation on locally available manuscripts and printed materials, and separate scholarly traditions developed in European countries, each with their own claims to affinity with Bartholomew. These include France, where he studied and where most of the Latin manuscripts reside; Germany, where he taught and wrote; Italy, birthplace of the Franciscan Order and location of the earliest vernacular translation; and England. Now, researchers have the benefit of easier access to manuscripts and incunables. In addition, they have the benefit of a century of insights and labours from other scholars and can gain a clearer picture of the context in which the compiler lived and worked. Over the past century, researchers have focused mainly on the identity and career of Bartholomaeus Anglicus; on the manuscript tradition of the Latin 'Properties' and the English translation, *On the Properties of Things*; on the nature of the text; and on the genre that comprises 'Properties' and other medieval compilations of knowledge. The accumulation of studies reflects changes in the way the modern world has responded to a medieval compilation of knowledge and its related concepts.

The search for the compiler and his work

In 1888 Léopold Delisle brought Bartholomew to the attention of European scholars when he catalogued and wrote about a set of singly-bound manuscripts in the Bibliothèque nationale, Paris, which all dealt with the properties of things. Delisle concluded that they were all 'du même genre', the aim of which was to use the observation of natural phenomena for the instruction and edification of the faithful. He recognised that they all dealt with properties of the natural world but included symbolic properties, leading to speculation on their medieval authorship and literary function.[1] Among them was a scarcely-known fourteenth-century allegorical treatise which he named *Proprietates rerum moralizatae*, 'The moralised properties of things', which bore an evident close relationship to another one, *De proprietatibus rerum*, 'On the properties of things'. Delisle argued that the former was derived from the latter and therefore the compiler of *De proprietatibus rerum* must pre-date the fourteenth century and could not be the supposed Glanville, known as a learned British author since Leland's time. Having thus shaken the basis of belief in Bartholomew's late-Middle English origins, Delisle further asserted from the internal evidence in Book 15's chapter on France that the compiler was a fellow Frenchman.[2]

A flurry of debate about the author and his country of origin, in German and French, followed Delisle's article. P. Perdrizet examined textual evidence for the English, not French, nationality of the author. H. Matrod gave an enthusiastic account of the Bibliothèque nationale's manuscripts of 'Properties' from a French Franciscan perspective, seeing Bartholomew as a popular guide into the 'garden' of science and Roger Bacon, on the other hand, as a direct investigator of nature. Matrod was convinced of Bartholomew's enriching influence on English culture, saying that Shakespeare, Jonson, Spenser, Marlowe, Massinger, Lyly and Drayton were 'all nourished by *De Proprietatibus*'.[3] In Germany, Anton Schönbach and Edmund Voigt turned their attention to the history of the manuscripts of 'Properties' and to the problems of textual consistency and affiliation.[4] T. Plassmann, also a Franciscan, to some extent quelled the argument about Bartholomew's origins, citing contemporary sources to establish that Bartholomew lived early in the thirteenth century, taught in Paris and worked in Magdeburg, and that only 'Properties' could be safely assigned to him.[5] Meanwhile in England, the antiquarian Robert Steele had published an 'epitome' of extracts from Berthelet's 1535 edition of Trevisa. The German scholars approached 'Properties' as philologists and codicologists, but prefatory comments by Steele and William Morris show that their interest in the work was largely political and aesthetic. Steele justifies his interest in Bartholomew's work by saying that 'Properties' was one of the documents 'by the help of which we rebuild for ourselves the fabric of mediaeval life'; Morris praises the 'quaint floweriness' of the language, fancifully modernised by Steele, and recommends the book as a corrective to 'the just-past epoch of intelligence dominated by Whig politics'.[6] Steele's book testifies mainly to a late-Victorian conception of the Gothic, but it did serve to maintain scholarly awareness, in the English-speaking world, of Bartholomew and his work.

After World War I, Gerald Se Boyar, an American Franciscan, reviewed the literature on 'Properties' in a seminal work that brought the topic into the ambit of English-speaking scholars. He aimed to make a careful study of the encyclopaedia as a whole and to fix its place in the history of the encyclopaedic writings of the Middle Ages.[7] Se Boyar was also keen to convince readers of a connection between Bartholomew and Shakespeare and to show 'that Shakespeare was at least familiar with the book, whether he owned a copy or not, and that it was an important reference book'.[8]

In 1952, Elizabeth Brockhurst followed the lead of Se Boyar's research but her resources were limited. Using only material in the British Library, she confined her analysis to parts of Book 1 of the English translation, and parts of Books 2, 3 and 4 from the Latin 'Properties'.[9] For Brockhurst, the only available printed version, other than the sixteenth-century editions in the British Library, was Steele's pastiche. Nevertheless, she adduced evidence for the work's popularity and for the continuity of its core content over time, situated the translation within the Trevisa canon, and described seven of the manuscripts of the English *Properties*. Her method and approach, given her lack of access to data, were narrowly focused upon textual affiliation and variation within a very small sample of manuscripts and incunables. In France, Pierre Michaud-Quantin was similarly constrained in the 1960s. He suggested that one must consider how the encyclopaedias answered the needs of readers in order to gain 'une perspective sur la culture et la mentalité du milieu dans lequel elles sont apparues'. But Michaud-Quantin has not space enough in a short article to do more than reinforce the notion that 'Properties' was a somewhat inadequate textbook of information.[10]

Over time, and in separate countries, research into the context in which the work appeared and the excavation of related documents have brought the compiler more clearly into focus. Most recently, Juris Lidaka has clarified the time and circumstances of composition, while Michael Seymour has fleshed out the few biographical details to create a speculative biography, and to reconstruct Bartholomew's use of literary sources.[11] The well-attested identity of the compiler as a Franciscan of a particular time and place is now sufficiently established to underpin further investigations of his work.

Later approaches

During the 1960s, work began in England and America on Michael Seymour's three-volume critical edition (1974–88) of Trevisa's translation.[12] Seymour's edition was a major achievement which made the work, with the addition of critical apparatus, accessible to scholars of Middle English. The research that was involved in achieving a 'best reading' of Trevisa's lost copy-text, and in tracing the Latin exemplars possibly available to him, also cultivated a still-productive research area into the manuscript provenances and affiliations. In addition, the team of editors involved in the project went on to provide much of the English-language literature on *Properties*, in further critical editions of manuscript sections of the work.[13]

In particular, it produced studies of John Trevisa and his work as a pioneer translator of serious prose works into the vernacular.[14] In the context of Lollard dissent at this time and of the contentious issue of Bible translation, Trevisa's work as a stage in the establishment of vernacular prose writing and his involvement in the translation of devotional prose works have been the subject of conjecture.[15] Together the comprehensive work of David Fowler on the life and work of John Trevisa, the Seymour edition of *Properties* and modern studies of late-fourteenth-century literary patronage in England and in France provide a clearer picture of the culture and the conditions of production within which *Properties* appeared in an English vernacular dialect.[16]

The quantity of research into the manuscript tradition of 'Properties' and *Properties* involved in the edition also led to studies of individuals and institutions that owned or bequeathed copies in France and England.[17] Seymour brought together evidence for ownership of 'Properties' in England and France on the basis of wills and library catalogues. Anthony Edwards took the search further, looking at contemporary writings showing evidence of other writers' direct knowledge of the work in the later Middle Ages. He concluded that 'Properties' and its translation came to be a resource freely mined by other writers, and he cites evidence from direct citations and borrowings found in late-medieval texts across a wide range of genres.[18] The important studies of the translation, the ownership and the borrowings, help to contextualise the work within a widening English readership of the later Middle Ages.

The modern edition of Trevisa's *Properties*, and the significant body of secondary literature surrounding it, open up the subject for research into the work's function for English readers, writers and sermon audiences of that era. However, while it is an essential basis for further research, Seymour's edition of *Properties* is haunted by the ghost of the lost exemplar towards which the editors aspire. The pursuit of a complete version of the text involves a particular approach and special skills, but it usefully draws attention to another possible approach: that of seeing the manuscript tradition as multi-stranded. In one strand, the work maintains basic integrity in its 19 Books, a repository of ancient wisdom maintained in ecclesiastical and academic libraries; in others, readers adapt it and abstract from it to meet new needs, and according to the methods of production available to them.

The question of genre

Because a number of compilations appear around the turn of the thirteenth century, coeval with the translations from Aristotle and the growth of secular colleges in Paris, they have been grouped together in the literature and labelled 'encyclopaedias'. Robert Collison lists 'Properties' as one of the medieval encyclopaedias that amass contemporary knowledge from the Christian, Arab and Buddhist medieval worlds.[19] K. W. Humphreys includes 'Properties' among the 'scientific books' held in the library of St Croce, Florence, in 1426.[20] An exhibition held in the Newberry Library, Chicago, to commemorate the 200th anniversary of the *Encyclopaedia Britannica*, includes Wynkyn de Worde's 'Properties' as the first printed example of the genre.[21]

In the introduction to their volume on Christian imagery, R. Kaske and his colleagues comment: 'During the past several decades, we have become increasingly aware of the allusive density of medieval literature, and of the extent to which much of its imagery depends on certain large bodies of traditional Christian learning.' While potentially of great value as a clue to the multivalent nature of medieval works, this density can be hard for us to penetrate.[22] To assist the reader in this task Michael Twomey, in an appendix to the volume, lists and describes compendia roughly contemporary with 'Properties' that he categorises as 'major' and 'minor' encyclopaedias.[23] He includes 'Properties' among the major works, along with Isidore of Seville's *Etymologiae*, Rabanus Maurus' *De rerum naturis*, Honorius Augustodunensis' *Elucidarium* and *Imago mundi*, the German *Lucidarius* (c.1190, a guide for the laity); Alexander Neckam's *De naturis rerum* and *Laus sapientie divine*; Thomas of Cantimpré's *Liber de natura rerum* and Vincent of Beauvais' *Speculum maius*. Twomey finds the 'minor' works harder to categorise, but includes Isidore's *De natura rerum*; Ps-Isidore's *De ordine creaturarum*; Bede's *De natura rerum* and *Summarium Heinrici*; Lambert of St Omer's *Liber floridus*; Hildegard of Bingen's *Physica* and *Causae et curae*; Pseudo-Hugh of St Victor's *De bestiis et aliis rebus*; *Secretum secretorum*; Arnoldus Saxo's *De finibus rerum naturalium* (mid-thirteenth century); Brunetto Latini's *Trésor*; *Book of Sidrach* (mid-thirteenth century, also called *Fountain of All Knowledge*); and *Placides et Timéo* (a platonic dialogue, c.1250–1300). He includes some of Bartholomew's near-contemporary sources, such as the work *Magnae derivationes* by Uguccione da Pisa (d.1210: 'an etymological dictionary with an encyclopedic range'). Twomey considers that this work formed the basis for the alphabetically organized *Catholicon* by Johannes de Balbis, completed in 1286.

Such a survey allows us to see Bartholomew's undertaking in the context of a widely felt impulse to compile useful knowledge, and to realise that although the compilers presented their work in different ways, they partook of the same pool of authorised knowledge, borrowed from each other, and shared the same general views about the value and purpose of their undertakings. This appendix is a useful database for the researcher, as it supplies an overview of each work's content and dissemination history and does indeed provide one kind of map of the genre.

The faulty encyclopaedia

As recently as 1987 a symposium held at Caen (published 1991) showed that the idea of the medieval encyclopaedia as a genre was still firmly in place.[24] Among the papers, Sylvain Louis summarises the French thinking at that time on 'Properties', while M. De Boüard sees the genre as the expression of a new phase of medieval natural philosophy, comprising two types of encyclopaedia: the scientific/objective, and the symbolic/edifying. He sees a 'liberating' change occurring, from the latter to the former, and remnants of allegorisation as 'contaminating' some of the 'scientific' type.[25] In English-language histories also, as an encyclopaedia 'Properties' fell short in the judgement of historians who tended to assess it by criteria we apply today to that type of work — impartiality, balance, order, consistency, factual accuracy and careful editing.[26] The earlier twentieth-century literature on the history of western science tended, therefore, to place 'Properties' and comparable works within the march of progress and to find them wanting. Lynn Thorndike expressed the view that writings such as 'Properties' represented a primitive stage of scientific thought, and their longevity was therefore deplorable. In his later work, reprinted in 1967, Thorndike reproved the late-medieval encyclopaedists for failing to 'advance'.[27] To Charles Raven, their works were inconsistent, repetitive, subjective, without original thought or analysis, and cluttered up with marvellous and legendary content.[28] Even more recently, Edward Grant stated: 'Without access to the hard core of Greek science, the Western world could not rise above the level of the Latin encyclopedists.'[29]

The world-book tradition

In the last decades of the twentieth century, the earlier assumptions about 'Properties' and its peers started to be questioned as historians rethought the nature of so-called medieval science as an enterprise in its own right and with a particular function in its own time. The contentious issue of genre arises in part from the fact that Bartholomew placed side by side the teachings of the Church Fathers and extracts from the works of Aristotle newly available in Latin — for him and his readers, the respectively old and revered, and modern and controversial. David Greetham examines 'Properties' as a specifically Franciscan work, addressing what he sees as a fundamental problem; namely, that Bartholomew is trying to provide biblical exegesis, practical information and affective stories all at the same time. Thus his work 'exemplifies the intellectual discomforts of the medieval philosophy of science'.[30] Greetham concludes, however, that the inherent contradictions within 'Properties' contributed to its popularity, and helped to transmit a 'tensioned and ambiguous' philosophy of nature through the course of the Middle Ages and into the sixteenth century. More recently, and in the context of an ongoing debate about the nature of medieval investigation of the natural world, David Lindberg concludes:

> Science was no more autonomous and isolated, no more situated in a social and institutional vacuum, during the medieval period than in more recent eras; and we cannot pretend to have fully grasped the nature and significance, or even the content, of medieval science until we have thoroughly contextualized it.[31]

Contextual elements relevant to this study include the role of the thirteenth-century church as the primary patron of learning and its efforts to combat Cathar heresy; changing techniques of book production; the expansion of the book market into the lay world; and the friars' pursuit of a philosophy of nature combining allegorical and classical elements. The troubles surrounding the Catholic church at the time were an important factor in the production of authoritative books; French and Cunningham show that the friars' compilations, particularly those of the Dominicans, were tools designed for waging intellectual war on the Cathars. This urgent ecclesiastical need for patronage and control through teaching had a gradual effect on the theory and practice of authorship and compilation.[32] In addition, the friars — particularly the Franciscans — were intent upon the study of the natural world as a way of understanding God. French and Cunningham also examine and elucidate the character and function of the friars' natural philosophy (which privileges light and its symbolic properties) in the context of the concerns of the church and of the Order. They conclude that Roger Bacon, for example, drew on 'Properties' to investigate physical phenomena, especially light, in order to align Aristotle's teaching with Franciscan beliefs and orthodox doctrine: 'The famous medieval conflict between "science" and "religion" is in fact a construct of the nineteenth century. The medieval discipline of natural philosophy, by contrast, was one in which nature was explored in the cause of defending Roman Catholicism — fighting heresy and promoting lay spirituality.'[33]

The inclusion of religious allegory in the medieval compilations, then, has been a problem for historians because it appears to muddy the springs of scientific thought and to contradict their assumed purpose. In the 1980s, 'Properties' and its encyclopaedic contemporaries became the subject of illuminating research in Europe. Christel Meier traces the sources, models and likely functions of the *compilatio* as a genre and suggests new ways of defining it in medieval terms, noting a discrepancy between the negative judgements of modern readers and the positive approval of medieval commentators. She suggests that we need to see the compilations not as high-medieval innovations, but as products of a long tradition dating from late antiquity and formed by minds already ripe. Their function was to act as combined library substitute, repository of knowledge and guide to salvation.[34] Heinz Meyer points out that the fourteenth-century derivatives of 'Properties', the *Liber moralizatae* mentioned above and the *Reductium morale* of Pierre Bersuire, testify that the properties of the material world as described by Bartholomew could indeed hold moral and ethical significations for the clerical reader and fulfil the criterion of moral *utilitas*. He asserts that the consistent body of marginal glosses occurring in early Latin manuscripts were an essential vehicle within the earliest manuscripts for the allegorical and moral meanings of the text. The later shedding of the glosses in fourteenth-century manuscripts indicates that readers became more interested in the work as a source of factual, rather than moralised, accounts of the properties of things. However, the complexity of 'Properties' forbids a simple antithesis between worldly and spiritual readings, and may offer a reason for its success under different conditions.[35]

The Journey of a Book

Compilatio and *utilitas*

Thanks to the work of Christel Meier, Heinz Meyer and others, the so-called encyclopaedias are now considered to be representatives of a long-standing medieval tradition of *compilatio* — that is, the encyclopaedic compilation made for a specific set of purposes and following certain scholarly conventions.[36] Meier concludes that compilers from Isidore of Seville in the seventh century, to Bartholomew and his peers in the thirteenth, take the Genesis account of creation as a temporal or conceptual starting point for a book of the world, and use a title such as *imago mundi* or *speculum mundi* to reflect that universal scope. Some compilers (such as Vincent de Beauvais) choose a six-day format that mirrors the six-day genesis of the created world; others (such as Bartholomew) order the content from Creator to created, incorporeal to corporeal, reflecting cosmic hierarchy. Meier notes that individual works give the impression not of chaos or lack of form but of a closed and complete order: the variety of things of all kinds appears as abundance and perfection, so that the 'world book' again resembles the world itself; like the world, nobody can grasp it all, but they can recognise that there is an ordering principle at work. In addition, a 'world book' that describes creation implies the inverse notion that the world is a book that we can read. The main reason for compiling given throughout the life of the genre is the work's functional and moral *utilitas* in leading to knowledge of God. She deduces that the fundamental criteria for a medieval world book are that it should function as a library substitute, as a repository of knowledge and as a guide to salvation; compilers should use the technique of excerption and maintain a tight connection with tradition.[37] In these conclusions and criteria, Meier provides us with a way of thinking about the compilation genre and about Bartholomew's task of aspiring, first and foremost, towards moral and spiritual usefulness.

Questions about the genre opened up by such reappraisal have been the topic of a major colloquium in the past decade.[38] Papers focus upon the significance and function of the 'encyclopaedias' in the intellectual life of the Middle Ages; not only European compendia of knowledge, but also Arabic and Jewish. The papers cover 'Definitions and theoretical questions'; 'Organisation of knowledge'; 'Epistemology of encyclopaedic knowledge'; 'Cultural and political uses'; and 'Reception and transmission of texts'. In this last category, Juris Lidaka takes 'Properties' as a case-study, and provides a résumé of recent findings concerning the compiler in his social and political context. Lidaka draws conclusions from a study of features of the Paris book trade that help our understanding of the work's earliest exposure to a widening readership.[39] Christel Meier's paper published in the same volume summarises and clarifies, in English, her theory of the functions and purposes of the world-book genre and the concept of moral utility that underpins it.[40]

At the time of writing, the most concentrated research on the genre, and on 'Properties' in particular, is being carried out by an international team of researchers based at the Universities of Münster in Germany, Orléans in France and Louvain-la-Neuve in Belgium. This project includes the preparation of a new edition of 'Properties' in parallel text (Latin and French), which will treat the marginal glosses as an integral part of the text.[41] At the Catholic University of Louvain, a team of researchers is currently studying 'encyclopedias as images of the world and as vehicles of change in Islamic and western thought in the Middle Ages'.[42] This includes examinations by Godefroid de Callataÿ into intellectual exchanges between east and west; studies of the bestiary and animal iconography by Baudouin Van den Abeele, who is also a participant in the new edition of 'Properties' mentioned above; and particular attention on the part of Jérémy Loncke to 'Properties' as a significant representative of the genre.[43] These and other researchers have spoken on Bartholomew's work and on other aspects of the encyclopaedic genre at colloquia held in 2003 and 2005.

Other corners of the field

It will be seen that European scholars have been interested in Bartholomew for a long time. But 'Properties' and its compiler are only one aspect of a much larger field of study that has been increasingly well-dug in recent decades: that is, the studies of what medieval texts can reveal about medieval 'science' — both as explanation of, and the practice of preserving knowledge about, the material world and its contents, predicated upon a belief in the world's purposeful creation by God. Meier's assessment of the major compilations as images of a world created and provided for by God, formulated as aids to salvation as well as learning, serve to validate this broader project. Any study, therefore, of medieval responses to 'Properties' must take into account seminal and ongoing researches into medieval concepts of knowledge and its moral utility; medieval literary theory; methods of codifying, organising and presenting knowledge in compilations of various kinds; and of the sources, content and forms of informational texts.

In particular, two related kinds of medieval compilation, each with its own manuscript tradition and its own specialist scholars, complement the discursive sources. One of these is the codification of medieval world history and Christian teaching represented in the works of art we know as *mappaemundi*, the development of which tends to parallel that of the world-book encyclopaedias. The other is the medieval body of received wisdom about 'things' made during the six days of Creation — animals, birds, fishes and plants — and their religious significance, embodied in the tradition of bestiary manuscripts dating from late antiquity to the fifteenth century. Recent studies in these areas, as well as this study of the reception of 'Properties', indicate that while there are obviously formal differences between maps, bestiaries and compilations such as 'Properties', they can all be seen as clerical productions directed towards the goal of preserving religious knowledge and teaching Catholic doctrine. Indeed, Margriet Hoogvliet has argued that maps and encyclopaedias should be seen as complementary and the name *mappamundi* applied to both.[44] Similarly, the bestiary literature has proliferated in recent decades.[45] Scholars conclude that animals and birds could be significant in the Middle Ages as objects of practical interest encountered in real life; analogues of humanity; players in the important historical events recounted in the Christian Scriptures; and visible signs of the 'invisible things of God' that the preacher needed to expound. Writers therefore valued an authoritative source-book on the symbolic properties of creatures. In clerical and secular adaptations of the later Books of 'Properties', that is, those about birds, plants and animals, we find Bartholomew described as 'Master of kind' and even as 'Bartholomew the bestiary'. As later chapters will show, this study is therefore also indebted to modern exponents of the bestiary and of medieval animal symbolism.[46]

To conclude this survey of the long-accumulated literature on Bartholomew and his work, it should be pointed out that our compilation here is one example of a textual type within an increasingly explored area. The earlier literature on 'Properties' is an invaluable resource in that so much groundwork has been done as a basis for fresh research into the compiler, the manuscripts and the translations, and the place these occupied in late-medieval English life and letters. Twentieth-century research into the context in which the work appeared, and the excavation of related documents, has brought the compiler more clearly into focus. Research into the genre of the thirteenth-century *compilatio* as a tool of the militant Catholic church, and as part of a wider exchange of knowledge between east and west, has improved our understanding of the genre's context and function. However, in the present century, important ongoing research is being shared and published in languages other than English. The important studies of the English translation, the later-medieval ownership of manuscripts and the literary borrowings from Bartholomew help to contextualise the work within a widening English readership of the later Middle Ages. The size and scope of the work has so far prevented the appearance of a detailed reception history, but the present study offers a limited contribution to such a project by examining, in English, the work's transmission and diffusion in a significant area of its medieval and early-modern readership.

NOTES

[1] Delisle, 1888, follows this clarification (p.352) with a description of Thomas de Cantimpré's *Liber de natura rerum*, also little-known at the time, and which he considered 'tout a fait digne d'être placé a coté du *De proprietatibus rerum*' (p.365); and with some 'opuscules' in manuscripts that seem to be related in character though fragmentary (pp.384–8). Delisle was regarded as the founder of the wealth and orderliness of the BN mss collection and his word carried weight: Blasselle, B. et J. Melet-Sanson, *La Bibliotheque Nationale, Mémoire de l'Avenir*, Paris: Gallimard, 1991, pp.67–8; Tesnière, M., *Creating*

French Culture: Treasures from the Bibliotheque Nationale de France, New Haven and London: Yale University Press, 1995, pp.xxxix–xl.

[2] Delisle, p.335; for the present study the ms of the *Moralizatae* (variously referred to in the literature as the *Liber moralizate, moralisate/ae, liber de moralitatibus* and henceforth referred to as LM) used is BNF Ms Lat. 3332.

[3] Matrod, p.478: 'sont tous nourris du *De Proprietatibus*'.

[4] Schönbach, A., "Des Bartholomeus Anglicus Beschreibung Deutschlands gegen 1240", *Mitteilungen des Instituts für Osterreichische Geschichtsforschung* 17 (1906): 56–62; Voigt, 1910.

[5] Plassmann, T., "Bartholomaeus Anglicus", *Archivum franciscanum historicum* 12 (1919): 68–109. Perdrizet, P., "Barthélemy l'Anglais et son description de l'Angleterre", *Journal des savants* 7 (1909): 170–5; Matrod, H., "Roger Bacon et Fr. Barthélemy D'Angleterre", *Etudes franciscaines* XXVIII (1912): 468–83; Plassmann, T., "Bartholomaeus Anglicus", *Archivum franciscanum historicum* 12 (1919): 68–109.

[6] Steele, Robert, *Medieval Lore from Bartholomeus Anglicus*, London: De la More Press, 1893, reprinted 1905, p.2; Morris, William, Preface, in Steele, pp.xii–xiii.

[7] Se Boyar, p.169.

[8] Se Boyar, p.168.

[9] Brockhurst, 1952; Seymour acknowledges Brockhurst's role in English-language studies of 'Properties', with a quotation from Chaucer: 'evere she roode the foremoste of oure route' (Seymour, 1975–88, Dedication).

[10] Michaud-Quantin, p.107. His examples are the works of Neckam, Bartholomew and Cantimpré, and the *Compendium Philosophia*, all 'little' by comparison with the work of Vincent de Beauvais.

[11] It has not been questioned (to my knowledge) that there was a sole maker. The fact that there is a preface attached to early manuscripts of 'Properties', in which a *compilator* sets out his intentions concerning the work as a whole, has allowed scholars to assume that a single mind and hand composed the 19 Books (as Salimbene had implied in the 1280s: see Chapter 1, note 6, above).

[12] Seymour, 1975–88.

[13] These and other unpublished PhD and MA studies of 'Properties' of which I am aware are: Keen, E., From Bartholomaeus to Batman: Four hundred years of the Properties of Things, The Australian National University, 2002; Lidaka, Juris, Bartholomaeus Anglicus' De Proprietatibus Rerum, Book XIX, Chapters on Mathematics, Measures, and Music: A Critical Edition of the Latin Text in England, Northern Illinois University, 1988, Clinton, 1982; Hamilton, Ruth Elaine, Of Fire and of Air: Notes and Commentary on Books 10 and 11 of John Trevisa's Translation of Bartholomaeus Anglicus' De Proprietatibus Rerum, Northwestern University, 1982; Hutchison, Ann McCall, An Edition of Book VI of John Trevisa's English Translation of De Proprietatibus Rerum by Bartholomaeus Anglicus, University of Toronto, 1974; Wallis, F., Structure and Philosophy in Mediaeval Encyclopaedias, McGill University, Montreal, 1974; Brockhurst, 1952.

[14] Especially, Lawler, 1983; Waldron, Ronald, "John Trevisa and the use of English", *Proceedings of the British Academy* LXXIV (1988): 171–202; Waldron, Ronald, "Trevisa's 'Celtic complex' revisited", *Notes and Queries* 20 (1989): 303–7; Waldron, Ronald, "Trevisa's original prefaces on translation: a critical edition" in *Medieval English Studies Presented to George Kane*, edited by E. D. Kennedy, R. Waldron and J. S. Wittig, Woodbridge: D. S. Brewer, 1988.

[15] See Fowler, D. C., "John Trevisa and the English Bible", *Modern Philology* 58 (1960): 81–98; Fowler, D. C., "More about John Trevisa", *Modern Language Quarterly* 32 (1971): 243–51; Fowler, D. C., "New light on John Trevisa", *Traditio* 18 (1963): 289–317; and Fowler, D. C., *The Life and Times of John Trevisa, Scholar*, University of Washington Press, 1995; Hudson, Anne, *Lollards and their Books*, The Hambledon Press, 1985, p.199, concludes that Trevisa's expressions on temporal power 'remain within the bounds of orthodoxy'.

[16] Invaluable studies of this context include Bennett, Michael J., "The court of Richard II and the promotion of literature" in *Chaucer's England: Literature in Historical Context*, edited by Barbara J. Hanawalt, 3–20. Minneapolis: University of Minnesota Press, 1992; Byrne, Donal, "Rex imago Dei: Charles V of France and the Livre des propriétés des choses", *Journal of Medieval History* 7 (1981): 97–113; Green, Richard Firth, *Poets and Princepleasers: Literature and the English Court in the Late Middle Ages*: University of Toronto Press, 1980; Scattergood, V. J., "Literary culture at the court of Richard II" in *English Court Culture in the Late Middle Ages*, edited by V. J. Scattergood and J. W. Sherborne, 29–43. London: Duckworth, 1983; Salvat, Michel, "Science et pouvoir á Mantoue et á Paris au XIVe siècle" in *L'Encyclopédisme. Actes du Colloque de Caen 12–16 janvier 1987*, edited by Annie Becq, 389–94. Paris: Éditions Aux Amateurs de Livres, 1991.

[17] Seymour, 1974, "English owners"; Seymour, M. C., "Some medieval French readers of De Proprietatibus Rerum", *Scriptorium* XXVII (1974): 100–2.

[18] Edwards, A. S. G., "Bartholomeus Anglicus, De Proprietatibus Rerum and medieval English literature", *Archiv* 222 (1985): 121–8.

[19] Collison, pp.54–63.

[20] Humphreys, K. W., *The Book Provisions of the Medieval Friars 1215–1400*, Amsterdam: Erasmus, 1964, p.114.

[21] Wells, James M., *The Circle of Knowledge: Encyclopedias Past and Present*, Chicago: The Newberry Library, 1968.

[22] Kaske, Groos and Twomey (eds), p.xvii.

[23] Twomey, 1988, pp.182–215.

[24] Louis, Sylvain, "Le projet encyclopédique de Barthélemy l'Anglais" in Becq, ed, pp.147–51.

[25] De Boüard, Michel, "Réflexions sur l'encyclopédisme médiéval" in *L'Encyclopédisme. Actes du Colloque de Caen 12–16 janvier 1987*, edited by Annie Becq, 281–290. Paris: Klincksieck, 1991, p. 284: 'dans la seconde moitié du XIIe siecle, les esprits étaient murs pour accueillir la 'philosophie naturelle" d'Aristote et de ses commentateurs arabes ... Le véritable "décollage" des sciences ne se manifestera cependant que dans le troisieme quart du XIIIe siecle.'

[26] For example, Brockhurst, 1952, pp.33–4, finds many 'faults of arrangement' and undue repetition; Long, 1979, pp.9–12, finds 'errors of fact' and lack of synthesis; Seymour, 1992, p.147, finds Bartholomew's treatment of some items 'unbalanced and disappointing'.

[27] Thorndike, Lynn, *Science and thought in the fifteenth century*: Columbia University Press, 1929, p.12.

[28] Raven, Charles E., *English Naturalists from Neckam to Ray*: Cambridge University Press, 1947.

[29] Grant, E., *Physical Science in the Middle Ages*, New York: John Wiley, 1971, p.13.

[30] Greetham, D. C., "On Cultural Translation: From Patristic Repository to Shakespeare's Encyclopedia" in *Voices in Translation: The Authority of "Olde Bookes" in Medieval Literature: Essays in Honor of Helaine Newstead*, edited by Deborah M. Sinnreich-Levi and Gale Sigal, 69–84. New York: A. M. S. Press, 1992.

[31] Lindberg, David, "Medieval science and its religious context", *Osiris* (1995), p.66.

[32] A. J. Minnis discusses the development of literary theories and methods during the thirteenth and fourteenth centuries in the context of demand for effective guides to the art of preaching and teaching: Minnis, A. J., *Medieval Theory of Authorship*, Aldershot: Wildwood House, 1984, pp.160–3.

[33] French and Cunningham, "About this book", front flyleaf.

[34] Meier, 1984, p.470; Meier, Christel, "Organisation of knowledge and encyclopaedic *ordo*: Functions and purposes of a universal literary genre" in *Pre-Modern Encyclopaedic Texts. Proceedings of the Second COMERS Congress, Groningen, 1–4 July 1996*, edited by Peter Binkley, 103–26, Leiden New York Cologne: Brill, 1997: Meier considers about 20 compilations plus their translations and revisions, including those by Hrabanus Maurus, Isidore of Seville, Honorius of Autun, Thomas de Cantimpré, Bartholomew the Englishman, Vincent de Beauvais, Brunetto Latini and Gossuin de Metz.

[35] Meyer, Heinz, "Bartholomäus Anglicus, De proprietatibus rerum: Selbstverständnis und Rezeption", *Zeitschrift für deutsches Altertum und deutsche Literatur* 117 (1988): 237–74; Meyer, 1990, p.313.

[36] Parkes, 1991, pp.52–60; Minnis, A. J., A. B. Scott and D. Wallace, *Medieval Literary Theory and Criticism, c.1100–c.1375: the Commentary Tradition*: Oxford University Press, 1988.

[37] Meier, 1984, p.470; for her argument in English see Meier, 1997; also Parkes, M. B., "The influence of the concepts of *ordinatio* and *compilatio* on the development of the book" in *Scribes, Scripts, and Readers: Studies in the Communication, Presentation, and Dissemination of Medieval Texts*, 35–69. London: Hambledon Press, 1991. See pp.52–4 on the concept of *ordinatio*; pp.58–60 on *compilatio* as a sophisticated scholarly tool in the thirteenth century; p.58 on Bonaventure's distinction between the *compilator, auctor, commentator* and *scriptor*. There were well-understood conventions to be observed by the *compilator*, including the stated aim of *utilitas*, the modest disclaiming of authorship, the appeal for correction or improvement, and the commending of his sources as superior authorities.

[38] Binkley, Peter, ed, *Pre-Modern Encyclopaedic Texts. Proceedings of the Second COMERS Congress, Groningen, 1–4 July 1996*, 103–26, Leiden New York Cologne: Brill, 1997.

[39] Lidaka, 1997.

[40] Meier, 1997. See also Ribémont, B., "On the definition of an encyclopaedic genre in the Middle Ages", in Binkley, ed, pp.47–61.

[41] Van den Abeele, Meyer et Ribémont, 1999.

[42] <http://cyclopes.fltr.ucl.ac.be/recherches/index.htm>, *Encyclopédies comme images du monde et comme vecteurs d'échanges intellectuels dans l'Islam et l'Occident au Moyen Age*, Projet F. S. R. de l'Université catholique de Louvain, Belgium, 2006.

[43] *Le discourse encyclopédique arabe et latin au Moyen Age: L'incorporation des saviors étrangers*, Louvain-la-Neuve, 14–15 novembre 2003; *Une lumière venue d'ailleurs: Héritages et ouvertures dans les encyclopédies d'Orient et d'Occident au Moyen Age*, Louvain-la-Neuve, 19–21 mai 2005; see <http://cyclopes.fltr.ucl.ac.be/colloques>.

[44] Hoogvliet, Margriet, "Mappae Mundi and Medieval Encyclopaedias: Image versus Text", in Binkley, ed, 63–74, pp.63–4; David Woodward and also Evelyn Edson examine the evidence for their didactic and symbolic functions: Woodward, David, "Medieval mappaemundi" in *Cartography in Prehistoric, Ancient and Medieval Europe and the Mediterranean*, edited by J. B. Harley and David Woodward, 286–370, Chicago and London: The University of Chicago Press, 1987, pp.287, 304; Woodward, David, "Reality, Symbolism, Time, and Space in Medieval World Maps", *Annals of the Association of American Geographers* 75 (1985): 510–21; Edson, Evelyn, *Mapping Time and Space: How Medieval Mapmakers Viewed Their World*, London: The British Library, 1997, pp.145–90; studies of the Hereford map elucidate in detail the relation of function to form and content in a particularly rich example: Harvey, P. D. A., ed, *The Hereford World Map: Medieval World Maps and their Context*; Westrem, Scott. D., *The Hereford Map*, Turnhout: Brepols, 2001. The essential descriptive catalogue and index to known maps is Déstombes, Marcel, ed. *Mappemondes AD 1200–1500*, Amsterdam: N. Israel, 1964.

[45] M. R. James (*The Bestiary*: Oxford University Press, 1928) drew attention to the genre in the pre-war period; Florence McCulloch (*Medieval Latin and French Bestiaries*, University of North Carolina Press, 1960), and later Willene B. Clark and Meradith McMunn (*Birds and Beasts in the Middle Ages: The Bestiary and its Legacy*. Philadelphia: University of Pennsylvania Press, 1989) elucidated their content and examined the teaching function of aviaries and bestiaries. Meanwhile, Francis Klingender (*Animals in Art and Thought to the End of the Middle Ages*, London: Routledge and Kegan Paul, 1971) produced a comprehensive, illustrated survey of evidence for the ubiquity and importance of animals and birds in medieval religion and art. See also Houwen, L., "Animal parallelism in medieval literature and the bestiaries: a preliminary investigation", *Neophilologus* 78 (1994), 483–96; Clark, Willene B., "The illustrated medieval aviary and the lay-brotherhood", *Gesta* XXI (1982): 63–74. Recently, Debra Hassig (Hassig, Debra, ed, *The Mark of the Beast*, London and New York: Routledge, 1999; and *Medieval Bestiaries: Text, Image, Ideology*: Cambridge University Press, 1995) has clarified the interplay between text and images in English bestiaries, and the way they can give us insights into social as well as spiritual concerns.

[46] Bestiary manuscripts typically include a frontispiece depicting Adam naming the beasts, a scene from apocryphal history which implicitly places the ensuing list of creatures in a broader narrative framework; that of creation and prelapsarian paradise: see Klingender, p.28. From this point of view, the encyclopaedic texts subsume the bestiary as the Genesis account of creation subsumes what God made on each of the six days: Keen, E., 'Separate or Together? Questioning the relationship between the encyclopedia and bestiary traditions', *Journal of the Australian Early Medieval Association*, vol.2 (2006) pp. 121–39.

Chapter 3. 'Properties' as a guide to salvation

The subject of this and the following chapter is a suggested way of reconstructing early perceptions of Bartholomew's work during the first phase of its life story. They can only be suggestions as we have no hard evidence for earliest readers' responses to the text, but our understanding of the medieval use of allegory can alert us to the need to look beneath the surface at both things and their properties as Bartholomew presents them.

Bartholomew summarises the contents of each Book in his preface.[1] The categories seem, on the face of it, clear and well-defined, leading modern readers to expect the kind of ordered and objective descriptions of things consistent with modern expository texts. These are not forthcoming, however, and commentators have expressed bafflement at Bartholomew's failure to keep to his stated categories in a rational manner. Léopold Delisle, for one, had referred in the 1880s to 'le désordre qui règne dans le *Proprietatibus rerum*'.[2] The following passage expresses a twentieth-century English researcher's frustration at the apparent incompatibility of chapter arrangements with the 'system' Bartholomew predicts in the *Praefatio*:

> This excellent system, which should be compared with those of contemporary encyclopedias, keeps Bartholomew from gross lapses into incoherence; but within its framework some faults of arrangement are apparent. Repetition is a common failure ... a more careful revision would have decreased the length of the book by eliminating duplications [such as the two chapters on bees] ... In Book XVIII the animals are not classed under species, but alphabetically, with their young distinguished separately; so that 'De bove' ... occurs at chapter xiii, 'De tauro' at chapter c ... Even more oddly, 'De cornu', of the horn, 'De ficario', of the seller of figs, and 'De bubulco', of the oxherd, occur among the animals. Birds and insects are classed together in Book XII, and reptiles with animals in Book XVIII; but their eggs receive consideration in Book XIX, among the assortment of objects which could not be fitted in elsewhere.[3]

Elizabeth Brockhurst was a pioneer of 'Properties' studies in England, and her thesis was seminally important in that it drew the attention of post-war English historians to Bartholomew and his compilation within an English manuscript tradition. I quote the above in order to emphasise the contrast with the approach taken in this chapter, which seeks to explain the work's organisation and content as appropriate for its own time and purpose. Although the work's allegorical nature has been acknowledged and discussed in recent years in several languages it still remains to describe Bartholomew's 'excellent system' in terms of his own day and readership, in English, and to incorporate Book 19 into the explanatory framework.

I propose that in Bartholomew's work moral and religious themes serve to link and underpin apparent confusion on the surface. These themes are appropriate to religious instruction: the positive aspects of spreading the Word; the passage of our lives and the need for submission to authority, and other virtues; the rewards of serving God; ways towards salvation. While making use of conventional models of piety and service, Bartholomew also expresses Franciscan philosophy and aims: in his attitude to the natural world and the role of the senses, and his evocation of an apostolic, non-enclosed form of religious work.

Foragers and gleaners

Brockhurst's concern over the duplication of chapters on bees provides a starting point from which to examine this apparent anomaly from a thirteenth-century clerical point of view. The image of the bee has an important unifying role in the work as a whole, and Bartholomew's attention to it is significant for our understanding of the work. In the first place, they were ubiquitous domestic creatures with an important economic role in lay community and monastery.[4] Debra Hassig notes in her study of twelfth-century English bestiary manuscripts that in medieval England 'every monastery and abbey had its own apiary, and many of the peasants who worked or rented Church lands also kept bees in order to pay part of their yearly rent in wax'.[5]

Buzzing about the meadows and vineyards, communally producing honey and wax for the careful apiarist, the bee is palpably an orderly, useful creature within a disciplined community of its own. Hassig finds that the communal bee could serve in the Middle Ages as an ideal type of civic order and usefulness, capable of extension into a range of associated ideas. The bestiary texts and illustrations emphasise the bee's associations of orderliness, organisation and a fair division of labour, while the communal ideal represented by the beehive describes a monastic situation of freedom in Christ under the lordship of the abbot, collecting the honey from flowers identified as the love of God. Bees as tractable producers of real honey and church candle-wax readily connoted an ideal of moral and civic order and *utilitas*, while their apparent sexlessness also signified chastity and the Virgin Mary.[6] Ivan Illich, in his study of Hugh of St Victor's treatise on monastic reading, *Didascalicon* (c.1128), states that 'since Christian antiquity, metaphors for spiritual experiences taken from the language of bee-keeping appear whenever new communities of monks grow out of old hermitages'.[7] Michael Twomey lists among the major encyclopaedias of the Middle Ages *Bonum universale de apibus*, 'the definitive medieval study of bees, which develops an extended allegory of spiritual authority'.[8]

According to Neil Hathaway, these major encyclopaedias are themselves justified in the very etymology of the term *compilatio*, which derives from *pilare*, 'to pillage'. Hathaway points out that Macrobius had expressed the idea of the moral usefulness of abstracting from others' works through an analogy with bees, nectar-gathering from others' fields: 'We should in a way imitate the bees which … pluck the flowers, and then whatever they are wont to bring back they divide up into the honeycomb, changing the varied liquor into one flavor by a certain mixture.' Here then are bees serving an allegorical and didactic purpose early in the medieval period. Hathaway argues that the analogy shed its pejorative associations with stealing as Christian writers, notably St Jerome, made use of it.[9] Hathaway's study indicates that by Bartholomew's time compilation was acknowledged as a useful didactic method that brought together, and made available, nourishing and palatable teachings already in existence.

Fertility and growth

The metaphor of nectar-gathering implies fertility and florescence, and opens pathways for medieval writers and readers into a broader moralised landscape of fields, ploughlands and vineyards and associated activities expressing the aims and nature of clerical endeavour: 'the Lord is to be praised', writes Gregory IX in 1233, 'for in this the eleventh hour He has led the Friars Preachers and Minors into His vineyard' to root out heresy. It is an extended metaphor that embraces realities of medieval economy in northern Europe, as well as scriptural parables such as that of the workers in the Lord's vineyard, and the parable of the sower.[10] As Elizabeth Freeman has demonstrated, it was possible for the Cistercian writer Hugh of Kirkstall, a daughter house of Fountains Abbey in England, to celebrate the success of Fountains Abbey using this complex metaphor drawn from writings of Bernard of Clairvaux, founder of his Order. Hugh, a near-contemporary of Bartholomew, wrote the following passage sometime between 1205 and 1226. The image is of vines, bees, seeds, harvest and procreation to signal the Cistercian Order's growth, industry, and success:

> Thus Newminster took its origin. This was the first shoot which our vine put forth; this was the first swarm which went out from our hive. The holy seed sprouted in the soil and, being cast as it were in the lap of fertile earth, grew to a great plant, and from a few grains there sprang a plentiful harvest. This newly founded monastery rivalled her mother in fertility. She conceived and brought forth three daughters, Pipewell, Sawley and Roche.[11]

The above quotation shows a writer combining well-understood metaphors of fertility to express the evangelising aims of the Cistercians in Bartholomew's time, but it also demonstrates an understood precedent that existed for scholars, whether mendicant or monastic, to use imagery of the vine, the beehive, the seed, the gleaner, the cultivation of fertile ground and of female fertility to denote the active work of spreading God's word, nurturing Christian souls and obtaining the rewards of salvation. Francis of Assisi had in some senses been a follower of Bernard, and Bartholomew testifies early on to the latter's importance as an authority.[12]

The properties of bees

In 'Properties' Bartholomew cites *Physiologus* and other sources in his two main chapters on the bee, but numerous brief mentions of it in other chapters serve to carry forward and remind us of Bartholomew's main teaching themes: those of authority, discipline and obedience to one's superiors; of useful, cooperative labour through one's lifespan; of the sweetness and nourishment of God's word flourishing in fertile soil; and of the Franciscan ideal of worship through sensory awareness of *natura*. These themes are intertwined with threads of imagery, including that of bees and other creatures in action; of the seasons and waxing and waning growth; of rest and refreshment; of rebelliousness and submission.

In the *Praefatio* Bartholomew situates himself and his work firmly within the established genre of *compilatio* as a 'gathering' or 'harvesting' of useful fruits of others' labours, by describing himself as a gleaner, the humble and impoverished one who gathers up the harvesters' leavings.[13] Like Hugh of Kirkstall, Bartholomew stresses the idea of genealogical descent and the passing-on of virtue when he refers, in Book 17's chapter on the vine, to the growing vine-shoot as the daughter of a fertile mother. Although, unlike Hugh, he repeats the mother-daughter comparison in several other Books and chapters on diverse topics, he was evidently familiar with the conventional metaphor and expected his readers to be.[14] We may reasonably infer an allusion within the text to the task of the compiler in the several chapters where Bartholomew describes bees gathering nutritious matter from flowers near and far.[15] Their wide range of associations mean that bees flit throughout the work, sometimes briefly referred to and at other times inviting meditation upon their significance to the reader. Bartholomew's own gathered wisdom on bees comes from Pliny, Virgil, Avicenna, Isidore, Ambrose and Aristotle, but his accounts vary in their emphasis and in the kind of analogy they create with human activity, and have a naturalistic quality that suggests they are also drawn from observation.

In the last chapter of Book 1 the allegory of the bee is put in place. Bartholomew introduces the idea of God as honey and sweetness: '[God] has many other names ... "dew and rain" because he makes the soul fruitful with virtues; "honey" for the sweetness that he puts into the soul of mankind.'[16] Then in Book 3, on the soul (including the *anima sensibilis* of the senses), Bartholomew cites the medical authority Constantine on diet: 'for sweetness is very nourishing, and easily assimilated by all the limbs'.[17] In Book 6 the bee serves as a simile that exemplifies the natural preferment of, and submission to, worthy lords among people: 'Ambrose says that among beasts *natura* sets the most noble and strong at their head, and makes kings and leaders among them, as happens among animals and birds and also among bees, which are controlled and led by [these leaders].'[18] In Book 9 on the properties of time, 'Summer feeds and satisfies bees that gather honey from flowers'. Whitsun, seven weeks after Easter, at the start of good, dry weather, is a time of seven-fold grace for Christians from the coming of the Holy Ghost. Military expeditions prepare for action and the bee is part of the general activity:

> And then is the time of all kinds of gladness, joy and mirth, for then all animals and birds are in greatest amity; it is a time of greenness, for then plants and woods come into leaf and growth. It is also a time of fragrance and sweetness from flowers in gardens, groves and meadows, when heaven dries up moisture in flowers and turns it into sweetness. Therefore as Aristotle says it is a good time to make honey, because bees frequent plants and trees on account of their flowers; honey collected in springtime is much sweeter than honey collected at harvest time.[19]

In Book 12, on flying creatures, Bartholomew describes the bee community as obedient to its king, each bee having its allotted task and returning to the hive at night. Some bees gather honey, some nurse the young, and some keep watch against predators.[20] In Book 17 bees and their work are a property of the summer vineyard and of the light-filled tree tops: 'Leaves clothe plants, fields, gardens and woods with beauty and make them delightful with the sweetness that they conceive from the dew of heaven. Therefore bees gather honey when flowers appear; it is a sign of the changing season, and gives hope of fruit.'[21] In Book 18 we are told that the bee deserves to be included among crawling creatures because it uses its legs, as well as its wings, to get along.[22] In this long chapter Bartholomew presents the bee as exemplary in its useful activity, purity and brotherly love. In a complementary chapter he tells how the drones, false bees that do not make honey, steal that of others, kill young bees and are cast out to die.[23] In Book 19, discussed more fully below, we find the products of the bees' industry listed as 'things' with properties we can taste and smell. Liquors, for example, are the natural or man-made products of animals and plants. Honey, he says, is made by the skill of bees from the dew of heaven that falls on flowers.[24] Following chapters are on the properties of honey, honeycomb, *mulsus* or Greek honeyed wine, mead, *claretus* or honeyed wine with spices, *oxymel* or medicated honey, beeswax, and the wax taper or candle.[25]

Much of this may be a matter of observation but, in the context of an allegorical trope where fertility, harvest and honey-gathering express pastoral values, can also be read as religious instruction or *exempla* for sermons. The manuscript glosses in the chapter *De Apibus* indicate that readers could and did associate the image of the bee with an ideal of clerical obedience, care and kindness, humility, contemplation and study. By contrast, glosses in the chapter on the drone bee, *De fuco*, warn against failure in clerical virtue: 'Be mindful of sloth'; 'Take note of humility; of contemplation; of him who comes to be a preacher through study'.[26]

The unstable world

The bee, then, is one of the joyful and salutary aspects of the physical world. Bartholomew does not deny the pleasures of the summer landscape; nevertheless, seasons and weather can cloud the real and the metaphorical landscape. He also has to address the world's wintery and fleeting aspects and to emphasise that the Christian's goal lies beyond this world and in eternity. In the lengthy first chapter of Book 8, Bartholomew sets out definitions of the physical world according to classical writers, in particular Aristotle and Plato, but concludes with Christian teaching derived from St Augustine:

> Although the universe is clothed with so many noble and diverse things by the might and virtue of God, yet as far as this lower world goes, it is totally subject to many faults and much wretchedness. Although this world seems to be father and begetter of bodies, yet it is the prison of spirits, and a most cruel exile for souls, and a place of very great suffering. For the world is a place of sin and guilt, of exile and pilgrimage, of sorrow and woe ... of moving and of changing, of flow and ebb, of decay and corruption, of disease and turmoil, of violence and destruction, of deceit and guile.[27]

According to Aristotle, however, heaven is simple; its movement is even, it is sober, steadfast and abiding, incorruptible and unchanging.[28] In Book 9, on time, Bartholomew tells us that changeableness on earth is caused by, but is different from, the movement of the spheres and takes six forms — generation, corruption, alteration, growth, diminution, and movement from place to place.[29] Nevertheless, in a spirit of Franciscan acceptance of *natura*, Bartholomew presents the change and decay we witness in the changing seasons as a cause for reassurance and joy. *Natura*, he tells us in Book 18, has reasons and remedies for all our discomforts.[30]

In 'Properties', representations of decay and destructiveness accompany and counterbalance those of growth and sweetness, and vice versa. We have seen that the ideas of movement, growth and activity inform the religious metaphors of the vine, the bee, and the mother and daughter, used in the Cistercian chronicle of Hugh of Kirkstall. The same sense of movement pervades 'Properties' in passages describing the actions and effects of people, animals, birds and fishes, plants and trees. These things become sources for positive-spirited meditation on life and death, fertility and salvation.[31] In Book 17 the well-filled panorama of rural labour in vineyard, woods, fields and ploughland can be joyously productive but its guardians have to be vigilant against foxes, caterpillars, nettles and briars. There are also weeds, bad soil, snakes and toads that hide in the foliage, and invading pigs and dogs.[32] The glosses show that destructive animals and weeds could denote moral hazards such as worldly, proud and secular people, as in the chapter on the bramble that snatches at the legs of the unwary walker: 'Take note of the worldly and proud; of the secular; of the sons and disciples of wicked men and heretics; of the works of the wicked; of greedy prelates.'[33] Nature, then, is a salutary reminder of our own vices as well as of God's providence. Brambles and pests are reminders of the way nature balances opposite properties, humours and elements in human life as in the cosmos. In Book 9, on the chapter on the Hebrew festival of the tabernacles, Bartholomew shows how the rewards of autumn balance those of spring: at this harvest festival, fruits are brought and houses decorated, but it is also a time of expiation and repentance. The harvest is gathered and the trees are dry and cold.[34] In Book 17, in the chapter 'On the tree-tops', Bartholomew delivers a sermon, with reference only to the authority of Isidore, on the consolations and hopes we can draw from the seasonal cycle of growth and decay. The leaves that shelter the bees 'are green and growing in spring and summer, fade in autumn, fall one by one as winter comes, and in the end rot into the ground. Leaves are, however, useful as medicine and fodder.' The growth of leaves, flowers and fruit provides protection, remedies, food and enjoyment. Isidore says they are like light: while they last they activate all our senses.[35]

Bartholomew stresses in the last chapters of Book 6 that, as the times of year balance each other, we must balance our diet and complement exercise with rest. As the year turns, so peace and quietness come at the end to crown the turbulence and laboriousness of life. Bartholomew describes the properties of complementary conditions, both general and specific: life and death; childhood and adulthood; male and female; lordship and servitude; waking and sleeping; exercise and rest; food and drink; and, in particular, things that accord with nature and things that are contrary to nature.[36]

Natura and remedies

Bartholomew's Franciscan presentation of *natura* has been the subject of scholarly discussion. In the 1980s, David Greetham commented upon the mix of observation and allegory in 'Properties', and the way Bartholomew emphasises the natural world as a source of both wonder and praise. He finds a pleasing tension in the work between its 'earthbound' appearance and its moralising function.[37] Peter Dronke's important study of *natura* as a Christian concept traces its development over almost 1000 years, from late antiquity to the time of Bernard Silvestris and the school of Chartres.[38] Roger French and Andrew Cunningham clarify the difference between the Franciscan and Dominican uses of the term *natura* and stress the fundamental importance to the Franciscans of particular biblical texts; above all, of Paul's epistle to the Romans: 'For the invisible things of him from the creation of the world are clearly seen, being understood by the things that are made, even his eternal power and Godhead.' The properties of 'the things that are made' need to be understood as a window into the eternal world. For example, as French and Cunningham explain, light is of extreme importance to the Franciscans as the seraphic illumination which had descended upon Francis on Monte Verna. Light was therefore the clearest expression of nature and the primary Franciscan symbol of the unity and power of God.[39]

In Book 2, Bartholomew devotes the second chapter to the properties of angels according to Pseudo-Dionysius, with some reference also to John Damascene, St Gregory and the Bible. He tells us that, according to Damascene, angels receive their light from God and reflect it upon those below. In this way they share with us the hidden sweetness of the goodness of God, received through contemplation and 'tasting' (*contemplando et gustando*).[40] In Book 3, he describes the soul first of all as receptive to divine illumination.[41] In Book 8, the subject of light receives specific and thoroughgoing treatment in a different context of knowledge, that of the earth and heavenly bodies. In the chapters on light in general, glowing light, light reflected and refracted, radiance, shadows and darkness, Bartholomew refers to a host of authorities, including Aristotle, Albumazar, Algazel, Augustine, Basil and Ambrose, to Calcidius' commentary on Plato's *Timaeus*, and to Pseudo-Dionysius *On the divine names*.[42] This is a broad gathering of medieval statements concerning a key phenomenon of the physical and theological universe, in which Bartholomew does not adjudicate but simply makes available the spread of opinion. He does, however, balance the authority of Aristotle with that of Pseudo-Dionysius and other Neoplatonic writers, drawing the reader's attention to the mystical and contemplative as well as physical properties of light. This would be appropriate for students familiar with the already-growing legend of Francis's encounter with the seraph on Monte Verna.[43]

This philosophy of nature, as that which our senses can apprehend as a first step towards God, is one which the Franciscan Bonaventure would later formulate in his *Itinerarium mentis ad Deum*. Bonaventure describes how the invisible things of God can be grasped intellectually through the senses, in contemplation of seven things: the origin, magnitude, multitude, beauty, plenitude, operation and order of the created world.[44] According to Seymour, there is evidence of personal communication between Bonaventure and Bartholomew in a letter of 1266 addressing the older man as *carissimo fratri Bartholomeo ministro Saxonie*. 'Properties' may well have been available to Bonaventure in Paris by this time.[45]

Bartholomew establishes early in the work the reassuring idea that life's dangers and difficulties are counterbalanced by providential supports and remedies. He develops the theme of instability, change, growth and decay with much emphasis on the fecund as well as the degenerate nature of the unstable physical world, but teaches that amid this fecundity it is essential to be discriminating. Some 'things' are harmful, others remedial, and there are those that give us a feeling of closeness to God. Some of them require that we do our bit to make them useful. Book 17 contains chapters on the products of plants that can be processed, such as strong planed timbers for building ships and houses; paper and straw; a medicinal kind of pesto made of burdock leaves, nourishing porridge, raisins; bread-grains, yeast, ointment, olives and their oil.[46] A long section of the Book is devoted to the distinctions that must be made between types of grapes and wine, some being beneficial but others spurious or harmful.[47] The glosses indicate that these chapters were particularly resonant with associations with the Eucharist. They include references to the passion and blood of Christ, to the elevation of the Host, and to the nourishment and growth of charity and virtue: 'Take note concerning the passion of Christ; the raising of the Host; the blood of Christ and its purity.'[48] Glosses on the grape include pointers to fullness and fatness belonging both to the grape itself and to the idea of Christian love.[49] Those on new wine point to novices, argument, and the danger of drunkenness and sensuality.[50] In Book 17 there are also chapters on places where plants grow: within hedges, in prepared fields, and densely in groves, according to the fertility of the place.[51] Bartholomew makes the chapter on the vineyard a focus for meditation on the plants, workers, good and destructive animals and sensory delights of the scene of earthly labour, while the chapter on the cellar tells us that the wine will be all the better for being kept in the cold and dark.[52]

Learning to submit

Plants, as well as bees and other animals, can remind us that we have to grow up, learn discipline from our elders and betters and face the ending of life's day. In Book 17, Bartholomew describes the properties of the root as the part of the plant that draws in nourishment to send to the leaves: roots vary in form; they accord with the nature of the ground in which they are hidden; a root is stronger the deeper it lies; it passes its quality on to the leaves and fruit of the plant, and thence to the seed; it can be edible, medicinal or otherwise useful. Bartholomew overtly likens the root of a plant to a nurse who nourishes the growing child.[53] The glossator points to another level of meaning available within this descriptive account: 'Take note concerning faith and humility; nurture and kindness; the study of the divine Word through reading and listening; the strength of charity; the remission of sin, the choice between good and bad.'[54] The glosses tell us, then, that for a thirteenth-century reader aware of the clerical connotations, the physical reality of a plant's root could serve to exemplify the professional virtue of providing good pastoral care. The glosses also show us that the underlying significance of the small boy resisting his mother's attempts to wash and comb him, described in Book 6, is similar to that of the colt resisting the bridle, described in Book 18.[55] Against Bartholomew's lively and evocative sketch of the mother and child the glossator strikes a sombre and warning note: '[T]ake note concerning those who will not be told about eternal life; those who chatter; those who will not submit to discipline.'[56] Against Bartholomew's lyrical description of the colt allowed to run freely with its mother until the time for training comes, the glossator warns: '[T]ake note concerning subordinates and novices; the wish of subordinates to be prelates; concerning preachers; why the world should be spurned.'[57] Both the small boy and the colt have properties that can point to an underlying lesson — that there are those who have not yet learned to submit to discipline, who are spiritually immature or recalcitrant, noisy or in a hurry, and who do not want to give up worldly things. Examples of wilfulness and discipline, teaching and learning, service and reward, authority and subordination, infancy, growth and maturity crop up again and again in the rest of the work, among the properties of creatures on earth and in the commentary alongside the text. The glosses help us to see how the text creates a web of connected spiritual meanings through the properties of diverse physical things: roots supply nourishment to the growing plant; mothers and nurses give nourishment and guidance to the growing child; the preacher supplies nourishment and guidance to the growing Christian soul. Humans, plants, animals, stones, birds and bees can all point to the same truth.

Lightening the burden

The reader can infer that there is both humour and reassurance to be found in *natura*, who, as Bartholomew mentions in Book 18, citing Pliny, makes marvellous beasts to entertain and astonish us.[58] In Book 17, playing on the word *virga* (rod or twig), Bartholomew links the ideas of florescence and of the Incarnation, a rhetorical device favoured by the Benedictine abbess and poetess Hildegard of Bingen a century earlier.[59] This wordplay reveals Bartholomew's use of literary concepts available in his time and place, but he concludes the chapter with a touch of punning humour and bathos: 'At the same time the rod is hateful to dogs and little boys, because it restrains their bad behaviour.'[60] Another example of his populist touch occurs in his references to the fox in Book 18 and elsewhere. Hassig discusses the array of significations that the image of the bestiary fox could carry, derived from scripture, folklore and daily life: sly hypocrisy, the guile of the devil seeking souls to devour; heresy.[61] Bartholomew's fox in Book 18 is derived from several sources, including scripture, the bestiary and folklore. In *De Vulpe*, Bartholomew reiterates the bestiary descriptions of the fox's crooked gait and untrustworthy ways, but also alludes to popular comic stories about the fox current at his time, recalling that the fox is helped by his friend the stag in his quarrel with the badger. In his chapter on the badger, Bartholomew evokes in a few words a vignette of the animal as a careful householder mindful of his stores, bothered by his greedy wife on one hand and by his impudent neighbour the fox on the other. Fox and badger are nevertheless allied in that they both live in dens and use their hairy coats to protect them against hounds.[62] In these two chapters Bartholomew is apparently alluding to the characters of fox, badger and stag from the *Roman de Renard*, making use of an existing bit of the popular tradition as it existed in his time and place that could engage both readers and sermon audiences.[63] In these examples Bartholomew seems to acknowledge that study, like other forms of labour, can be arduous and that the reader, like the music-loving ox, works better with a bit of cheerful encouragement. The glossator, however, sternly reminds the reader of the fox's connotations of hypocrisy, heresy, greed and guile: 'Take note of the cunning and hypocritical; of entrapments; against the gluttonous.'[64]

Rest and reward

As mentioned above, our to-ing and fro-ing from place to place is one of the six kinds of movement listed by Bartholomew as symptomatic of this world's instability. In the work as a whole, the reader's attention is constantly drawn to images of rest and refreshment after labour or travel. Secular workers and travellers — the labourer, overseer, household servant, builder, land surveyor, foot-traveller, seaman and so on — populate the text, as well as animal workers such as the bee, ox, ass and dog. Among flying creatures, the dove carries letters for long distances at great personal risk; the crane flies far, calls loudly, watches sleeplessly and is ready for battle; the hen looks after her chicks and the bee works all day at a range of tasks. Work can be painful but rewarding: Bartholomew describes the ox as a good animal but one that suffers a lot from outward and inward causes; it has to look at the ground because of the yoke but it loves its fellow, and is loved and cared for by its master. The companion chapter on the ox-herd fills out the picture of obedient labour. Here, Bartholomew gives the reader a glimpse of the ploughman at work, yoking and driving his oxen to and fro, but coaxing them with whistling and songs and giving them refreshment at the end of the day.[65] There is a strong narrative feel to these chapters on the patient ox and the whistling ploughman going about their work, inviting the reader to recall experience of pain and weariness, solace and friendship, as well as of actual labour in the fields.[66] The glosses confirm that clerical readers could understand the imagery of the plough to be about their own work, trials and rewards; glosses on the ox include: 'Take note concerning the prelate's piety and compassion; of the work of prelates and scholars; against those who disparage prelates; of the martyrs; of confessors and their office; of preachers; of preaching.'[67] Glosses on the ox-herd emphasise the disciplinary role of the prelate over subordinates: 'Take note concerning the office of the prelate; of the correcting guidance of prelates; of the correction of subordinates.'[68] We can see why Bartholomew could place *bubulcus* next to *bos* in Book 18; from the preacher's point of view, as well as the ploughman's, they form a team.

In Book 9, evening is described as the time when watchmen take their place on walls and turrets, and when working men and animals are rewarded, paid and allowed to rest. The whole chapter on evening is a naturalistic description of the day's end — shadows lengthening, nocturnal creatures emerging, plants closing, moisture rising, the chilling of the air on the skin, flocks being gathered in and watches set. The homely phrase 'In the evening dogs can hardly be told from wolves' implies both physical and spiritual danger.[69] Here are opportunities for the reader to meditate on the close of life. In the work as a whole the repeated references to evening, with its properties of obscurity, imminent danger and need for refuge, keep readers aware of the ending of life and of the uncertainty of what comes after: will they have earned salvation and reward in the Lord's mansions, or a painful and ignominious casting-out?[70]

The lord's familia

The setting of the parable of the workers in the vineyard was especially meaningful since the narrative had some real-life parallels in thirteenth-century rural life.[71] In Book 6 of 'Properties', Bartholomew takes us indoors, into the manorial household, where we find lord and lady, children, guests and servants. These include not only male workers such as the manservant and steward but also the nurse, the maidservant and the midwife. Here, he presents a sequence of chapters dealing with the most universal and commonplace experiences — those of childhood, of work, domestic relations, mealtimes and bedtimes, sports and pastimes, sleep and dreams — beginning with the first chapter on death, *De morte*, and ending with rest, *De quiete*.[72] The midwife swaddles the newborn infant, the child wilfully struggles under his mother's hand as she tries to wash him, the daughter is cherished by the father, the negligent servant is punished and the good steward rewarded. The image of the maidservant beaten for misbehaviour contrasts with that of the servant or guest in the house of a good lord; rewarded, feasted and secure.[73] The domestic household depicted is strongly hierarchical, with lord and lady presiding over ranks of servants. The range of *dramatis personae* in Book 6 could have allowed readers of all social backgrounds to identify with Bartholomew's normative portrayals of servanthood in the lord's *familia*.

Book 6's chapters on meal-times make palpable the physical and spiritual rewards of belonging to, and serving in, the well-run abode of lord and lady. In *De prandio*, 'On the mid-day meal', Bartholomew tells us that food is prepared;

fellow diners (*conviviae*) are called; forms and stools are set in the hall; trestles, cloths, towels are organised. Guests sit down with the lord at the top of the table, and no-one sits down until the guests have washed their hands. Mothers and daughters take their place, and retainers take theirs. Spoons, knives and salt-cellars are set on the table, then bread, drink and various dishes. Menials and servants cheerfully bring dishes and drinks and joke amongst themselves. There is music. Fruit and *épiceries* conclude the meal, then tables are cleared and moved from the centre of the room; hands are washed and dried. The lord and the guests say grace, and drinks go round again. Finally, everyone goes to rest or back to their own homes. Bartholomew does not need to cite any external authorities, but could be drawing on experience of secular occasions to describe lunchtime in a prosperous household.[74]

Throughout 'Properties', Bartholomew implies the goal of arrival, rest and reward. Whether they be workers in the household or travellers emerging from the thickets and arriving at the walls before the gates close, all can have a share in the lord's feast at the end of the day. Bartholomew puts this reassuring idea clearly in place in Book 6, where he describes the evening meal at the lord's house.[75] Here, all is decorous conviviality, sensory enjoyment, relaxation and rest. There are people, colours, music, candles, lights, delicious food and wine, and darkness and moths are shut out. All ranks are present, and again it is, in a sense, a scene which the reader can concretise from actual experience, whether sitting at the head or the foot of the table (above or below the salt, as the saying goes) or serving up in the kitchen, and be fully involved in mind, body and spirit. At the same time, early in the chapter Bartholomew makes explicit reference to the Old Testament story of the feast of Ahasuerus, foreshadowing the New Testament promise of the 'many mansions' prepared for the faithful.[76] Such descriptions allow the reader to reflect on actual life and service within the manorial household, but also on an ideal of life spent in the service of God.

Bartholomew keeps familiar images of service and lordship before the reader from first to last. In Book 1, on the properties and names of God, he puts in place an ideal of lordship drawn from the most authoritative sources: for Damascene, God is perfect unity, light itself, a mystical circle; St Bernard describes God in terms of fruitfulness, benevolence and loving rule; the blessed Dionysius (St Denis) describes God as the father of fathers, shepherd of his flock, only describable by figures of speech.[77] Book 2 then presents the orders of good angels as ideal servants of God, and Lucifer as the archetype of the disobedient servant.[78] The idea of good and bad governance recurs in Book 5, where the soul is described as ruler of the body, and the limbs and organs have separate tasks; if the head is well disposed or distempered, all the limbs follow suit.[79] In Book 6, chapters on good lordship and good service spell out the ideal relationship, while chapters on bad lordship and bad servants present the reverse.[80]

In Book 6 the notion of lordship and service is extended to the mutual relations of man and wife in a colourful and courtly passage. The man woos a bride, gives gifts in exchange for her, takes her into his house and bed, looks after and corrects her, and makes her mistress over his money and *familia*; he takes care of her interests just as much as his own.[81] The economic concerns of the *dominus* and *domina* are referred to in the chapter on the good servant, who, among other virtues, is meek but eager to procure the profit of his lord; he takes more heed to multiply and grow his lord's goods and cattle than his own, for in multiplying his lord's cattle he procures his own profit. A good servant is careful to give an account of what he has taken and delivered of his lord's goods and cattle, for he hopes to have payment and reward for good stewardship.[82] This normative but lively picture of the *familia*, complete with marriage, money and orderly housekeeping, not only recalls scriptural parables of good service but also seems appropriately evocative for the Franciscan committed to a life without fixed abode or domestic comfort. Bartholomew's description of the man wooing, wedding and bedding the bride might have suggested a compensatory vision for the celibate Christian cleric, one that we know was promoted by Bernard of Clairvaux in his imagery of the mystical espousal to the church celebrated in the *Song of Songs*.[83]

The celibate servant

For the compiler and his contemporaries, the *familia* could be a religious as well as a secular institution, manifest in the religious orders and houses. It was also a visionary one, where Father, Son and Holy Spirit were joined by the Virgin as Christ's mother and the church as his bride. In the womb of the Church lay souls waiting to be nurtured by priests and preachers. The emphasis on feminine forms of service in Book 6 and elsewhere in 'Properties' can be seen as appropriate for male religious in the light of this medieval trope, and of recent studies of female and male fertility as a complex metaphor for the pastoral role of the clergy.[84] Taking this further, the glosses confirm that readers could draw from certain chapters the idea that physical procreation could be joyfully embraced as a metaphor for clerical office. Some indicate, for example, that clerical readers could see their own relationship with Christ, their own spiritual nurture and their own office reflected in the figure of the nurse: 'Take note concerning Christ; of the teaching of the masters; of the office of prelate and of subordinates.'[85] In the following chapter on the midwife, the glossator infers the ideal compassion of preachers as they help to bring forth Christian souls from the womb of the church: 'Take note of preachers and their office; of compassion; of the prelate and the preacher.'[86] The inclusion in Book 18 of chapters on the feminine or female, on gestation and on the foetus are thus by no means anomalous in the context of this metaphorical understanding, as the glossator makes clear in relation to the foetus: 'Take note concerning sons in the womb of the church.'[87]

In such positive representations of clerical and pastoral office we can discern what, in effect, appears as an idealised third gender — the celibate creature who performs both masculine and feminine roles. In the chapters cited above and elsewhere, Bartholomew subtly reinforces the idea that preaching can be both nurturing and fertilising. In Book 13's long last chapter on the properties of fishes, he cites Aristotle on the ways fishes reproduce: 'For certain [fishes] are engendered through coitus and emission of sperm, as Aristotle says.'[88] The gloss alongside makes clear the implied analogy with spreading the word: 'Take note concerning the preacher.'[89] In Book 12, on flying creatures, Bartholomew emphasises the cock's masculine properties of vigour, aggressive display and male ardour but also feminine compassion; and in the case of the hen, feminine properties of submissiveness to the male, modesty and maternal love. The glosses indicate that these properties could pertain to preachers. Those against the chapter on the cock include: 'Take note concerning the labour of the good and of works of piety; of the compassion of women.'[90] Glosses against the chapter on the hen include: 'Be on your guard against vain glory; take note of compassion; of pastoral care.'[91] In the chapter on the castrated capon, Bartholomew portrays a creature in which both masculine and feminine properties are absent or subverted; the capon is fleshy but sexless, and neither defends nor nurtures. In the end it is good only for taking to the oven and eating.[92] The glosses confirm that mere inactive neutrality could be associated (as in the case of the drone bee) with ineffective, carnal and useless clerics and hypocrites, and warn of their ending. On the other hand, the properties of familiar creatures such as the ox or bee could imply an active role for the celibate, and the clerical life could be envisaged as a productive, rewarding, procreative state embracing the best of men's and women's sexual roles. To be merely neuter was to be useless, but the preacher, like the un-mated nurse, could be a privileged surrogate mother.[93]

Travelling through the world and the book

I have argued that Bartholomew's early readers could interpret the properties of things in the everyday world — fishes, farmyard poultry, the ploughman and his team, bees and other creatures — as reminders of the preacher's role, vows and hopes of heaven. However, while the image of the bee was ideal for the monastic worker, enclosed in a hierarchical community and separated from the world, Franciscans entering into apostolic missionary work had no such assurance of subsistence or protection. They were committed to a life of homelessness as well as celibacy. Bartholomew's recurring mentions of *peregrines, viatores, transeuntes, ambulantes, navigantes* and *remiges* (pilgrims, wayfarers, travellers, walkers, mariners and rowers) seem appropriate to the needs of students who expected to be literally exposed to perilous contact with the world in a way that enclosed monastic *laborantes* were not.

Bartholomew's description of the migratory crane in Book 12 tends to support the view that while the moralised image of the bee matched beautifully the ideals of *opus Dei, castitas* and *stabilitas* of the enclosed Orders, the mendicants needed a more adventurous metaphor to express their aims. The crane's bestiary character suited the Franciscans in some of its features: according to the bestiary the crane looks after its brothers, obeys and follows its leader on long journeys, is grey in colour, has a loud voice, fights pigmies armed with arrows and keeps watch holding a stone in one claw.[94] Bartholomew in *De grue*, 'On the crane', refers to bestiary authorities but he restricts his account to the strength of the crane's voice and the wings, the urge to seek far places, the orderliness of the brotherhood and especially the office of the leader, who is replaced if he grows hoarse, and the bird's vigilance and defensive strategies.[95] In an early manuscript of 'Properties', against the first line of the column text the glossator has put: 'Take note concerning the lord's ascension.'[96] From this we might reasonably infer an analogy between this bird's strong upward flight and Christ's Ascension from Mt Olivet.[97] But if we consult the early-fourteenth-century *Liber rerum moralizatae,* the collection of preaching *exempla* based on parts of 'Properties', on the moral properties of the crane, we find that the Franciscan compiler of this later work expands on the gloss to convey a wider meaning relevant to his Order. The redactor first repeats Bartholomew's account and then enlarges upon the significance of the crane's large wings, strong voice and lofty flight in search of distant places:

> The crane, briefly, is found among the authors to have these conditions or properties. First, as Ambrose says in the *Hexameron*, it is a bird of large wings and strong flight, seeking the high air like a pilgrim seeking those regions. It signifies powerful prelates or [ ] great and famous contemplatives, as was Paul, who was snatched up suddenly towards a beam of light and into Paradise, where he heard the words of the archangel which it is not lawful to hear in this place. It was written of the blessed Francis who, on such strong and powerful wings, [ ] was many times suspended in rare and sweet contemplation, and indeed the Seraphim irradiated him with glory so that he might become altogether one with God, with whom he is now become like a bird of the angels.[98]

This passage in the later work tends to confirm that, for Franciscan readers especially, the strong upward flight of the crane could connote an ideal of ecstatic contemplation and the light-filled apotheoses of the Order's spiritual great ones, recounted in scripture and legend: that of St Paul ('caught up to the third heaven' in a vision) and of St Francis (lifted up in ecstatic contemplation on Monte Verna).[99] It strongly suggests that the later work might provide important

'Properties' as a guide to salvation

complementary data for the study of 'Properties'; it also reminds us that the full freight of meaning of the glosses may now be lost, along with stories they could once evoke.

We need not assume that medieval readers read 'Properties' from Book 1 to Book 19; the sequence of Books and chapters may reflect a thinking and organising process rather than a set plan for the reader. Nevertheless, the reader, too, can be considered as a kind of traveller through the book. As Roger Chartier observes, reading can be seen as a kind of work and a kind of travel.[100] In the thirteenth-century context, 'Properties' as a 'world book' also implies a journey for the reader through the properties of created things, just as the world itself is a place of *peregrinatio* or pilgrimage.[101]

A respected precedent existed in the words of St Augustine for seeing, within every actual or contemplated journey, a pilgrimage towards our true home that is not of this world:

> Suppose, then, we were wanderers in a strange country, and could not live happily away from our fatherland, and that we felt wretched in our wandering, and wishing to put an end to our misery determined to return home. We find, however, that we must make use of some mode of conveyance, either by land or water, in order to reach that fatherland where our enjoyment is to commence ... Such is a picture of our condition in this life of mortality. We have wandered far from God; and if we wish to return to our Father's home, this world must be used, not enjoyed, so that the invisible things of God may be clearly seen, being understood by the things that are made — that is, that by means of what is material and temporary we may lay hold upon that which is spiritual and eternal.[102]

Bartholomew reminds the reader from time to time that we are all pilgrims through life and, like travellers by land and sea, are at risk of getting lost in the dark or in bad weather, of arriving late, being distracted, encumbered or poorly prepared. In Book 1, Bartholomew tells us that God is announced by many names, including way, life and truth.[103] The notion of the travelling and endangered soul is introduced at the beginning of Book 3, on the soul and reason. Here, Bartholomew describes a difficult concept in concrete terms: 'For [the soul] is one with the body as a driving force is one with a moving object, and as the sailor is one with his boat.'[104] Thereafter the reader is given glimpses, scattered in several Books, of the fallible wayfarer and the frail mariner on dangerous routes, threatened by many hazards but aided by stars, islands, winds, floating spars or stabilising barnacles on the hull. In Book 9 we are reminded that although daylight turns to darkness the movement of the heavens can give light and guidance to travellers: '[I]n the darkness of night wayfarers and mariners easily miss the right way, unless they are guided by the movement and position of the stars.'[105] In Book 13's chapter on the sea, discussed more fully in the next chapter, Bartholomew warns that the inadequately captained ship may come late to the harbour.[106] In Book 17, brambles are troublesome to passers-by, they spread everywhere, blunt the knife, catch at the feet and clothing, scratch the hands.[107] The short phrases, plentiful verbs, graphic details, recognisable brambles and memories of the sensations of such an everyday experience, all invite the reader to identify with this walker. In Book 17 we also see the walker in a dark wood, where the light is dim and robbers lurk waiting to rob or strangle the passer-by. The properties of dense woods include both dangers and delights for the traveller: on the one hand pagan rites are enacted in their darkness, snakes lurk, there are many paths, and it is easy to be led astray by false signs and pointers made by robbers. On the other hand, birds find shelter there from predators, and bees find hollow trees in which to hide their honey.[108] These are all things that we know and experience as part of active daily life and work. As on any cross-country excursion, the traveller through the world — or vicariously through the world book — needs to have faith and rely on guiding signs, but may find sources of enjoyment along the way. The reader can pick up references to them throughout the compilation — but all paths lead to Book 19.

Book 19: Coming full circle

The unassuming rubric of Book 19 has given the impression of a casual ragbag of leftover topics.[109] While the topics have an undeniably bric-a-brac appearance at first sight, I would argue that they combine to create a single overarching idea: that earthly things can lead us to an understanding of heavenly things and to reconciliation with God. The final Book deals with the ways in which we perceive through our senses 'the accidents of matter' in terms of colour, flavour, shape, weight, number and sound. The chapters on colours, tastes and smells, sounds, quantities and vessels implicitly refer back to experiences of vineyard and manorial hall. We have seen that Books 6, 9 and 13 reinforce the idea of homecoming, rest and reward at evening. Books 12 to 18 itemise the raw materials of the lord's feast: foods and drink, timber, flax, dyes, clays, metals, shells, leather, candle wax and more. Book 17 refers to a wide range of plant foods, cooking and processing, growers and harvesters, and the properties of grapes and wines. Book 19 then anatomises the lord's feast in its chapters on colour, taste and smell; milk and milk products; honey and beeswax; vessels and money; order, measure and music, and the senses through which we perceive and evaluate all these. As we have seen, the bee is an idealised worker in constant motion, and in Book 19 the products of the bees' activity are itemised as those which can be tasted, eaten and drunk, and above all used to make light.[110] Bartholomew recounts how beeswax candles illumine those things which are hidden in darkness. They have three properties: material, use and shape. The material is three-fold: wick, wax and flame; they are pyramidal in shape. Carried before lords, they are used to light the way.[111] The final Book of 'Properties' offers the reader a sense of purpose to the bees' industry in this description of the end-product, the light-giving candle, with its three-fold qualities emphasising the religious and platonic associations of the number three and the triangle.[112]

Good doctrine and good works

Book 19 brings together in its chapters the diversity of 'things' and the many distinct tasks and processes they impose on us. At the start of its chapters on numbers, weights, measures and unity, Bartholomew cites *The Book of Wisdom* on God's ordering of creation: 'For it is not said in vain, "You have made all things in number, weight and measure."'[113] We see how material 'things' involve work in their production, processing and use; their properties have to be taken into account in a practical way. Clothes have to be dyed, pigments ground, food cooked, wax made into candles. Oil has to be put into lamps, milk made into junket, butter, cheese. The chapters on milk inform the reader that it can come from mammals in general and, in particular, from camels, cows, goats, sheep, asses, mares and pigs.[114] It can be turned into buttermilk, butter, fresh cheese, matured cheese and curds.[115] This is matter of fact, but the glossator points to the teaching of doctrine (*doctrina*) as the real subject of the chapters. Like milk, Christian teaching can be sound and nourishing, warm, pure and refreshing, flavoursome, unwholesome and bad, or just right. It can be flavoured or suspect; and like the flow from the teat, the ideas and words of preachers who at first have a lot to say can gradually dry up.[116] Bartholomew devotes considerable space to eggs and their properties — not only the eggs of birds, but also of ants and spiders, turtles, dragons, toads, locusts, snakes, gryphons, crabs and crocodiles. Eggs can be cooked but may be digestible or indigestible, according to the creatures from which they come.[117] The glossator shows us that Bartholomew's odd-seeming lists of eggs, far from being anomalous, can be understood as signifiers of salvation through good works, though not all works are necessarily good. The glosses on eggs include: 'Take note what the works of just men ought to be like; concerning the fertile soil of grace and devotion; how vainglory destroys works.'[118] Doves' eggs can signify the works of the simple and good; eagles' eggs those of the powerful, and also Christ in the heart; dragons' eggs, however, are a warning of those with power and hidden malice; spiders' eggs signify the lazy works of hypocrites and heretics, and the eggs of ants are like those of the poor.[119] While it seems safe to conclude from the annotations that the chapters on milk, eggs, honey and wax could hold spiritual and liturgical associations, it is not possible here to fully unravel the symbolic causes, conditions and effects of the other material items mentioned in Book 19.

The chapters on tastes, aromas and foods should remind us that this was a literary culture in which Hugh of St Victor and Bernard of Clairvaux had portrayed reading as chewing, tasting and swallowing for the replenishment of the soul.[120] Bartholomew makes palatable doctrines that were complex, controversial and highly scholastic. The term 'accident', for example, had a far-from-casual philosophical meaning which, in the context of contemporary debate about the transformation of matter, Thomas Aquinas (1225–74) expounded in the articles of his *Summa Theologica*. Chapters in Book 19 treat materials which, like the Eucharist, involve changes: butter, cheese, curds and whey are all essentially milk; honey, mead, candle-wax are all essentially that which bees make. There is also a chapter on change itself: 'On coagulation'. Spiced and sweetened wines are still essentially wine. It is surely no accident that Bartholomew reiterates examples of the transformation of matter at a time when the relationship between a thing's inner substance, or *substancia*, and its outer appearance, or *species*, was a highly important issue for the church.[121] For Bartholomew, writing when Aristotelian philosophy appeared to be at odds with the church's teaching and when the nature of transubstantiation was the subject of much debate, the 'appearance of those things which are of frequent use' and their physical properties were important and controversial.[122] Beneath appearances and properties lay the possibility of a conversion to something useful and even divine. In Book 19's accounts of the conversion of milk into butter, junket and cheese; of beeswax into candles; of honey and wines into medicines, we may justifiably infer an allusion to the spiritual transformation believed to be effected at the Mass.

Choosing the right path

The work as a whole, then, presents a conflation of joyful rewarding feasts: the actual, the scriptural, the liturgical and the eschatological. But first it is necessary to arrive and to be judged. In Book 19 Bartholomew describes different kinds of road, footpath and track, with their uses and hazards, making clear that before arriving at the desired refuge the traveller has a choice of paths and the chance of further danger from robbers at the crossroads.[123] Glosses against this chapter indicate choices of career available to medieval readers — religious or military, for instance — and the need to follow example and advice: 'Take note concerning the multiplicity of ways; of precepts and advice; of the path of religion; of the path of the warrior.'[124] It is as if the compiler, having brought the reader to this final stage, leaves it to him or her to decide what happens next. The reader's identification with the traveller comes to a logical endpoint.

Harmony and reconciliation

In Book 19, the themes of work and of travel culminate in images of movement towards God, of judgement, but also of communion, light and harmony. As we have seen, the reader can become an imaginary participant in the lord's feast, drawing on memory to savour the light of candles, the taste of honey, milk, butter, cheese, eggs, amid the clutter and clatter of vessels and the harmonising effect of music. One effect on the reader of Book 19 is of a climax to the diversity of properties and things in creation, a confusing cacophony of artefacts, substances and conflicting sense impressions. Out of this diverse clutter, Bartholomew draws an elegant effect of closure by returning to his original theme of heavenly unity and perfection, in his praise of the divine properties of the numbers one and three and of the circle, as they represent the Trinity and the perfection of God. In the last Book, Bartholomew returns to a paradoxical analogy with which he begins, bringing the work itself full circle. In Book 1 he had described God in philosophical terms as universal and infinite creator: 'God is the sphere of intellect whose centre is everywhere, and indeed its circumference is nowhere ... thus God brings forth his creations and also confines them.'[125] He repeats this near the end of Book 19: 'God [says the philosopher Secundus] is the intellectual circle, whose centre is everywhere, and circumference nowhere. From which it is clear that the meaning of that circle glimmers in all creation.'[126] In his description of the properties of the circle and the number one, Bartholomew also unites the practical with the theological functions of the work and brings together as compatible and complementary his Christian and pagan sources, citing both Aristotle and Hermes Trismegistos in support of Christian teaching. He concludes, through the technicalities of musical harmony, on the note of cosmic unity with which he began: music reconciles the oppositions and calms the strife caused by the six kinds of movement on earth. It comforts rowers, makes all kinds of labour bearable and encourages warriors.[127] The word *remiges*, rowers, conveys a sense of physical labour and also recalls the above-mentioned description of the soul which, starting out early in Book 3, is at one with the body as a mariner is at one with his boat. In this focus upon arrival, reconciliation and harmony, Book 19 seems to remind the reader of his or her spiritual goal — what Sylvain Louis refers to as 'ce qu'il faut atteindre'.[128] This effect of wholeness endorses Christel Meier's conclusion, noted in the previous chapter, that a characteristic of the world-book genre is the demonstration of underlying order and logic beneath the apparent chaos of the world.

To sum up and conclude this chapter: Bartholomew's image of the world, far from being a static account of the properties of things, is dynamic in that it contains many descriptions of people and things in action and rest, growth and decay, transit and flux. The six kinds of movement afflict the earth and living things, but *natura* providentially mitigates their effects and balances decay with growth; harm with remedy; discord with harmony, the unstable with the stable. What is more, our senses allow us to enjoy and praise God's creation and thus to begin an ascent towards Him, reminded by the properties of natural things that rest and reward await the penitent. Overall, Bartholomew makes strong contrasting statements about the coldness, instability and trouble of the physical world, set far from the sun, as in the preamble to Book 8; and about the joy and solace to be gained from things put into the world at Creation: light, stars, air, water, land, and the plants and creatures that 'adorn' these elements.

The medieval *compilatio* implied a long-established pastoral metaphor of gathering, as bees gather honey or gleaners gather corn. Bartholomew builds upon these familiar analogies to engage the reader imaginatively in the idea of earthly labour as preparation for heavenly salvation. Fragments from an implied larger narrative — in particular, those of the worker and the traveller, and of the ranks of the *familia* at their occupations, indoors and out — invite meditation upon narratives from the Christian Scriptures. Recalling the parable of the workers in the vineyard, the ox and oxherd, the bee, the vine, and the good servant all serve as models for material and spiritual labour, reward, fertility and fruition, and thus their recurring presence in the work can be seen as logical and necessary for its didactic purpose. Although this underlying logic in the work is not immediately apparent to us today, we can work towards it with the help of the glosses, and through an awareness of the parables of salvation available to Bartholomew and a segment of his readers. While the thirteenth-century marginal glosses confirm that busy clerics could find in 'Properties' a handy guide to exegesis, the narratives suggest that they could also ruminate upon the fundamental Christian themes of repentance and salvation as they dipped into the work in a spirit of contemplation. Approaching 'Properties' as a thematic and multivalent work places Book 19 in a fresh light. In the last Book, Bartholomew focuses the reader's attention on the significance of our senses and how the myriad distinctions we make in everyday experience can teach us about salvation. He brings home the message of St Paul to the Romans: 'For the invisible things of him from the creation of the world are clearly seen, being understood by the things that are made, even his eternal power and Godhead.'[129] Earthly products and processes remind us of spiritual ones, and lead us back into the narratives of working, feasting at the Lord's table, and travelling through life. Numbers, shapes and music remind us of heavenly order and spiritual harmony with God. It may be scarcely possible for a modern reader to elucidate Book 19 as a whole, but it calls for a more satisfactory modern interpretation as a fitting culmination, rather than a tailing-off, of 'Properties'.

While the trope of the vineyard and the beehive represented an ideal of pastoral labour appropriate for cloistered religious, those who sought to follow the apostolic example of St Francis and St Paul might, as the evidence of the *Liber de moralitatibus* suggests, identify their role-models as strong-winged cranes with loud voices, and prepare themselves likewise to make long journeys into the unknown. The explicit moralisations of the selected topics in this later adaptation of 'Properties' tend to confirm the view that the glosses in 'Properties' were made as a scholarly aid or index rather than as a full explanation of the significance of the column text. In the next chapter we will consider 'Properties' as a map and guide to survival in the world and to salvation beyond it.

NOTES

[1] DrP, *Bartholomaei Anglici, in suos De Proprietatibus Rerum Libros, Praefatio*, pp.1–3.

[2] Delisle, p.362.

[3] Brockhurst, 1952, pp.33–4.

[4] Duby, Georges and Cynthia Postan (trans), *Rural Economy and Society in the Medieval West*: University of South Carolina Press, 1968, pp.116 foll.

[5] Hassig, 1995, p.51.

[6] Hassig, 1995, pp.49–52, p.215, n.10. Klingender (pp.354 foll) illustrates the association between bees and the Virgin with twelfth-century rolls of the *Exultet*, the hymn of thanksgiving sung during the blessing of the Easter candles attributed to St Augustine, which includes a long passage in praise of the bees.

[7] Illich, Ivan, *In the Vineyard of the Text: A Commentary to Hugh's Didascalicon*: University of Chicago Press, 1993, p.55 n.19.

[8] Twomey, 1988, p.198.

[9] Hathaway, p.25 and n.30.

[10] Pope Gregory IX in the Bull *Benedicimus Deum coeli*, 1233: Landini, p.64. Duby, pp.137–41, describes the spread of viticulture in France during the eleventh–twelfth centuries and the involvement of all ranks of workers, clerical and lay, in this economy.

[11] Freeman, Elizabeth, "Meaning and multi-centeredness in (postmodern) medieval historiography: the foundation history of Fountains Abbey", *Parergon* n.s.16, no.2 (1999): 43–84, pp.66–8; see also Barney, Stephen A., "'The plowshare of the tongue': the progress of a symbol from the Bible to Piers Plowman", *Medieval Studies* 35, no.263 (1973): 261–93; and Dolan, T. P., "The plowman as hero" in *Heroes and Heroines in Medieval English Literature*, edited by Leo Carruthers, 97–103, Cambridge: D. S. Brewer, 1994, on agricultural imagery in medieval religious texts.

[12] DrP, Bk 1, cap xvii, p.13: *Quomodo Bernardus describit Deum*, (*Deus est foecundans ad fructum*).

[13] DrP, *Praefatio*, p.3: *picae quae effugerunt manus metentium*.

[14] DrP, Bk 17, *De proprietatibus plantarum*, cap cxviii *De Propagine*, p.900. See also Bk 15, cap xxviii *De Brittannia*, p.638; Bk 14, cap xxxvii *De Monte Sion*, p.613; Bk 6, cap vii *De Matre*, p.241 and cap viii *De Filia*, p.242; Bk 19, cap viii *De Opinione eorum, qui ponunt lucem esse de substancia coloris*, p.1146.

[15] DrP, Bk 18, cap xi *De ape*, pp.1013–9; Bk 12 cap iv *De Apibus*, pp.520–4; Bk 9 cap v *De aestate*, p.442; cap xxxi *De Pentecoste*, p.466.

[16] DrP, Bk 1, cap xxi *De diversis Christi nominibus*, p.17. Author's paraphrases here and below.

[17] DrP, Bk 3, cap xx *De Gustu*, p.71. See Illich, p.55, on the metaphors of tasting and cud-chewing (*ruminans*) used by Hugh of St Victor and others to express the experience of monastic reading as a 'carnal activity' in which God's power is felt as sweetness.

[18] DrP, Bk 6, cap xviii *De bono Domino*, p.254.

[19] DrP, Bk 9, cap v *De Aestate*, p.442; cap xxxi *De Pentecoste*, pp.465–6.

[20] DrP, Bk, 12 cap iv *De Apibus*, pp. 510–24.

[21] DrP, Bk 17, cap lxxiii *De Flagellis*, pp.849–50.

[22] DrP, Bk, 18 cap xi *De Ape*, p.1013.

[23] DrP, Bk 18, cap liii *De Fuco*, pp.1073–74.

[24] DrP, Bk 19, cap li *De liquore* , p.2182.

[25] DrP, Bk 19, caps lii-lx *De liquore in speciali et primo de melle; De Favo; De Mulso; De Medone; De Clareto, De Oxymelle; De Cera; De Cereo*, pp.1183–9.

[26] Wellcome Inst. ms 115, f.79r: *Nota contra ociosos; Nota de humilitate; Nota de [ ] contemplationes; Nota que per studium reditus est ad predicationem*.

[27] DrP, Bk 8, cap i *Quid sit mundus*, pp.371–2. Author's paraphrase.

[28] DrP, Bk 8, cap ii *De coelorum distinctione*, pp.374–5.

[29] Preamble to Bk 9 *De proprietatibus Temporis*, p.434: *Et sunt sex species motus, scil[icet] generatio, corruptio, alteratio, augmentatio, diminutio, secundum locum mutatio, ut dicit idem.*

[30] DrP, Bk 18, *Prooemium*, p.974.

[31] See, for example, DrP, Bk 17, cap lxxiv *De Fructu*, p.851; cap lxxv *De Germine*, p.853; cap lxxxi *De Grana*, p.859; cap cxviii *De Propagine*, p.900; cap xxxvii *De Radice*, p.915; cap cxlix *De Spina*, p.928; cap clvi *De Semine*, p.932; cap clxxv *De Virga*, p.946; cap clxxvi *De Virgulto*, p.947.

[32] Chapters on specific pests occur in Books 17 and 18, and troublesome birds in Book 12; see, for example, Bk 17, cap clxxx *De Vinea*, pp. 952–3; cap cxciii *De Urtica*, pp.965–6; cap clxx *De Tribulo*, pp.942–3.

[33] BNF Lat. ms 67098 f.198r: *Nota de mundanis et superbis;Nota de secularibus;Nota de filiis et discipulis malorum et hereticorum;Nota de operibus malorum;Nota contra hereticos; Nota de cupidis prelatis.*

[34] DrP, Bk 9, cap xxxii *De Scenopegia*, pp.466–7; see also cap vii *De Autumno*, p.443–4; cap xxxiii *De Encania*, pp.467; Bk 6, cap xxix *De quiete*, pp.275–6; Bk 8, cap xlv *De Tenebra*, p.433.

[35] DrP, Bk 17, cap lxxiii *De Flagellis*, pp.849–50.

[36] DrP, Bk 6, preamble, p.231; cap xxix *De quiete*, p.275.

[37] Greetham, D. C., "The concept of nature in Bartholomeus Anglicus (floruit 1230)", *Journal of the History of Ideas*, XLI (1980), pp.663–77.

[38] Dronke, Peter, "Bernard Silvestris, Natura, and personification" in Dronke, ed, *Intellectuals and Poets in Medieval Europe*, 41–61. Rome: Edizione de storia e letteratura, 1992.

[39] AV, *St Paul's Epistle to the Romans* 1:20 (although BA would have known the Vulgate version of the Scriptures the AV is cited here for the convenience of readers). French and Cunningham, pp.210–11, 221: after BA's time the Franciscan writers Bonaventura, Grosseteste (not a member of, but sympathetic to, the Order) and Roger Bacon relied especially on the work of Pseudo-Dionysius in their studies of the spiritual and mystical properties of light; see also Illich, p.20, on the scholastic notion of *lumen oculorum* and reading as a recovery of light lost at the Fall.

[40] DrP, Bk 2, cap ii *Quid sit Angelus secundum Damascenum*, p.21. See n.17 above.

[41] DrP Bk 3, cap iii *De Anima*, p.46: *Anima est substantia insubstantia incorporea, intellectualis, illuminationis a primo ultima relatione perceptiva. Ex qua diffinitione primam & praecipuam cognoscimus rationalis animae proprietatem, spiritus enim humanus mediante prius angelos, est divine illuminationis receptivus.*

[42] DrP, Bk 8, cap xl *De Luce & eius proprietatibus*, pp.425–30; cap xli *De Splendore*, p.430; cap xlii *De Lumine*, pp.430–2; cap xliii *De Radio*, pp.431–2; cap xliv *De Umbra*, pp.432–3; cap xlv *De Tenebra*, p.435.

[43] Brooke, Rosalind B., ed, *The Writings of Leo, Rufino and Angelo Companions of St. Francis*, Oxford: The Clarendon Press, 1970, pp.6, 8, 340–1 and passim.

[44] Boas, George, *St. Bonaventure's Itinerarium Mentis in Deum: The Mind's Road to God*, Indianapolis: Bobbs-Merrill Educational Publishing, 1953, p.12.

[45] Seymour, 1992, p.4.

[46] See, for example, DrP, Bk 17, cap clxii *De Tabula*, p.937; cap clxiii *De Trabe*, p.938; cap clxvii *De Tigno*, p.939; cap cxxvi *De Papyro*, p.906; cap clvii *De Stipula*, p.935; cap ciii *De Myrrho*, p.880; cap xciii *De Lappate*, p.870; cap lxv *De Frumento*, p.842; cap clxxxiii *De Uva passa*, p.955; cap cxi *De Olea*, p.887; cap cxii *De Oleo*, p.890; cap cxiii *De Oleastro*, p.890; cap cxiv *De Olere*, p.892.

[47] DrP, Bk 17, caps clxxvii–cxc *De Vite, De Vite agresti, De Vitulamine, De Vinea, De Uva, De Uva immatura, De Uva passa, De Vino, De Vino rubeo, De Vino novo, De Vino condito, De Vino acetoso, De Vinacio, De Vinaria*, pp.948–64. In cap clxxix *De Vitulamine*, p.952, BA cites the *Book of Wisdom*, Hrabanus Maurus and St Augustine on the spurious or bastard vine, and the need to be able to distinguish it from the true vine; Hugh of St Victor had used the idea of the vineyard, grapes, vine supports, sticks and building materials as a complex analogy for the reading and learning process as gathering and building, in his treatise on reading and preaching, the *Didascalicon* (cited in Hassig, 1995, p.59, n.47).

[48] BNF Lat. ms 67098, f.201r; see DrP, Bk 17, cap clxxxiv *De Vino*, pp.956–8.

[49] BNF Lat. ms 67098, f.200v; see DrP, Bk 17, cap clxxxi *De Uva*, pp.953–5.

[50] BNF Lat. ms 67098, f.202r; see DrP, Bk 17, cap clxxxvi *De Vino novo*, pp.960–1.

[51] See, for example, DrP, Bk 17, cap clii *De Sepe*, p.930; cap cliii *De Sude*, p.931; cap cxlii *De Saltu & eius proprietatibus*, p.922; cap clxxx *De Vinea*, p.952; cap cxc *De Vinaria*, p.964.

[52] DrP, cap clxxx *De Vinea*, p.952; cap cxc *De Vinaria*, p.964.

53 DrP, Bk 17, cap cxxxvii *De radice*, pp.915–8.

54 BNF ms 67098, f.191v: *Nota de fide et humilitate; Nota de benignitate; Nota de studio et auditu verbi divinis; Nota de fortitudine caritatis; Nota de remissione peccatoris; Nota de societate bona et mala.*

55 DrP, Bk 6, cap v *De Puero*, pp.238–40; Bk 18, cap xi *De Poledro*, pp.1058–60: *Sed in fine labori exponitur & loris, & capistris coarctatur, a matre subtrahitur, ubera fugere non permittitur, suaves cursus facere multipliciter informatur, & ut dicit Isido. lib. 14. aurigis exponitur, quadrigis & curribus subiicitur, equestri militiae deputatur, variis fortunae fortibus pauper equi filius propagatur.*

56 BNF Lat. ms 67098, f.52r: *Nota de illis qui non auratur de eternis; Nota contra amatores mundi; Nota contra ingratos; Nota contra stultos consiliarios; Nota contra garrulos; Nota contra non recipientes disciplinam.*

57 BNF Lat. ms 67098, f.223r: *Nota de subditis et noviciis; Nota de affectu subditorum esse prelati; Nota de predicatoribus; Nota quare mundus est contempnendus*

58 For example, DrP, Bk 18, cap lxxvii *De onocentaur*, p.1097.

59 For example, in "Antiphon for the Virgin II", Bowie, Fiona and Oliver Davies (eds), *Hildegard of Bingen: An Anthology*, London: Society for the Propogation of Christian Knowledge, 1992, p.7.

60 DrP, Bk 17, cap clxxv *De Virga*, p.946: *Item virga canibus est odiosa & parvulis, quia virga eorum insolentia coercetur.*

61 Hassig, 1995, pp.62–71.

62 DrP, Bk 18, cap cxii *De Vulpe*, pp.1127–8; cap ci *De Taxo*, pp.1118–9.

63 This story was popular in France and England from about 1150 and gathered additions and retellings throughout the thirteenth century. In the various versions of the story, the fox is a murderous and lecherous deceiver, perversely admirable in his cunning and bravado. He comes into regular conflict with his partner-in-crime, Grimbert the badger, with his lord, Noble the lion, and other retainers such as Brichemer the stag and Chantecler the cock: Varty, Kenneth, *Reynard the Fox; a Study of the Fox in Medieval English Art*: Leicester University Press, 1967. In Books 18 and 12, BA includes properties of the badger, fox, stag, lion and cock that together evoke these popular characterisations.

64 BNF Lat. ms 67098, f.238r: *Nota de dolosis et ypocratis; Nota de insidiis; Nota de hereticis; Nota contra gulosas.*

65 DrP, Bk 18, cap xii *De Bove*, pp.1019–21; cap xiii *De Bubulco*, p.1021.

66 Duby, pp.103–16, 201–2, discusses the evidence for the varied status of the ploughman relative to other labourers in eleventh–fourteenth-century England and France, the nature of his task, and the use of both oxen and horses as draught animals.

67 BNF Lat. ms 67098, f.214v: *Nota de pietate et compassione prelatis; Nota de labore prelatorum et doctorum;Nota contra illos qui detrahunt prelatis; Nota de utilitate prelatorum; Nota de martyribus; Nota de confessoribus et eorum offici; Nota de predicatoribus; Nota de predicatione.*

68 BNF Lat. ms 67098, f.215r: *Nota de officio prelatis; Nota de correctione prelatorum; Nota de correctione subditorum.*

69 DrP, Bk 9, cap xxiii *De Vespera*, p.457: *Lupi a canibus in vespera vix discernuntur, vigiles & custodes propter latronum insidias & hostium insultus in muris & turribus flatuuntur, in vespera autem laborantes remunerantur & quieti exponuntur.* 'Entre chien et loup' ('between dog and wolf'), a French colloquialism for twilight, suggests that BA is using a homely idiom here.

70 See, for example, DrP, Bk 18, cap xxvi *De aliis proprietatibus Canum*, p.1041; cap vii *De Asino*, p.998.

71 Duby, pp.28–39, analyses data concerning the manorial economy and *familia* in thirteenth-century France and England.

72 DrP, Bk 6, *De proprietatibus Aetatum*, pp.231–76.

73 See Goodich, Michael, "Ancilla Dei: the servant as saint in the late middle ages" in *Women of the Medieval World*, edited by Julius Kirshner and Suzanne F. Wemple, Oxford: Basil Blackwell, 1985, on the ambivalent associations of *ancilla*, the maidservant.

74 DrP, Bk 6, cap xxii *De prandio & convivio*, pp.264–5; see Woolgar, C. M., *The Great Household in Late Medieval England*: Yale University Press, 1999, Chapter 5, "The rhythms of the household". Woolgar's reconstruction of later-medieval mealtimes, *prandium* and *cena*, drawn from English household accounts, corresponds closely with the material details in *De prandio* and in cap xxiii *De cena*, pp.265–6. Reynolds, Susan, *Kingdoms and Communities in Western Europe, 900–1300*. Oxford: The Clarendon Press, 1984, pp.122–54, discusses corporate life in the medieval villa, castella, manor or nucleated settlement, that functioned 'like a miniature kingdom'; Freed, pp.65–9, suggests that Magdeburg *studium*, located

75 DrP, Bk 6, cap xxiii *De cena*, pp.265–6.

76 AV, *Esther* 1:5–8; *Gospel of St John* 14:2.

77 DrP, Bk 1, cap xvi *De proprietatibus divinae essentiae*, p.12; cap xvii *Quomodo Bernardus describit Deum*, p.13; cap xx *De nominibus transsumptis*, p.15.

78 DrP, Bk 2, cap xix *De malis Angelis*; cap xx *De angelis perversis*, pp.40–5.

79 DrP, Bk 5, *De dispositione membrorum*: cap i *De membrorum proprietatibus in generale*, pp.114–9; cap ii *De proprietatibus capitis*, p.122.

80 DrP, Bk 6, cap xviii *De bono Domino sive dominio*, pp.253–5; see Reynolds, pp.321–3, on the collective nature of the ideal medieval manorial community and its designation by John of Salisbury (c.1115–1180) as *respublica*, a term used by BA at the start of this chapter on good lordship: *Sine enim dominio non posset stare salva respublica, nec esset humana societas pacifica vel quieta* ('For without lordship a *respublica* may not stand in safety, nor can human society be peaceful or quiet').

81 DrP, Bk 6, cap xiii *De Viro*, p.246: *eam dominam pecuniae suae et familiae facit, deinde non minus uxoris suae quam suiipsius causam vel etiam curam gerit*.

82 Bk 6, cap xvii *De conditionibus boni servi*, pp.251–3.

83 Riehle, Wolfgang, *The Middle English Mystics*, London: Routledge & Kegan Paul, 1981.

84 Wessley, Stephen, "Female imagery: a clue to the role of Joachim's Order of Fiore" in *Women of the Medieval World*, edited by J. Kirchner and S. Wemple, 161–78. Oxford: Basil Blackwell, 1985; Bynum, Caroline Walker, *Jesus as mother: Studies in the spirituality of the High Middle Ages*: University of California Press, 1982. Moses, David, *Notes and Queries* 50:1 (2003), 11–13, discussing BA's apparently anomalous inclusion of *De femina* in Bk 18 on animals, takes a different approach; he finds it logical that BA closely follows Aristotle and 'defines the animal by reproductivity at its most instinctive and functional, rather than at its most reasonable level'.

85 BNF Lat. ms 67098, f.52v: *Nota de Christo et prelato; Nota de doctrina magistrorum; Nota de officio prelati et subordinates;* see DrP, Bk 6, cap ix *De Nutrice*, p.242.

86 BNF Lat. ms 67098 f.54r: *Nota de predicatoribus et eorum officio; Nota de compassione; Nota de prelato et predicatore*. See DrP, Bk 6, cap x *De Obstetrice*, pp. 242–3.

87 BNF Lat. ms 67098, f.226r: *Nota de filiis in utero ecclesiae;* see DrP, Bk 18, cap xlix *De Foetu*, p.1070.

88 DrP, Bk 13, cap xxvi *De piscibus*, p.580: *Quidam enim generantur ... per coitum et spermatis emissionem. Unde dic. Arist. li. 5.*

89 BNF Lat. ms 67098, f.127r: *Nota de predicatore..*

90 BNF Lat. ms 67098, f.117r: *Nota de labore bonorum et operibus pietatis; Nota de compassione mulierum;* see DrP, Bk 12, cap xvi *De Gallo*, pp.535–6.

91 BNF Lat. ms 67098, f.117v; see DrP, Bk 12, cap xviii *De Gallina*, pp.537–8.

92 DrP, Bk 12, cap. xvii *De Gallo gallinaceo*, p.537.

93 Goodich, 1985, p.122, notes that the nurse's position in the medieval household was that of a privileged surrogate mother in charge of other domestics.

94 Readers familiar with the bestiary and teaching aviary would know the Christian iconography of the crane 'in its vigilance' against attack, especially by pigmies with arrows: see McCulloch, pp.33, 37–8, 105–6. Flocks of migratory cranes, which are large and make a strident sound, were formerly plentiful in northern Europe and illustrations suggest that people of south-east England were familiar with them: Klingender, pp.414, 491; Yapp, 1985, pp.12–13; Yapp, W. B., "Medieval knowledge of birds as shown in bestiaries", *Archives of Natural History* 14, no.2 (1987): 175–210, pp.179–81.

95 DrP, Bk 12, cap xv *De Grue*, p.534. See DrP, Bk 18, cap lxxxiv *De Pygmeis*, p.1102.

96 Wellcome ms 115, f.81v: *Nota de assencione domini*. St.Bonaventure writes of his own vision of the winged seraph on Monte Verna: 'I immediately saw that it signified the suspension of our father himself in contemplation': Boas, p.4.

97 AV, *Acts of the Apostles* 1:9–12.

98 BNF lat. 3332, ff.62v–63r. *Grus has conditiones sive proprietates invenitur breve in auctores. Primo enim ut dicit ambrose in exameron est avis magnarum alarum et fortis volatus aeris alta petens ut indeat ad quos velit peregrine per regiones. Significat prelatos potentes vel [ ] contemplationes magnos et eminentes qualiter fuit paulus qui raptus fuit ad telum celere et in paradisum ubi audivit archangeli verba quae non licet hic loqui. Scriberetur de benedicto francisco qui tam fortes et potentes alas [ ] suspendebatur multotiens*

rara contemplationis dulcedine et etenim lucifir radiabatur fulgoribus ut indentur totus in deum abfortus et iam quiscum avis angelorum effectus. Author's paraphrase. Square brackets indicate undeciphered text.

99 AV, *II Corinthians* 12:1–4; R. Brooke, 1970, pp.340–1.

100 Chartier, Roger, "Labourers and voyagers: from the text to the reader" in *Readers and Reading*, edited by Andrew Bennett, 132–49, London: Longman, 1995, pp.132–3.

101 DrP, Bk 8, cap i *Quid sit mundus*, p.371.

102 Green, R. P. H., ed, *Augustine: De Doctrina Christiana*, Oxford: The Clarendon Press, 1995, pp.15–6; Zacher, Christian K., *Curiosity and Pilgrimage: the Literature of Discovery in Fourteenth Century England*, Johns Hopkins University Press, 1976, pp.42–4, 169 nn.16–26, quotes this passage (trans. Shaw 1883) and refers to other biblical texts from which medieval writers drew the symbolism of the *viator in peregrinatione*; he concludes that 'Christianity defined the unstable, mobile quality of human existence as a choice of alternative directions and goals. Impelled by curiosity, man could make the world his destination; impelled by an awareness of his true homelessness, he would make the other world his destination.'

103 DrP, Bk 1, cap xxi *De diversis Christi nominibus, quibus nuncupatur*, pp.16–7.

104 DrP, Bk 3, *de proprietatibus animae rationalis*, pp.45–81; cap iii *De Anima*, pp.46–8: *Quia unitur corpori, scilicet, ut motor mobili & nauta navi*.

105 DrP, Bk 9 cap xxiv *De Nocte*, p.456: *in nocturnis tenebris ambulantes vel navigantes, de facili deviant, nisi eorum via per motum & siderum situm dirigatur*.

106 DrP, Bk 13, cap xxi *De Mari*, p.575.

107 DrP, Bk 17, cap clxx *De Tribulo*, p.942.

108 DrP Bk 17 cxlii *De Saltu & eius proprietatibus*, pp.922–3.

109 For example, Brockhurst, 1952, p.34; also Lidaka, 1996, p. 403 on Bk 19 as 'a hodgepodge of many topics'; Twomey, 1988, p.173, describes Bk 19's contents as 'a variety of minor subjects'.

110 DrP, Bk 19, caps lii–lx, *De Liquore in speciali & primo de melle; De Favo; De Muso; De Medone; De Clareto; De Oxymelle; De Cera; De Cereo*, pp.1183–9.

111 DrP, Bk 19, cap lx *De Cereo*, p.1189: *Nam agens in lychnum mediante cera convertit utrunque in suam similitudinem: unde & in dispari natura mirabilem inter se habent aptissimam unionem*.

112 BA sets out these at length in Bk 19, cap cxvi *De Ternario*, p.1223; cap cxxvi *De Tertia divisione totium numeri*, pp.1229–33; cap cxxviii *De Figura Trianguli*, pp.1236–8. Hassig (1995, p.57, pp.217–8) notes the absence in the bestiaries of the identification of the Virgin Mary with the chaste bee and Paschal candles, following Ambrose in *De virginibus*; BA alludes to these candles in DrP, Bk 9, cap xxx *De Paschate*, p.465: *In hac die ignis novus acquiritur, benedicitur, & ad accendendum Paschalem cereum custoditur, deinde Paschalis cereus erigitur, & a Diacono benedicitur & accenditur*. For eleventh-century ms examples of the association between bees and BVM, see Klingender, p.248 and Figs. 154, 155.

113 DrP, Bk 19, cap cxiv, p.1219: *Omnia fecisti in numero, pondere & mensura, sicut dic. Sapien.cap.11*.

114 DrP, Bk 19, *De rerum accidentibus, in quo coloribus, odoribus, saporibus & liquoribus agitur*, caps lxi–lxix, pp.1189–96.

115 DrP, Bk 19, caps lxx–lxiiii, pp.1197–1201.

116 BNF lat. ms 67098, ff.251r–252v: *Nota de dulcetudine et puritate doctrinae apostolicae; Nota de sana doctrina; Nota quod in cordibus sociorum apostolicorum est decoctum lac doctrinae; Nota quod dulci doctrina et pura anima reficitur; Nota de illis qui predicant; Nota contra malos doctrines [sic]; Nota de doctrina poetarum et philosophorum; Nota de illis qui in primo multum et sepe predicant et postea paulatim cessant*.

117 DrP, Bk 19, caps lxxvii–cxiii, pp.1205–19.

118 BNF ms lat. 67098, f.254v: *Nota qualia debent esse opera justorum; Nota de humore gracie et devotionis; Nota qua vana gloria corrumpit opera*.

119 Ibid, ff.256r, 256v: *Nota de operibus simplicium et bonorum; Nota de potentibus mundi; Nota de Christo in corde; Nota de magnis et potentibus et eorum occultata malicia; Nota de operibus otiosis ypocratarum et hereticorum; Nota de operibus pauperibus*.

120 Illich, pp.54–7.

121 The first canon of the Fourth Lateran Council of 1215 declared that Christ's body and blood 'are truly contained in the sacrament of the altar under the *species* of bread and wine, the bread being transubstantiated into the body and the wine into the blood by the divine power': Rothwell, Harry, ed. *English Historical Documents* 1189–1327, Vol III. London: Eyre & Spottiswood, 1975, pp.643–4.

122 DrP, Bk 19, *Prooemium*, p.1133.

[123] DrP, Bk 19, cap cxxx *De mensura spacii localis*, pp.1247–8.

[124] Wellcome ms 115, f.192v: *Nota de multiplice via; Nota de preceptis et consiliis; Nota de via preceptorum; Nota de via religionis; Nota de via militari*.

[125] DrP, Bk 1, cap xvi *De prop. divina essentia*, p.12: *Deus est sphaera intellectualis, cuius centrum ubique est, circumferentia vero nusquam … ita Deus deducit creaturas & limitat & finit eas*. Author's paraphrase.

[126] DrP, Bk 19, cap cxxvii *De mensura et pondere*, p.1235: *Deus, inquit [secundus philosophus] est intellectualis circulus, cuius centrum ubique est, circumferentia vero nusquam. Ex quo patet, quod ratio circuli relucet in qualibet creatura*. Seymour (1974–88 iii, p.323) identifies *philosophus* here as Hermes Trismegistos, a supposed sage and writer of antiquity.

[127] DrP, Bk 19, cap cxlvl *De tintinnabulo*, pp.1258–60; cap cxxxi *De musica*, p.1251.

[128] Louis, p.149.

[129] AV, *St Paul's Epistle to the Romans* 1:20.

Chapter 4. The world and the journey[1]

Bartholomew was writing and teaching in the 1220s and '30s, only a few years after the death of St Francis. As a Franciscan *lector*, he had the task of transmitting an ideal of homeless mendicancy in town and countryside without appearing to challenge the orthodox ideal of a religious life. Before this, the Benedictine ideal of separation from the world through monastic enclosure had underpinned religious life for five centuries. Although the Minorites shared vows and preaching objectives with their colleagues in the Benedictine and Cistercian Orders, the early years of Francis' Order were nevertheless politically precarious as factions differed in the interpretation of Franciscan poverty and their involvement with laity aroused disapproval. Because Francis had shunned the security of religious enclosure, his ministry appeared to some to be an unseemly immersion in the secular world and its temptations.[2]

This chapter looks at how Bartholomew weaves into his work a persistent strand of encouragement and information about physical travel across land and sea among alien races, and about spiritual pilgrimage through worldly life, through the subtle use of stories and images taken from both Christian and pagan sources. In this capacity, Bartholomew's work can be seen as being closely allied to contemporary graphic compilations or *mappaemundi*. Like the maps, 'Properties' testifies to contemporary interest in the extent of Christendom and the known pagan lands, the perceived limits of the physical world, and in rumoured places and peoples existing beyond them, perhaps awaiting salvation. Both kinds of text enabled the preacher or reader to travel in spirit to both centre and rim of Christendom.

The Fourth Crusade (1204) to the Seventh (1270) took place during Bartholomew's lifetime. The actuality of the Holy Land inspired people to travel towards the centre of Christendom as crusaders or pilgrims; either literally, or vicariously by means of devotional texts. In addition, known pagan lands beyond the borders of Christendom were the focus of crusade and mission, inspiring movement in a direction away from the Mediterranean centres.[3] This chapter examines 'Properties' as a guide and textual map to peoples and places and to survival in the world. It looks at how Bartholomew builds upon the eschatological theme of journeying and labour in 'Properties', discussed in the previous chapter, to create a densely illustrated image of the world in senses described by Meier: as source of information, site of world history and course of preparation for Judgement.

The Journey of a Book

Pilgrimage, crusade, mission, mendicants

The first task, though, is to summarise the context of expansion and mission in which Bartholomew was working. The historical record of mission, pilgrimage and crusade shows that in Bartholomew's time certain kinds of travel were a legitimate part of the religious life.[4] The record shows a double focus on Christendom: at its heart in Jerusalem and Rome, sites of crusade, pilgrimage and political struggle; and at its fringes where expansion and control were issues for the church. The Fourth Lateran Council of 1215, at which Innocent III authorised the Order of Preachers under Dominic and the Minorites under Francis, had demonstrated papal commitment to action against heretics in Europe and infidels abroad. The church was supporting the forceful conversion of Cathar heretics in southern France (initially by Cistercians) as well as a crusade against the Moslem presence in Jerusalem and the Holy Land. The church was also becoming aware that the Mongol empire was expanding westward.[5] At the Franciscan General Chapter of 1219, groups of friars had assembled to travel to Germany and eastern Europe, Spain and north Africa.[6] In the 1220s, Francis and Jacques de Vitry, bishop of Acre, hoped to undertake conversion of the Moslem world and in 1223 Pope Gregory IX had sent Franciscan envoys to meet both Moslem and Mongol rulers.[7]

Crusades against the Cathars and Slavs would take preachers into barely penetrated regions in the mountain areas of Europe as well as to the fringes of the unknown lands to the east. The steppes of Russia, the Crimean peninsula, Armenia and the Caucasus were all zones of missionary activity by the mid 1240s.[8] Dominic's main concern became the Cathars in southern France, but Dominican preachers were also involved, from before 1221, in converting the Prussians, Hungarians and Russians. While the Dominicans were trained clerics who met the Cathars with their own weapons of scholarship and reasoned argument, the Franciscans were strongly associated with the laity and the towns, and used affective, dramatic methods and the example of their own poverty to teach the Gospel.[9]

The figure of Francis himself provided followers with the ideal of an evangelist who confronted the dangers of seas and mountains in a physically frail body and received divine confirmation of Christ-like power. In 1219-20 Francis, sick and nearly blind, had made an arduous journey across the Mediterranean on a mission to convert the Moslem Sultan, travelling to Ancona, Crete, Cyprus and Egypt.[10] He died in 1226, and his supposed feats immediately became part of the body of legend that attached to his sanctified image. The belief persisted that he had achieved a light-filled apotheosis attended by Seraphim, and received miraculous stigmata, on Monte Verna in Italy.[11]

John of Plano Carpini, an early associate of Francis of Assisi who had taken a leading part in the establishment of the Order, became Guardian of the new province of Saxony in 1222. Later, according to his companion and chronicler Giordino of Giano, he sent friars all over northern and eastern Europe, to Bohemia, Poland, Hungary, Denmark and Norway. With his companion, Lawrence of Portugal, Carpini himself left Lyons in April 1245 as envoy of the Apostolic See to the Tartars and other nations of the east. He returned to Lyons in November 1248 and shortly afterwards began writing his *Historia Mongolorum*.[12] Louis IX sent two more Franciscans, William of Rubruck and Bartholomew of Cremona, from Acre to Mongolia in 1253 in the hope of gaining Mongol conversions and support against the Moslem world.[13] Although Carpini and Rubruck were travelling eastwards close to the time when Bartholomew was compiling 'Properties', their travel accounts did not circulate until after the middle of the century and would not have been available in time for inclusion. For us today, they form a background to the life of Bartholomew and of those for whom he wrote; they also testify to an increasing attention to the fringes as well as the heart of Christendom during those years.

The belief that Christians lived in the fourth or last age of the world, and that the age would soon end as prophesied, added an additional sense of urgency to the idea of global conversion. While missions endorsed by the pope may have been politically motivated they could be justified in scriptural terms as helping to fulfil the prophecy of St John in *Revelation*: 'And I saw a new heaven and a new earth: for the first heaven and the first earth were passed away; and there was no more sea.' Meanwhile, the properties of earth, water and weather in the existing sinful world were realities with which the missionary preacher might have to contend.

Bartholomew and the sea

Bartholomew brings the idea of mission vividly before the reader through two reiterated sets of images, each of which carries an accessible moral subtext. One of these involves realistic and dramatic descriptions of the ocean; the other evokes well-known stories about archetypal travellers over land and sea.

In long chapters on the sea and on fishes in Book 13, Bartholomew compiles empirical-seeming descriptions of the ocean as a heaving mass of water, speculations on the nature of saltiness, descriptions of lunar influence and tides, the sea bed and sea monsters, and the great variety of the underwater world of fishes. In *De mari*, Bartholomew paints a vivid picture of the open sea, with its dangers to sailors: waves, weather, monsters, sandbanks, sea-sickness, distance from land. He cites Aristotle and others on the medicinal properties of sea water, its incessant motion and changeable colours under different winds. Both fog and wind are perilous to those coming towards shore and a ship may be imperilled or late coming to harbour if it is weak, overloaded or poorly steered.[14] He goes on to depict some formidable dangers to shipping: the rock Scylla and the whirlpool Charybdis that nearly destroyed Odysseus; hidden rocks, sandbanks, and an indeterminate hazard where the bow gets stuck and the stern breaks, called *bitalapsum;* and uneven deeps and shallows called *sirtes*.[15] These were real hazards which any prospective traveller needed to be aware of, and Bartholomew devotes a separate chapter to the Sirtes in Book 15, treating them as a named location off the coast of Egypt and citing their etymological meaning of drawing or dragging.[16]

Some of these dangers, then, were and are real enough. Bartholomew states: 'These are dangers for men who sail on the sea, both the Mediterranean and Ocean', but in the midst of describing them he pauses to say that, while many common things are known about the sea, he wants to make sure that his readers have matter with which to persuade simple men of spiritual and hidden truths.[17] In other words, he's talking about the moral as well as physical dangers that the traveller might encounter. The glossator's copious comments confirm that readers could draw deeper connotations of the commotion and dangers of worldly life from under the surface description. They warn that *sirtes* point us to the lure of worldly wealth that can wreck one's hopes of salvation: 'Take note of the condition of the worldly; of the rise and fall of the worldly man; of love of the world and its danger; be on your guard against riches.' At the start of the chapter on the sea, where Bartholomew describes the continual movement, waves and storms, the glossator has written: 'Take note of the condition of the worldly.'[18] Comments against the ensuing column text on rocks and wild weather include: 'Take note concerning usurers and rich men ... concerning the pride and self-importance of the wealthy ... of the infirmity of the body and soul ... of mortal sin.' Against the monsters Scylla and Charybdis, the glossator warns of the changeableness of the world, and its strong appeal: 'Take care against prosperity and adversity in the world; against love of the world and its danger.' Where Bartholomew cites Aristotle on the way the sea becomes changeable in colour in the 'dog days' after the rising of the dog-star *canicula,* the glosses include: 'Take note of Antichrist.'[19] Bartholomew's chapter on the open ocean, *pelagus*, describes a dangerous shoreless waste, very deep and constantly in motion, home of whales and other monsters, windy and full of spray, changing colours, and the din of crashing waves; the glossator likens these to 'worldly tumult' and 'the mutability of worldly things'.[20] A warning against the fatal attraction or 'drawing' implied in the etymology of *sirtes* appears again in Book 18 in Bartholomew's chapter on the siren, the monster that seeks to destroy mariners by luring them off course with song, holding out false promises and arousing their lust.[21] The glossator sees them as reminders of love of the world; the desire of the flesh, lust of the eyes and pride of life; and as warnings against envy, pride and hypocrisy.[22] Within the sea lurk creatures of all kinds, just as people of all kinds inhabit the world.[23] These glosses demonstrate a reader's contemplative response to a dynamic description of physical experience. They also show us a stage in the process by which the sea — unstable, stormy and full of monstrous danger — became such a fruitful metaphor in the later Middle Ages for the world of secular society.

We have seen that Bartholomew's own justification for his work, that the things that are made show us the invisible things of God, recalls Augustine's teaching. He repeats this statement in Book 8 on the sublunary world.[24] Similarly, he seems to refer to St Augustine's mention of a necessary mode of conveyance near the start of his own literary undertaking. As stated earlier, he explains in Book 3 that the soul is said to be one with the body — but guides it, as a sailor is one with a ship — a non-bodily substance ruling the body.[25] For the Franciscan student such a reading could be appropriate as an Augustinian vision of spiritual pilgrimage; but Bartholomew also provides reminders of the need for courage and faith. In Book 8, the North Star, *stella maris*, reassures those who look on its fixedness, and guides the mariner.[26] In Book 13, Bartholomew describes the little fish *aphorus* as very small but full of virtue because it clings to a ship and holds it still and steady in the midst of storms, as Isidore says. Ambrose and Bede say that these fish use stones to help them stabilise ships with a strength beyond their own; they warn sailors to be ready for the coming tempest.[27] In Book 15, the island resists the onslaught of waves.[28] In Book 17, a plank of wood can save the shipwrecked sailor.[29] Like the glossator, Bartholomew seems to encourage the reader to identify with the sinner aware of being perilously exposed on the open ocean of worldly life.

Stories and travellers

In this setting, the reader's imagination is free to place historical and legendary travellers who found or lost their way on the sea — Noah, for example, whose story came to exemplify faith and the promise of salvation.[30] Hugh of St Victor had written his treatise on the meaning of Noah's Ark, *De Arca Noe Mystica,* in the previous century, and in the religious drama of the guilds, which developed their full complexity during the fourteenth and fifteenth centuries, Noah and his family become exemplary as well as entertaining figures.[31] The main ingredients of the Noah story are woven into the fabric of 'Properties': Noah's freight of animals and birds in Books 12 and 18 on those topics; the olive tree and the ship-building timbers in Book 17 on plants; the whole sea-going experience of waters and tempests in Book 13; Mount Ararat and Armenia in Books 14 and 15; the rainbow in Book 8 on earth and heaven.

Legends about archetypal travellers — sinful, heroic, misguided and repentant — were available to Bartholomew and his students from the Christian Scriptures, but also from Christianised Homeric legend and from classical history. Bartholomew's graphic description of the sailor in the empty ocean amid wallowing waves could evoke not only the contemporary example of St Francis and scriptural figures such as Noah or the Apostles, but also the pagan figures of Odysseus and Alexander the Great, whose stories had been adapted by Christian writers. The twelfth-century writer William of Conches is explicit about the allegorical significance for the Christian of Odysseus/Ulysses and elements of his story: 'By Ulysses you must understand the wise man (*sapiens*) whom Circe, that is, abundance of earthly possessions, does not succeed in transforming.'[32] Or, as Gerhard Ladner has put it:

> ... the Fathers of the Church could beautifully interpret the heroic travels of Ulysses as a type of the Christian's journey through terrestrial life. Ulysses had himself tied to the mast so that he would not be lured to disaster by the songs of the Sirens. Similarly, the Christian stranger on earth, the *peregrinus*, could be said to travel through strange and awesome seas in a ship, which is the Church, affixed to the mast of the Cross, absorbing the sweet and far from meaningless Siren songs of the world, without being deflected from the right course.[33]

Readers could infer allusions to the *Odyssey* in the monsters Scylla and Charybdis mentioned above, but also in an allusion to the homecoming Odysseus's welcome by his dog: 'Guard dogs can live longer, fourteen or sometimes twenty years, as in Homer.'[34] In *De Aeolia*, 'an island of Sicily', Bartholomew alludes obliquely to Odysseus's misadventure on that island by simply saying that the island was named after Aeolus, whom 'poets had made up to be god of the winds'.[35]

Like Ulysses/Odysseus, the figure of Alexander the Great (356–323 B.C.) had been annexed by earlier Christian writers as an exemplar of Christian vices and virtues, representing the *curiosus*, *gyrovagus* or restless traveller interested in seeing the world for its own sake but saved by the wisdom he eventually gained.[36] Literary evidence indicates that stories about this itinerant everyman, repeatedly being taught Christian virtues of humility, patience, poverty and penitence through his worldly successes, encounters and errors, were popular in Bartholomew's time. His arrogant curiosity and pursuit of worldly experiences took him beyond the bounds of normal travel and into contact with exotic and unnatural creatures including Amazon women and sirens.[37] It has been suggested that in Christianised versions of the Greek account Alexander embodied the worldly traveller subject to the 'lust of the eyes' and 'pride of life' warned against in the first epistle of John.[38] The Alexander stories that existed in the thirteenth century show that the non-Christian hero was strongly associated in Christian imagination with key locations on the map of the world, especially the earthly Paradise into which he tried to force an entry, and its antithesis, Babylon, the city identified in Scripture with the 'mother of whores and abominations of the earth', where he died.[39]

Bartholomew makes numerous allusions to Alexander in different Books. In Book 15's chapter on 'Amazonia' he tells us about the tribe of homicidal women, their taming by Hercules and Achilles, and how Alexander, after demanding tribute, learnt a lesson of humility from the Amazon queen.[40] In the chapter on Persia, Bartholomew refers to the treasure left behind by Alexander in the city of Elemayda.[41] In Book 17, on plants, he notes that there are rushes in India big enough to make boots with, as both Pliny and the Alexander story testify.[42] He alludes to Alexander's victory in India after which he crowned his soldiers with ivy, since it was sacred to Bacchus and to Mars.[43] However, after describing the vigour and usefulness of the palm tree found throughout Syria, Egypt and Palestine, he concludes dryly that, according to Pliny, some of Alexander's soldiers choked on unripe dates.[44] And in his chapter on the properties of red wine, Bartholomew tells how the mighty Greek spurned the warning of the wise Adronites and, being drunk, slew his friend.[45] In this Book we also find a comment on Alexander's legendary association with the stag, which Bartholomew says is evidently long-lived since those given gold collars by Alexander were found still living a hundred years later.[46] In Book 18's chapter on the dog, he reminds us that the king of Alania (a pagan area on the eastern boundary of Christendom) sent Alexander a cross-bred tiger-dog, so strong it could overcome a lion and an elephant.[47] Bartholomew adds a final sentence at the end of *De sirena* saying that such monsters can be read about in the history of Alexander the Great.[48] This cryptic reference to Alexander's underwater encounter with sirens, one facet of the Alexander story available to his contemporaries, illustrates the way Bartholomew gives his Christian readers the opportunity to dwell upon a whole set of adventures and resulting wisdoms gained by a pagan hero. In the Christian context of idealised spiritual pilgrimage, Alexander represents the opposite of the ideal; but his story also holds out the hope of salvation for the worldly person who learns and repents.

Stories were a valuable resource for the preacher as a way of engaging the attention of listeners even if they were, as Bartholomew himself puts it, 'pagan follies', *error gentilium*. He also points out in his chapter on Suecia, home of legendary Amazons, that we ought to believe pagan writers, *scriptores historiae tam Graecorum quam Romanorum*, who describe the Swedes as *gens valde robusta*, feared by Alexander the Great and Julius Caesar: as Jerome said, we may trust the sayings of poets and writers which do not harm the faith or contradict known truth.[49] Moreover it is possible that pagan stories could serve the purpose of heightening the clarity of the sacred through contrast with the profane. Bartholomew's many references to Alexander reinforce the suggestion that pagan stories provide contrasting figures which set off the virtues and significance of the church's objects of veneration. David Williams considers Alexander the Great a heroic but physically grotesque figure, both a builder and a destroyer, as an example of the didactic use of contrast and paradox in Christian teaching:

> It is not impossible that in Alexander the Great the people saw shadows of a prototype of Jesus, a manifestation of the paradox of divinity in

which the unnatural, even monstrous, combination of distinct natures, human and divine, unite in a single being. This certainly was the perception of, at least, the thirteenth century Armenian scribe [Ps. Callisthenes] who openly compares Alexander to Christ and who attaches to his poem a plea to be excused for this audacity.[50]

How else, the reasoning might be, to represent Christ and the Apostles but by antithesis? Evelyn Edson notes that for Lambert of St Omer in the twelfth century Alexander was a unifier of the physical world, compared to Christ as unifier of the spiritual world; and that Bartholomew's English contemporary Matthew Paris (d.1259) depicts Alexander and Christ enthroned together.[51]

A striking example of the use of contrast and paradox occurs in Bartholomew's introduction to the properties of the earth in Book 14. Bartholomew starts by citing Isidore: the earth is situated in the middle of the heavens, equidistant from all furthest points, signifying both its unity and its variety.[52] He explains the names given in other times and places to earth: *terra, humus, tellus, ops, arida, solum*, signifying her attributes; in old time she was called 'Ceres mother of gods', and 'Goddess Vesta'. He then describes a great seated female figure wearing a turreted crown, placed on a chariot, accompanied by submissive lions and cocks, holding in one hand a key, in the other a percussion instrument; the charioteers brandish naked swords.[53] Peter Dronke, in his chapter entitled "Bernard Silvestris, Natura, and personification" on the philosophy of the school of Chartres, notes that some scholars well into the thirteenth century did represent Earth and *natura* as a personified figure derived from the Roman goddess Terra or Tellus, a *magna mater* who nourishes and protects all.[54] This dramatic identification of the Christian ideal with the pagan image may therefore have been less surprising to medieval clerics than it is to us.

Bartholomew partly explains his inclusion of the pagan goddess among the properties of *terra* by saying that her attributes signify the seasonal round and the yearly rituals of ploughing and harvest 'under the cover of stories', *sub integumentum fabularum*.[55] Peter Dronke locates the device of *integumentum fabulae* within the twelfth-century School of Chartres and the philosophy of Bernard of Salisbury: through this device a legendary narrative can encase sub-textual meaning, which it is then up to the commentator to reveal.[56] In this instance the glossator is a 'commentator' who reveals a deeper meaning available to his contemporaries, lying beneath the description of the pagan earth-mother. The glosses point to the example of the Christian church and the Virgin Mary, to her faith and hope, her fullness of grace, her excellence, ripeness and stability; and to her total devotion to her Lord, in striking contrast to the personification of *terra* described in the column text.[57] The reader could draw both characters at once from the same page — the pagan story could be a paradoxical cover for, and vivid antithesis of, the image of the church (*ecclesia*) as bride and mother of Christ.[58] We might conclude then that this outwardly pagan and surprising passage in Book 14 could serve as a pause for reflection, not only upon the fertilising properties of religious life and the harvest of souls but also upon the virtues of Mary, her example to men and women, and her identification with the church as holy and fertile mother. At the same time, the chapter in Book 14 describing the fruitful properties of the earth prepares the way for Book 15 on the properties of places and peoples found upon its face — some still waiting to be sown with the word of God.

Book of the world, map of the world

Places and peoples known or rumoured to exist appear on world maps made during the Middle Ages. Scholars conclude that large *mappaemundi* such as those from Hereford (c.1280) and Ebstorf cathedrals (c.1300), and the tiny Psalter Map (c.1260), found in a small book of psalms for private devotion, were in effect compilations of theology, history and empirical knowledge, on the theme of salvation, for contemplation of the overarching meaning of the sites of original sin, redemption and judgement. They might serve a public or private teaching function.[59] Maps therefore parallel Bartholomew's textual image of the world: as a repertoire of places and peoples found within the mental horizons of the thirteenth-century Christian west; as a store of exemplary histories and legends; as an ordered hierarchical image of the cosmos; and as an object of contemplation for the Christian *peregrinus*. As David Woodward notes, the term *mappamundi*, or 'map of the world', could be used in the Middle Ages in an additional metaphorical sense, or to describe a purely textual account of the world.[60] A textual account of the world is precisely what Bartholomew builds as he takes us from Book 8 on the cosmos to Book 18 on land creatures. Margriet Hoogvliet argues that although many extant maps occur in world book texts, they are not simply illustrative or interchangeable but complementary: the name *mappamundi* belongs rightly to both; and the strong association between maps and texts 'can provide us with some clues for a reconstruction of the spiritual meaning of the medieval maps of the world'.[61] It seems reasonable to suppose that, conversely, our awareness of the forms, content and function of the maps can help us reconstruct the spiritual meanings underlying the properties of things amassed by Bartholomew from his sources.

Early 'Properties' manuscripts do not contain drawn maps but, from their presence in some of Bartholomew's main patristic sources, it seems reasonable to conclude that the compiler would have been familiar with earlier examples of the tradition.[62] Many of the *imago mundi* texts contain maps, the *Imago Mundi* of Henry of Mainz (floruit 1098–1156) being seen as a prototypical example from the twelfth century.[63] Each map is different but, since the maps were graphic representations of historical, geographical and exegetical knowledge, each map-maker had to find ways of encoding within the orthodox scheme, or *imago mundi*, far more information than could be fully depicted or described in the space available. The density of the maps, like that of 'Properties', suggests that a good deal of imaginative re-creation was expected on the part of both viewers and readers. Within this group, the English Psalter Map is most nearly contemporaneous with 'Properties' and comparable as a book for individual devotional reading (Figure 3).[64] Whether a map was made for public or private use, it was normal to depict the theme of Judgement in the area immediately inside the frame or edge of the page. In the Psalter map *recto*, the iconography of the Last Judgement is limited to the figure of Christ, but the dragons below could be reminders of the power of Satan to destroy faith — and on the *verso* of the map Christ's feet rest firmly upon them (Figure 4).[65] The Psalter map depicts earth as a circle within the rectangular page.

Divine and eternal beings, God and his angels, occupy the space outside the circle of the earth and within the rectangular frame. Books 1 to 4 of 'Properties' provide the conceptual framework for the whole work, as the rectangular frame or page does for the Christian cosmos depicted in the map. Bartholomew places God (Book 1) and the angels — good and bad — (Book 2) in the dominant position at the head of the work. Books 1 and 2 correspond to the area outside the circle of the world but within the rectangular frame of the map, embracing and dominating the sublunar world.

Book 3 presents the human soul at the start of its journey through the world and towards God. Book 4, on the four elements and four humours, is consistent with the symbolism of the number four embedded in *mappaemundi* and tetradic diagrams.[66] Book 4 can also be seen as the centre of a group of seven Books; between the first three Books that deal with the divine, and Books 5, 6, and 7 that deal with the corporeal aspects of the world.

In Book 8, Bartholomew describes the world at the centre of the spheres and furthest from heaven of all the heavenly bodies.[67] Books 9, 10 and 11 can be likened to the first or outer circle of the map, where the motion of the sublunary world creates the flow of time (Book 9) and the vicissitudes of temperature (Book 10) and winds (Book 11) that we experience.

The world and the journey

Figure 3: The Psalter Map, British Library Additional Ms 28681, f.9 *recto*. Circa 1260.

The map is a miniature occurring in a Book of Psalms, but it is thought that it could be a copy of larger-scale maps commissioned by Henry III for the walls of Westminster Abbey.
Used by permission of the British Library.

Figure 4: The Psalter Map, British Library Additional Ms 28681, f.9 *verso*. Circa 1260.

The features depicted on the map, and the places listed on its reverse side, represent the basic repertoire of a *mappaemundi* of 1100–1300 and coincide closely with those named in 'Properties' Books 13, 14 and 15.
Used by permission of the British Library.

Creatures of air, the subject of Book 12, are the 'ornaments' of that element.[68] At another level, Book 12 is a list of *distinctiones* into which the symbolic significance of individual birds could be read by those versed in them. It also serves to deepen and expand on the idea of the soul on its journey, and even (like the crane, the swift and the homing pigeon) to symbolise the viewer as *peregrinus* in the world and in the book.[69]

Book 13 on the element of water can be compared to the area on the *mappaemundi* where bodies of water and rivers are predominant features, with the Nile and the Mediterranean separating the world into its three divisions. In this Book, Bartholomew includes the rivers Nile and Danube; and the four rivers that come out of Paradise — Physon (or Ganges), Gyon, Tigris and Euphrates. These, with the rivers Dorix and Jordan, each have a chapter in Book 13. Here, he describes their passage from Paradise in the East, into the Red Sea, through Mesopotamia, Babylon and Armenia; the Jordan flows through Palestine, past Jericho and into the Dead Sea. The rivers Albana and Pharphar flow through Syria and Damascus; the river Gazan flows into the Red Sea; and Chebar, with its sedges and willows, is where God's people sat down and wept by the waters of Babylon. The Dead Sea, Lake Tiberias and Genesar 'pond' each have a chapter. The Mediterranean has a chapter, *De mari magno*, in which Bartholomew draws a verbal map of the coastline and the countries of its margins, including a paragraph on the Red Sea and its environs.[70] A characteristic feature of contemporary maps is the Ocean that rings the world, dotted with islands, named and unnamed. Bartholomew refers to 'the waters which surround the sides of the earth' at the start of Book 8 on the cosmos. As we have seen, he describes properties of the ocean in general in the chapter *De mari* in Book 13; and the properties of the island in general, as well as known and rumoured islands such as the Cyclades, Ireland and Thule, in Book 15 on provinces and peoples.[71]

Books 14 and 15 treat the land features of the maps; the mountains, valleys, islands and provinces. In Book 14, the chapter that follows *De terra* is *De monte*, dealing with mountains, the salient feature of the earth's surface, and also caverns, caves and deserts. Bartholomew's list of mountains encompasses those shown on the maps that were the scene of scriptural events and a goal of pilgrims. Among these are Mounts Ararat, Bethel, Golgatha, Hebron, Carmel, Lebanon, Moria, Nebo, Oreb, Sinai, Syon and Ziph.[72] He also includes some mountains important in classical writings, such as Mount Olympus. Having dealt with important specifics on the map of the world, both Christian and pagan, Bartholomew treats the properties of general features that result from the lumpy surface of the earth, namely hills and valleys, hollows and caves.[73]

In Book 15 Bartholomew starts with the division of the world among Noah's three sons according to the Gloss on *Genesis* and other patristic sources, and graphically represented in tri-partite ('T-O') medieval maps.[74] In the Psalter map and others of this group, the division of the world into three is implicit in the vertical and horizontal divisions made by the Mediterranean Sea and the river Nile. In the chapter on Armenia, he mentions that this is where the Ark came to rest, having already referred to the legend of the Ark's inaccessible remains in the chapter on Mount Ararat in Book 14.[75]

Other key places we find on maps are the earthly Paradise, Jerusalem and Babylon. Bartholomew describes the earthly Paradise as 'a place in the east', but he then draws on scriptural and legendary sources, including the story of Alexander's journey to Paradise.[76] Bartholomew presents the properties of Jerusalem in *De Iudea*: 'In the centre of Judea is the city of Jerusalem, as if it were the navel of all this country and land, and it is rich with all kinds of richness.'[77] In his chapters on Babylon and Chaldea, Bartholomew includes the gathering of giants after the flood and the building of the Tower of Babel; the drama of Semiramis, the rise and fall of the Assyrians, and the foundation of Rome; the captivity of the Jews under Nebuchadnezzar and Babylon's destruction by the Medes and the Persians under Darius. He describes the fertility and richness of the Mesopotamian region and the contrast after its destruction: '[T]he place that Babylon was in is desert and contains nothing but monsters.'[78]

Book 6, on life, death and tasks, is one site for meditation on the theme of our mortality. Book 9 is another. In Book 9, on time, Bartholomew had already pointed to Babylon as the city representing the heathen and false homeland that entraps us in this earthly life. In the chapter on the church's feast of Septuagesima, he says that the 70 days before Easter signify the 70 years in which the children of Israel were enslaved in Babylon, but also prefigure 'the time of our life while it is subject to sin or pain'. At Easter, 'alleluya' is sung to celebrate the release of mankind from the slavery of sin by Christ's passion, even though hardship and pain persist, 'as the people of Israel made joy and mirth because they were coming into Jerusalem, but nevertheless they suffered sorely from the hardness of the way'.[79] Here, Bartholomew brings to the surface the idea of this life as a journey towards the true homeland or *patria* in which we each play the role of traveller. Like the Children of Israel, we should rejoice that we are on the way home but remain somewhat sad at the thought of our enslavement. In Book 15, the topics of Paradise and of Babylon, as named places on the world map, offer another point of entry into this principal theme. Books 16, 17 and 18 treat (only partially alphabetically) the properties of and distinctions between things of earth — namely rocks and gems, plants, and creatures with legs — maintaining the dual focus on the earth as both delightful vineyard and place of toil and travail.

In Book 19, Bartholomew returns to the overarching idea of the divine framework that holds the world; the rectangle signifies the universal church and the firmness of the faithful person:

> For the form of the quadrangle is the most stable and firm, and it signifies the utmost stability of the universal church and the firmness of the faithful soul, as much in spiritual strength as in knowledge and doctrine; and since it is length, breadth, height and depth it embraces all things holy.[80]

This description of a fundamental, universally enclosing form is consistent with the rectangular frames of the Psalter and most other maps, within which God and his angels dominate and surround the round world within.[81]

To sum up this chapter: stories of travellers such as Odysseus, Noah and Alexander the Great, encoded on medieval maps and alluded to in 'Properties', were an effective — and affective — means of teaching Christian doctrine and preparing students for missionary work. Bartholomew's images of the land, the seas and the traveller are consistent with his role as a Franciscan *lector* in a frontier area. They draw attention to exotic peoples and places in a positive spirit; encourage reflection on historical events recorded in the Bible that prefigure personal and world salvation; and embody the idea of the reader's own life as a pilgrimage. The glosses indicate that the properties of land and the sea could signify, for near-contemporary clerical readers, the spiritual growth and nurture provided by the church, and spiritual dangers of the world. Special dangers could serve as warnings against worldly perils that could only be survived with divine help and moral strength. This commentary, and our awareness of the literary device of *integumentum*, suggests that Bartholomew's stories about non-Christian places, peoples and adventurers were justified as entertaining and engaging vehicles for Christian teaching.

The narrative devices that link and cross-cut the sequence of Books add to its effectiveness as a teaching and learning tool and help us to form a picture of the mental horizons of the compiler and his students. 'Properties' can give us a clue to the freight of meaning potentially available to the reader of such an outwardly expository text. That is not to say, of course, that the encoded meanings are fully recoverable by historians. We can at least deduce from 'Properties' something of the depth and intricacy of an intellectual system that patterned the world qualitatively rather than quantitatively, in an effort to impose order on the intractable diversity of things and their properties within a balanced and providential whole. Bartholomew's sustained, overarching themes of pilgrimage and salvation show us something of the meaning, for medieval people, of the concept of *imago mundi*.

The Journey of a Book

NOTES

[1] Parts of this chapter have appeared in Keen, Libby, "Under cover of stories: Bartholomew the Englishman and the world of land and sea" in *Our Medieval Heritage*, edited by Linda Rasmussen, Valerie Spear and Dianne Tillotson, 94–108, Cardiff: Merton Priory Press, 2002.

[2] Mendicants and missionaries were vulnerable to charges of being inquisitive sightseers (*gyrovagi*): Zacher, 1976. Smalley, Beryl, "Ecclesiastical attitudes to novelty c1100–c1250" in *Church, Society and Politics*, edited by Derek Baker, 115–6. Oxford: Basil Blackwell, 1975, finds that the church's attitude to the new during the thirteenth century gradually came to accommodate the friars.

[3] Dawson, Christopher, *The Mongol Mission: Narratives and letters of the Franciscan Missionaries in Mongolia and China in the Thirteenth and Fourteenth Centuries*, London: Sheed and Ward, 1955.

[4] Southern, R. W., *The Making of the Middle Ages*, London: Hutchinson, 1953, pp.211–2; Phillips, J. R. S., *The Medieval Expansion of Europe*, Oxford University Press, 1988, pp.83–4.

[5] Sources include letters from the Emperor Frederick II to the kings of England and France proposing common action against the Tartars; and Bulls from Pope Innocent IV to the Emperor of the Tartars, carried by envoys who later wrote of their experiences: Dawson, p.xi.

[6] Moorman, pp.48–59. Africa south of the northern coastal area was almost unknown to Europeans in the Middle Ages, leading to conjecture about rumoured monstrous races inhabiting the interior: Phillips, pp.143 foll.

[7] French and Cunningham, Introduction; Phillips, pp.260–78, includes a comprehensive bibliography of both primary and secondary sources on medieval discoveries and theories concerning the inhabited world.

[8] Phillips, pp.83–4: 'In the 12th c. there was the movement of crusaders and settlers into the Baltic lands of Prussia and Livonia ... Throughout the period of the most intensive European missionary work in Asia there was ... a parallel movement going on within certain parts of Europe itself.'

[9] Brooke, 1975; Brooke, Rosalind B. and Christopher Brooke, *Popular Religion in the Middle Ages*, London: Thames and Hudson, 1984, p.140; Phillips, pp.15, 84.

[10] Moorman, pp.48–59.

[11] Brooke, Rosalind B., ed, 1970, pp.337, 341.

[12] Salimbene, who met Carpini after his return in 1245, records that he often heard him describe his experiences as a traveller and as a guest of the Great Khan: Dawson, pp.iv–viii; p.2. Carpini had taken a leading part in the establishment of the Franciscan Order in western Europe: Phillips, pp.73–82 and foll; Dawson, pp.xv–xviii. Salimbene states: 'In the time of Pope Gregory IX rumors first went abroad about the Tartars, and several Popes sent messengers to them. These Friars Minor returned from the Tatars [sic] without any harm, and they reported many things about them, which I heard with my own ears' (cited by Baird, pp.200–01).

[13] Phillips, pp.7–16. Dawson, p.88, says, 'Hardly anything is known about this great man except what he tells us in his book. The dates of his birth and his death are unknown, but he seems to have been a much younger man than John of Plano Carpini.'

[14] DrP, Bk 13, cap xxi *De Mari*, pp.569–75.

[15] The Sirtes, Major and Minor, were, and are, areas of shoals and currents off the North African shore in areas now known as the Gulfs of Sidra and Gabès: Westrem, pp.338–9. See Fig. 1. In the mid-sixth century Procopius had described the Greater and Lesser Sirtes as currents with a fatal shoreward drag on ships, requiring special skills and poles to navigate them: Stewart, Aubrey, ed, *Procopius of Caesarea (c560 AD): Of the Buildings of Justinian*, London: Palestine Pilgrims' Text Society, 1896, pp.157, 160. Thanks to Norman Lewis for this reference.

[16] DrP, Bk 15, cap cli *De Syrtibus*, p.702; BA cites Isidore and Sallust as his authorities.

[17] Bk 13, cap xxi *De Mari*, p.572: *Praeter istas autem maris proprietates sunt quaedam aliae communes, et omnibus fere notae, quas tamen propter simplices bonum putavi hic apponere, ut materiam habeant aliqua mystica, per earum similitudinem simplicibus suadere.*

[18] BNF Ms Lat. 60798, f.124v–125v: *Nota de statu mundanorum; Nota de prosperitate & adversitate mundi; Nota de amore mundi et eius periculo; Nota contra divitiis;* Alain de Lille (d.1203) had listed the sea as a symbol of the mundane world: Migne, Jacques-Paul, ed, *Patrilogiae cursus completus*, Vol.210. Paris, 1882, 685–10–12.

[19] BNF Ms Lat. 60798, f.124v–125v: other glosses against *De mari* include *Nota de mundanis; Nota de mutabiliente mundanorum; Nota de amore mundi;* beside the lines on Scylla and Charybdis, *Nota de*

prosperitate & adversitate mundi; Nota de amore mundi et eius periculo; beside mention of 'Syrtes' or 'Sirtes', *Nota contra divitiis*. Williams, David, *Deformed Discourse: The Function of the Monster in Mediaeval Thought and Literature*: University of Exeter Press, 1996, pp.183–5, interprets the significance of Scylla and Charybdis in Christian thought as warnings against the sexual voracity of women.

[20] DrP, cap xxiii *De pelago*, p.577; BNF Ms Lat. 16098, f.126r: *Nota de mundanorum mutabilitate; Nota de tumultu mundana*.

[21] DrP, Bk 18, cap xcv *De sirena*, p.1113.

[22] BNF Ms Lat. 67098, f.235r: *Nota de amore mundi; Nota contra invidioses & superbos; Nota contra ypocriticas; Nota de concupi[scentia] carnis et occulorum & de superbia vite*.

[23] DrP, Bk 13, cap xxvi *De Piscibus*, pp.578–87. In BNF Ms Lat. 16098, ff.126v–127r, the glossator interprets kinds of fish as types of people; for example, the first gloss is *Nota de studentibus*.

[24] DrP, Bk 8 *de proprietatibus Mundi et corporibus coelestibus*, cap i *Quid sit Mundus*, pp.367–72: *restat ut ad proprietates mundi sensibilis, quantum nobis datur desupermanus apponamus, ut materiam divinae laudis ex proprietatibus operationum possimus elicere conditoris. Invisibilia enim Dei per ea quae facta sunt intellecta conspiciuntur, ut dicit Apostolus*.

[25] DrP Bk 3 *de proprietatibus animae rationalis*, cap iii *De Anima*, pp.46–8: *Quia unitur corpori, scilicet, ut motor mobili & nauta navi, & secundum hoc diffinitur a Remigio sic: Anima est substantia incorporea, regens corpus. Et ab August. de anima & spiritu*.

[26] DrP, Bk 8, cap xxxiiii *De Polo*, p.421.

[27] DrP, Bk 13, cap xxvi *De Piscibus*, p.584.

[28] DrP Bk 15, *de proprietate Provinciarum*, cap.lxxxii *De Insula in Salo sita*, p.667.

[29] DrP, Bk 17, *de proprietatibus Plantarum*, cap clxii *De Tabula*, p.937.

[30] AV, *Genesis* 6–9.

[31] See Edson, pp.159–63, on Hugh of St Victor's *De Arca Noe Mystica* (1128/29) as a treatise on salvation; on Noah in medieval drama, see Davies, R. T., *The Corpus Christi Play of the English Middle Ages*, London: Faber and Faber, 1972, pp.15—44.

[32] William of Conches, *Commentary on Boethius, The Consolation of Philosophy*, cited by Minnis, Scott and Wallace, eds, p.129.

[33] Ladner, Gerhart B., "*Homo viator*: medieval ideas on alienation and order", *Speculum* 42.2 (1967): 233–59, p.237.

[34] DrP, Bk 18, cap xxiv *De Cane*, p.1037: *Alii autem canes ut custodies domorum & civium vivunt diutius, quia quatuordecim annis & aliquando viginti, ut dicit Homerus Item li.8*. Author's paraphrase.

[35] DrP, Bk 15, cap lv, p.652: *quem poetae finxerunt deum fuisse ventorum*. Author's paraphrase.

[36] Zacher, pp.34–5, p.166 n.63.

[37] Kratz, Dennis M., *The Romances of Alexander*, New York: Garland Publishing Inc., 1991; Bunt, Gerith H. V., *Alexander the Great in the Literature of Medieval Britain*, Groningen: Egbert Forsten, 1994, pp.6–7; Stoneman, Richard, ed, *Legends of Alexander the Great*, London: Everyman, 1994. Latin recensions of the Greek history of Alexander appropriated by both Jewish and Christian writers were highly popular in BA's time, such as that derived from the early-fourth century *Res Gestae Alexandri Magni* of Julius Valerius. By the thirteenth century, various versions of the legend existed which made use of Alexander as a moral example to be both observed and shunned by the Christian. Alexander's travels served to bring notions of marginal and monstrous races into the Christian image of the world: Woodward, 1987, pp.286–370.

[38] AV, *I John* 2:15–18: 'Love not the world, neither the things that are in the world. If any man love the world, the love of the Father is not in him. For all that is in the world, the lust of the flesh, and the lust of the eyes, and the pride of life, is not of the Father, but is of the world.' Zacher (p.3) sees this text as fundamental to the medieval trope of *peregrinatio*: 'As one of the earliest Christians expressed it, man must decide between this world and the homeland of the Father; the choice is either *mundus* or *patria*.'

[39] AV, *Revelation* 17:5.

[40] DrP, Bk 15, cap xii *De Amazonia*, p.629. Here BA refers to a legendary letter of reproof from the queen of the Amazons to Alexander, which taught the hero a more humble chivalry. According to Seymour, 1992, p.160, BA's account of the Amazons 'apparently derives from the unidentified version of the story of Alisaundre'.

[41] DrP, Bk 15, cap cxix *De Persida*, p.687.

[42] DrP, Bk 17, cap cxxvi *De Papyro*, p.906.

⁴³ DrP, Bk 17, cap liii *De Hedera*, p.833.

⁴⁴ DrP, Bk 17, cap cxvi *De Palma*, p.898.

⁴⁵ DrP, Bk 17, cap clxxxv *De Vino rubeo*, p.959. Drunkenness was a problem for the church at this time, the 4th Lateran Council urging temperance among clerics: Williams, Jane Welch, *Bread, Wine & Money: The Windows of the Trades at Chartres Cathedral*: The University of Chicago Press, 1990, p.99. Salimbene is an eager witness to clerical appreciation of good wine, both white and red: Baird, p.xii.

⁴⁶ DrP, Bk 18, cap xxx *De cervo*, p.1046; see Bath, Michael, "The legend of Caesar's deer", *Medievalia et Humanistica* 9 (1979): 53–66, on the evidence of a tradition concerning the hart's longevity, derived originally from Homeric and Roman legend. BA's oblique reference to the story suggests that it was known in his time and place and already associated with Alexander.

⁴⁷ DrP, Bk 18, *de proprietatibus Animalium* cap xxiv *De cane*, p.1036; Bk 15, cap xi *De Alania*, p.628; Matthew, p.185.

⁴⁸ DrP, Bk 18, cap xcv *De sirena*, p.1113: *De talibus monstris legitur in historia Alexandri Magni*. Alexander's descent to the depths of the sea, and his soldiers' encounter with predatory river-women, are described in *Historia de Preliis Alexandri* (tenth century): Kratz, pp.74–6.

⁴⁹ DrP, Bk 15, cap cliii *De Suecia*, p.704: *Poetarum et scriptorum scriptis et dictis fidem adhibere convenit, quororum relatio fides, moribus non preiudicat, nec veritate cognita contradicit*. Sweden had been more resistant to conversion than other Scandinavian countries, and Christianity was not well established there until the early twelfth century: Phillips, p.33.

⁵⁰ D. Williams, pp.183–5; in his Introduction (pp.4–5) Williams proposes that Christian Neoplatonism validated the grotesque and monstrous because the only way to describe God was through what He is not, citing Ps-Dionysius' *On the Divine Names*: 'Indeed, the inscrutable One is out of the reach of every rational process.'

⁵¹ D. Williams, p.249. Edson, pp.103, 111 & p.182 nn.46, 47.

⁵² DrP, Bk 14, *De proprietatibus Terrae* cap i *De Terra*, p.588.

⁵³ DrP, Bk 14, *De terra et eius partibus* cap i *De Terra*, p.590: *In signum autem tantae foecunditatis et virtutis facta est ei magna imago foeminea, et alma mater nuncupata, cum turrita corona, posita super currum, cui leones domiti subiiciebantur. In una manu portabat clavem, in alia tympanum sive cymbalum. Cuius aurigae vibrabant gladios gestabant, et galli matronam sedentem in curru subsequi fingenbantur.* Klingender (p.247) describes an image of the *Magna Mater* that combines *Terra*, Vesta and Ceres in an early-eleventh-century copy of Hrabanus Maurus' *De Universo*. This work and its imagery derive from Isidore of Seville, BA's cited source in *De Terra*; as Donald Byrne has shown, this description suggested to later fourteenth-century illustrators the Roman ceremony of Cybele. The figure of Earth depicted in Ms Cod. Guelf, f.176, and BNF ms fr.22531, f.216 to illustrate DrP, Bk 14 in French translation is that of Cybele; in the sources Galli were her eunuch priests, and it was BA who first rendered them as cocks: Byrne, 1978, pp.159–61.

⁵⁴ Dronke, Peter, *Intellectuals and Poets in Medieval Europe*, Rome: Edizione de storia e letteratura, 1992, pp.47–51.

⁵⁵ *His & aliis multis modis describuntur proprietates terrae sub integumentum fabularum, sicut ibidem recitatur ab Isidore*: DrP, Bk 14, cap i *De Terra*, p.591.

⁵⁶ Dronke, p.63: through the device of *integumentum fabulae* 'le sens profond est enveloppé par la narration fabuleuse — c'est donc au commentateur de le découvrir'. See also French & Cunningham, pp.57–9, on the thirteenth-century concept of pagan thought as a useful appropriation, analogous to the 'Egyptian gold' stolen by the departing Israelites.

⁵⁷ BNF Ms Lat. 16098 f.129r: the glosses include *Nota de ecclesia sive virgine benedicta; Nota de fide et spere virginis benedicte; Nota de gracie plenitudine; Nota de eius singulare excellentia; Nota de marie maturitate; Nota de eius intentione tota relata in domino; Nota de fidei et gracie sue stabilitate.*

⁵⁸ Dronke (p.52) examines the identification of *Terra* with *Ecclesia*, the church, in the work of Bernard Silvestris: 'The reason Tellus can have such nearness to divinity, and can become deeply comparable to Ecclesia, is that the sense of a whole Christian cosmos brought to renewed life — which the shining words of the Exultet convey — transfigures Tellus and Ecclesia equally. Their connotations, that is, move ... as close as possible to those of rejoicing living beings.'

⁵⁹ See Edson, pp.111–7 and Fig.6.3, p.114, for a discussion of the Hereford map as an image of the world 'strictly disciplined and subdued in the service of a greater world order'. For recent analyses of the Hereford map as a teaching tool, see Westrem, 2001. See also Woodward, 1987; also Klingender, p.247, on the *mappamundi* in the Montecassino ms of Hrabanus Maurus' *De Universo*. Whitfield says

(p.14): 'In constructing a world map, the essential principle was to adhere to a tradition. This is not to say that the medieval world map remained static and repetitive; on the contrary the extant maps show a multitude of variations. But the structure remains the same, and the variations are elaborations from literary and religious sources, not geographical developments.' Edson, pp.145–63, explores the spiritual function of maps with reference to the variations they display on a basic repertoire of forms and content.

[60] Woodward, 1987, p.287; see Westrem, pp.xxxiv–vii, on the recently-discovered *Expositio mappe mundi* and its relation to the Hereford map as an explanatory text.

[61] Hoogvliet, pp.63–4.

[62] Déstombes, p.189: The Wolfenbüttel codex Helmst. 442 (fourteenth century) contains 'Properties', a *Chronica Mundi*, a map of Palestine and a world map, suggesting that the compiler of this codex associated 'Properties' with the history and geography of the physical world. Thanks to Julie Hotchin for information on this codex.

[63] Edson, pp.11–3, and Woodward, 1987, pp.291–313, trace changes and elaborations on the earliest examples from late-Roman and early patristic manuscripts, the so-called T-O maps, showing the tripartite division of the world, Asia, Europe and Africa, between the three sons of Noah. See Woodward, 1987, p.312, on the confused identities of Henry of Mainz and Honorius of Autun; and pp.334–42 on the significance of Noah in the development and symbolism of the maps.

[64] On the Psalter Map (c.1250), see Déstombes, pp.168–70; Whitfield, pp.18–9; Woodward, 1987, pp.327–50; <www.bl.uk/onlinegallery/themes/mapsandviews/psaltermap.html>. Déstombes, loc.cit., describes this map in detail and notes its affinities with the Ebstorf and Hereford maps. He refers to the work of Konrad Miller, who transcribed all the names on the Psalter map in *Die ältesten Weltkarten* vol III (1895).

[65] Hassig, p.50, concludes that the dragon was 'bestiary devil par excellence', citing (p.246 n.20) the iconography of the dragon in Apocalypse illustrations.

[66] Sears, Elizabeth, *The Ages of Man: Medieval Interpretations of the Life Cycle*, Princeton University Press, 1986, pp.16-20; Woodward, 1987, pp.335-6.

[67] DrP, Bk 8, cap i *Quid sit mundus*, pp.367–72.

[68] DrP, Bk 12, preamble, p.507: *Ad ornatum autem aeris, pertinent aves et volatilia, ut dicit Beda*.

[69] Klingender, pp.402–51, discusses and illustrates the abundant use of birds to signify human souls in Apocalypse and other manuscripts. On the use of moralised birds as a teaching tool, see Clark, Willene B., "The illustrated medieval aviary and the lay-brotherhood", *Gesta* XXI (1982): 63–74. Cf. DrP, cap xv *De grue*, pp.534–5; cap xxi *De hirundine*, pp.539–40; cap vi *De columba*, pp.524–7.

[70] DrP, Bk 13, pp.569–75.

[71] DrP, Bk 8, cap i *Quid sit Mundus*, p.368: *Aqua quae terrae latera circumcingit*; Bk 15, cap lxxxii, *De insula in Salo sita*, pp.667—668.

[72] DrP, Bk 14, pp.596–616.

[73] While general at one level, these may have had a specific application to Franciscan readers. BA stresses the emotional responses to the mountain top and to the dark place as shelter or as danger. The chapter on the mountain (DrP, Bk 14, cap ii *De monte*, pp.595–6) concludes with a description of the valley as refuge for hunted animals that come down from the heights. Against this the glossator had written *Nota quod religio est refugium peccatorum*. The glosses against the passage describing the light on the mountain tops include *Nota de contemplativis, Nota de exemplis bonis, Nota contra superbos* (Meyer, 1988, pp.246–8). They are consistent with the recorded significance of wilderness, mountains and caves for the early Franciscans seeking casual shelters, and especially of Francis's reported sojourns on Monte Verna: see R Brooke, 1970, pp.337, 341.

[74] DrP, Bk 15, cap i *De Orbe*, p.624; Woodward, pp.301–2 and passim.

[75] DrP, Bk 15, cap v *De Armenia*, p.626: *Et dicitur Ararath mons, in quo Archa Noae post diluvium requievit*; Bk 14, cap.iii *De Ararath*, pp.596–7: *Ararath mons est Armeniae altissimus, in quo archa post diluvium requievit, ut dicit Isidor & usque hodie lignorum archae vestigia in eiusdem montis vertice adhuc apparent*.

[76] DrP, Bk 15, cap cxii *De paradiso*, pp.680–3. Bartholomew may have drawn on the Jewish story of Alexander's journey to Paradise found in the *Iter Alexandri ad Paradisum* which, it has been argued, was known widely in northern Europe in the Middle Ages: see Bunt, p.11. Lascelles, Mary, "Alexander and the earthly Paradise in mediaeval English writings", *Medium Aevum* 5 (1936): 31–47; 79–104; 173–88, demonstrates that the story of Alexander in Paradise was familiar to medieval English writers. Greetham, 1980, discusses Bartholomew's sources for and treatment of the properties of Paradise.

[77] DrP, Bk 15, cap lxxvi *De Iudea*, pp.663–4. Author's paraphrase.

[78] DrP, Bk 15, cap xxii *De Babylonia*, pp.635–6; cap xxxiii *De Chaldea*, pp.640–1: *Locus autem ubi quondam fuit Babylon, est desertus, et nihil continet nisi bestias monstrosas.*

[79] DrP, Bk 9, cap xxvii *De Septuagesima*, p.459: *In his autem 70 annis captivitatis babylonicae praefigurabatur totum tempus vitae nostrae, quam diu culpae subdimur atque poenae.* The number 70, as the allotted span of life, has its own cluster of associations, including the parable of the vineyard: Sears, 1986, pp.80-1. Landini (pp.24–5) notes that the passage in *Luke* 10:1–5, taken to denote the number of workers to be sent forth into the field, was one of the Gospel texts upon which Francis reputedly founded his Order.

[80] Bk 19, cap cxvii *De numero quaternario*, p.1223: *Forma autem quadrangula maxime stabilis est atque firma, et ideo maxime stabilitatem signat universalis ecclesie et firmitatem fidelis anime tam in virtutibus quam in scientia et doctrina, que comprehendit cum omnibus sanctis que sit longitudo, latitudo, sublimitas, et profundum.*

[81] The large Hereford map's upper edge is peaked, which strictly speaking makes it a rectangle surmounted by a triangle containing a circle.

Chapter 5. 'Properties', salvation and social order in late-medieval England

This chapter and the next look at 'Properties' on the next major stage of its journey through the Middle Ages. This is the later-medieval context of war, famine and plague in which noble lay patrons commission prose translations of 'Properties' into vernacular European languages; in which manuscripts of the Latin text, in whole or in part, proliferate in Europe; and in which readers and writers refer to Bartholomew as an authority on the properties of the natural world.

We saw in the last chapter that in the first half of the thirteenth century the Catholic church was facing great challenges to its authority from opponents and detractors from outside and from within. In the Friars Minor it had an evangelising brotherhood with a mandate to travel, however arduously, and committed to preaching without payment. With the papacy's support, small groups of friars made their way across Europe, across the English Channel and thence across the Irish Sea. The friars first arrived in England in 1224 and in Ireland by 1230.[1] Little more than a decade later, Bartholomew's finished work could have been available to support the Order's efforts.

The time and the manner of the first arrival and dissemination of 'Properties' in England are matters of speculation, but need to be seen in the context of the church's insistent focus upon preaching and scholarship at a time of social upheaval, when the secular and regular clergy were perceived to be performing poorly. Its reception and transmission over the thirteenth and fourteenth centuries must also be seen against the background of the long-term effects of the Black Death that were undermining traditional social norms; of recurrent warfare between the kings of England and France; and of the competitive culture of Christian chivalry, with its supporting texts, that was shared by the inter-related nobility of both countries. This chapter examines how far Bartholomew's world-book could have found a ready reception among English speakers, listeners, writers and readers during these troubled times: whether they were the poor, finding solace in its homely *exempla*; or the wealthy, responding to its endorsement of a divinely ordered system of status, and to its possibilities as a material commodity.

The friars in England

We have a partisan record of the arrival of the first friars in England in the account of the English Franciscan Thomas of Eccleston (floruit 1240–50), who records, barely a generation after the event, that in the early years of the Order in England, the friars received support from clerics and laity who supplied plots of land and recruits. Countess Loretta, 'a noblewoman who lived as an anchoress at Hackington', cherished the friars 'and discreetly exercised her influence' to obtain favour for the four Friars Minor and five lay-brothers who arrived at Canterbury in 1224.[2] From the start, the brotherhood of Minorites comprised a novel type of educated religious available to aid the devotions of noblewomen as well as men. Kings Henry III and Edward I gave money to the Order, and over three reigns Queen Eleanor of Provence, Queen Margaret and Queen Isabella of England founded and financed the London Greyfriars and their church.[3] Favours were forthcoming from clerical and lay sources — for example, from Simon of Langton, brother of the Archbishop of Canterbury — and from Sir Henry of Sandwich, a wealthy merchant who gave land to the friars in 1225. Eccleston tells us that recruitment to the Order gathered momentum across all ranks.[4] By 1240, when Bartholomew was completing 'Properties' in Magdeburg, at least 29 English houses had been established; the first in the west midlands, followed by the south-east.[5]

With them the friars brought their training in preaching, their knowledge of popular stories and songs, and their experience of how to communicate with people of all ranks. Whether they brought books, we do not know. There is an absence of firm information about the first copies of the Latin 'Properties' to arrive in England, when they were brought, and whether by Franciscan preachers. At the time of the friars' first arrival in England the Order was still grappling with the practical and ideological problems of absolute poverty and the use of books. It was not until the end of the century that papal directives legitimised the owning of property, including books, for the Minorites' use, bringing them into line with the Dominicans. It is reasonable to speculate that 'Properties' may have come to the notice of English readers through preachers from the continent, where it had been available for copying under the Paris *pecia* system at the end of the century.[6] 'Properties' was a suitable, available work that met the needs of students, chaplains and preachers, providing *exempla* and stories with which to enliven their teaching. It also met the needs of scholars for a comprehensive, authoritative world book and useful compendium of sources.

The friars were initially welcomed as chaplains in the households of wealthy laity and as sympathetic pastors of the poor. These are two possible points of entry for 'Properties', both orally and as manuscripts, into wider circulation in England. One can imagine the difficulty of taking even Bartholomew's handy compendium on a long journey, but an illustration in a manuscript of Rubruck's journey to the land of the Tartars shows two friars with staves, each with a book slung on his back, suggesting that books were carried far afield in this way.[7] It is on record that in the fourteenth century Charles VI of France gave a safe-conduct to a Minorite who had bought four books in Paris, including

'Properties', and who wanted to return with them to London.[8] By the mid-fourteenth century, and possibly earlier, 'Properties' was a valued possession and reference work held in several private, college and monastery libraries in England. Its content was thus available to clerics of different levels of education, and to laypeople within the social networks that had access to these libraries.[9] Thomas Eccleston records that in the 1240s lecturers were appointed at the Franciscan houses and '[g]radually the gift of learning spread abroad over the whole English province'.[10] This implies the kind of network of exchange, borrowing and bequest that broadens the readership of a valued work.

Social order and disorder

There is evidence that at the time of the friars' establishment in the British Isles, events were challenging the ideal of a triple-layered organisation of society described by a fourteenth-century sermon writer: 'For in erthe byn iij degrees of folke and all schuld loue God aboue all thynge. Telynge and laborers is on of tho. Lordes and ladies is anoþer. And men and wemmen of the Churche is the thridde.'[11] Maurice Keen summarises the documentary evidence that conditions in late-medieval England placed strains on this system, as each estate suffered a long build-up of economic and demographic distress produced by war, taxation, famine and the long-term effects of the Black Death over the course of the fourteenth century. As the population fell, wages rose, demesnes became unprofitable to farm, and labourers and lords had to re-negotiate longstanding labour relations. In addition, as the lower ranks gained economic strength following the worst of the plague years, recorded legislation shows efforts to keep them in their place, while the regular and secular clergy, including friars, were perceived to be in decline.[12] The friars themselves came under attack for failing to live up to the apostolic ideal, and for usurping the pastoral and clerical work of the clergy.[13] At the same time, economic changes were adversely affecting relations between landlords and their dependents. More specifically, Paul Hargreaves has examined causes and effects of tensions during the 1380s between the monks of Worcester Priory and its peasants, concluding that such tensions could be of a longstanding nature but were exacerbated by the tendency of peasants after the Black Death to appropriate chattels attached to peasant holdings, and in many cases to abscond with them. The more oppressive the conditions of tenancy, the more peasants resorted to flight. This helped to effect changes in the character of medieval property relationships.[14] E. B. Fryde finds a very similar response to harsh treatment on the Norfolk estates of Margaret Beaufort: account rolls and court rolls for the 1370s to 1390s show tenants choosing to flee with the estate's chattels rather than to pay dues, to the detriment of the estate.[15] The eighteenth-century chronicler of the Berkeley family and its estates in the west of England, John Smyth, records how in the mid-1380s Lord Berkeley, like many other lords of manors, turned to leasing out his lands 'instead of manureing his demesnes in each manor with his own servants, oxen, kine, sheep ... under the oversight of the reeves of the manors'.[16] Under such conditions longstanding bonds between lords and labourers broke down: in response, the wealthy sought greater distinction of rank by means of new sumptuary laws, and the display of lineage through the tools and texts of chivalry and the making of parks. Enclosures for sheep-pastures and sumptuous parklands, however, caused additional suffering and resentment as tenant farmers were evicted.[17]

'Properties' moralised

Whether or not writers name Bartholomew, we know that 'Properties', with its affirming, normative representations of labour and reward, of lordship and the *familia*, would have fitted the social concerns of English landowners in the fourteenth century. 'Properties' preserved, and made available for preachers and readers, a fundamentally simple and understandable image of hierarchy upon which later interpretations could be based. Bartholomew's descriptions of familiar animals such as asses, oxen and bees fitted the fourteenth-century convention of depicting agricultural labour as a metaphor for Christian life on earth. They also supplied models of harsh treatment. We might wonder, but cannot prove, whether exploited workers identified, through the medium of the mendicant's sermon, with Bartholomew's accounts of the serving woman bought and sold like a beast; with the victims of bad landlords who unfairly exacted tallages; with the dog, an excellent servant to his lord, ending his days lying on the dunghill; and with the overworked, abused and unrewarded ass, who even has his rough but serviceable coat taken from him after death.[18]

Echoes of, and references to, Bartholomew do occur in new writings, although it is not possible to say whether writers knew the work directly. A. S. G. Edwards notes that there is a mention in the popular *Ayenbyte of Inwyt* (1340), by the Benedictine Michael of Northgate, of 'a great scholar ... called Bartholomew'.[19] Baudouin van den Abeele has analysed manuscripts of sermon material, the *Stella Clericorum,* that testifies to the later use of animal *exempla* from 'Properties' and from Cantimpré's *De natura rerum* as sources for preaching.[20] More than half of the *Contes Moralisés* of the Franciscan preacher and writer Nicolas Bozon (d. c.1340) are thought to be based upon Bartholomew's descriptions of the properties of animals and birds in Books 18 and 12, and of everyday life in Book 6. Another of Bozon's sources, identified by Lucy Toulmin-Smith, is a 'sevenfold Treatise of the Moralities of the heavenly bodies, of the elements, of animals, fish, trees or plants, herbs, and precious stones'.[21] This is the *Proprietates rerum moralizatae* (or *Liber moralizate*) mentioned in Chapters 2 and 3 above.[22] Toulmin-Smith observes that Bozon deals with 'the moral aspects of all sorts of affairs in everyday life' including social relations: 'Evidently a man of experience among various orders of society, his sympathies are manifestly on the side of the poor against their oppression and robbery by rich masters and lords, while many of his stories are pointed against the great and powerful.' However, Bozon distributes blame or admonitions to all classes; several of the *contes* treat relations between servants and masters, admonishing faults in both high and low, but not advocating a change in the status quo.[23]

Gregory Kratzmann and Elizabeth Gee demonstrate connections between collections of *exempla* made in the early fourteenth century in response to preachers' needs for sermon material. These include the Anglo-Norman *Contes moralisés* and the Latin *Dialogus creaturatum moralizatus*, and the earlier *Proprietates rerum moralizate* mentioned above.[24] 'Properties' is a chief source for these three works, but how directly is not clear except perhaps in the case of the *Moralizate*, which clearly has close links to the glosses in 'Properties' (see Chapter 3). It is now agreed that the *Moralizate* is a late-thirteenth-century or early-fourteenth-century abridgement of 'Properties' that highlights its Franciscan teaching, possibly in the light of Bonaventure's *Itinerarium mentis ad Deum*, since the author gives it a carefully organised seven-fold form.[25] In it, the writer has abstracted passages from 'Properties' Books 8, 4, 12, 13, 18, 17 and 16 and arranged them into seven tracts, explaining the moralised properties or *conditiones* of the heavenly bodies; elements; birds; fishes; animals; trees and plants; and precious stones. John Friedman notes the utility of its detailed index, which names the included subjects and also their *conditiones*: 'Thus the user of the LM may find an item in the work according to the letter or to the spirit.'[26] The *Dialogus* also has seven parts: on the heavenly bodies, the four elements, birds, fish, animals, plants, and gemstones. Like 'Properties', it had a long life. Translated into English as *Dialoges of Creatures Moralysed,* it went into print in Holland, copiously illustrated with woodcuts, in 1480 and 1530, probably for an English market and probably as a tool for preachers and as recreational reading for laity.[27]

The writers of later works on salvation such as *Jacob's Well, The Litil Tretys on the Seven Deadly Sins, The Prick of Conscience, The Cloud of Unknowing*, and *Destructuorium Viciorum* may also have been indebted, knowingly or unknowingly, to Bartholomew. At least some of them seem to use the glosses as well as the column text of 'Properties'. Bartholomew's learned yet lively *exempla* found their way into recorded sermons such as those of John Bromyard, Thomas Wimbledon, John Waldeby and other popular preachers.[28] These and, no doubt, as yet undiscovered sources testify that while there was much new Latin and vernacular writing in later-medieval England, at the same time established Latin compendia of authorities, including 'Properties', were being preserved, owned, read and borrowed from on both sides of the English Channel, as Seymour's studies of ownership have shown.[29] We must conclude that their content fed into the pool of ideas available to writers, preachers and artists making new works for their own time. As Michael Twomey points out, a reception history of a medieval compilation such as 'Properties' is not likely to reveal clear lines of derivation; it should take into account the fluidity of medieval texts and their intertextual exchanges over time.[30]

Labouring and voyaging

The fourteenth-century Franciscan author of the sermons found in the *Fasciculus Morum* is another preacher who demonstrates that certain moralisations preserved in 'Properties' had become part of a pool of conventional imagery available to writers. He includes at least one passage that is extremely close to Bartholomew's wording, although without any such acknowledgement. Apparently echoing 'Properties' Book 13 on the sea, the preacher elaborates on the trope of the pilgrimage of the soul in his example of the person who 'has his own body for his ship in which he carries a most precious merchandise, namely his soul ... Reason, our captain, sits at the stern, which means that he must remember the wretchedness of his beginning. The mast in this ship is hope.' The world is an ocean of danger for the soul: 'Hidden rocks and sandbanks, sirens, Scylla, Charybdis, currents of pitch are the dangers at sea to be feared.'[31]

Similarly, the author of *Dives and Pauper* uses the imagery of the sea voyage to illustrate how a person, like a steersman:

> ... must stondyn in thee last ende of his schip & of his lyf and thinkyn of hys deth and of his ende, how mischeuouslyche & how perlyously he shal wendyn henys, & how, whiþyr, ne whanne woot he neuere; & in that maner he schal best steryn the schip of his lyf to the sykir hauene of heuene blysse.[32]

The two authors just quoted may not agree about why one should sit in the stern of the boat, but their common use of the allegory shows its currency and its flexibility. 'Properties' need not have been the only available source of the idea of pilgrimage across the sea of worldly life. Indeed, it has been suggested that by the end of the century the trope of the ship of the soul was a worn cliché in the mouths of Franciscan friars.[33] At any rate, we know from maps, misericords and other graphic representations that fourteenth-century and later viewers could contemplate perdition in the forms of the siren, or of Scylla and Charybdis, whether or not they were directly acquainted with Bartholomew's work.[34]

The parable of the vineyard, which as we saw earlier is such an important source of Bartholomew's imagery, became another well-worn but very flexible source of representations of labour, reward and lordship.[35] It appears as a motif in fourteenth-century devotional literature, but it also provides a setting in poems and sermons for dramatisations of labour relations between ranks. In the poem *Pearl* and in other devotional works, it becomes a vehicle for doctrines about grace, eternal life and mystical *unio* with God.[36] As in Gower's *Vox Clamantis* and Langland's *Vision of Piers the Plowman,* we find the figure of the ploughman and his co-labourers the ass, the ox and the dog used to represent ideals of obedient service and the subversion of those ideals. We can see from many literary examples that the figure of the ploughman with his oxen, itself a microcosm of hierarchy, provided an extremely adaptable and powerful image that could represent the Lord and the preacher or Langland's Christian seeking Do-well; but also the ordinary labourer in the field, the oppressed labourer feeding the spendthrifts of the land.[37] In a late-fourteenth-century Lollard sermon, God Himself is 'an erþe tilier ... in whose teme alle Cristen men shulden draw as oxen, vnder þe softe and liȝt ȝocke of loue'; but the preacher, though unworthy, is himself 'set here at þis tyme to dryue þis worþi teme' of parishioners with the goad of sharp sentences.[38] Recalling Bartholomew's vignettes of the ox and the ox-herd in Book 18, we can see how they can represent different ideals of labour from the perspective of the different estates.

Models of good behaviour ...

In the context of protracted unease following the death of Richard II in 1399 we find the writer of *Dives and Pauper,* in about 1410, drawing on 'Properties', either in the Latin form or in Trevisa's translation, for examples of proper relations between high and low. He dwells upon the mutual obligations of each and the necessity for each to maintain his place for the support of the whole social structure — it is Pauper who preaches, and Dives who learns, analogous perhaps to those of the first estate who instruct those of the second. The treatise is organised as a sequence of sermons or meditations on each of the Ten Commandments. The writer may have been a Franciscan friar, and another proper relation implicit in this treatise is that of preacher and audience. The sermon on each commandment contains colourful examples, parables and stories from the Old Testament and other sources. On the precept 'Thou shalt not kill', *Pauper* refers to Bartholomew as 'Master of Kind' when citing him on the properties of the insinuating adder:

> Also flatereris ben lykenyd to a neddere þat is clepyd dipsa, whiche, as seith þe Maystir of Kende, libro xviii, he is so lytil þat þou a man trede þeron he may nout sen it, but his venym is so violent þat it sleth a man or he felyth it & he dyyth withoutyn peyne.

> Also, flatterers are likened to the adder that is called *dipsa*, which, as the Master of Kind says in Book 18, is so little that a man may tread on it without seeing it, but its venom is so violent that it kills a man before he can feel it and he dies painlessly.[39]

Later in the same Commandment, he uses an example from Bartholomew to illustrate harmony and discord in Christian life, referring back to Bartholomew's biblical source:

> Tellyt þe Mayster of Kende, lib.xviii, þat þouȝ þe harpe be wel stryngyd with stryngis mad of a schep & þer be on stryng þat is mad of a wolf set in þat harpe it schal makyn alle oþere at discord, so þat þei schul nout mon acordyn whil it is þere, & it schal fretyn on two alle þe oþere cordis. Ryȝt so, þey man or woman kepe wel alle þe comandementis as to manys syȝthe, ȝif he breke on he is gylty of alle in Godis syȝthe, as Sent Iamys seith.
>
> The Master of Kind, in Book 18, says that even if a harp is well strung with strings made of sheep gut, if there is one string made of wolf gut set into that harp it will make all the others out of tune ... Just as, though a man or woman keeps all the Commandments well in the sight of mankind, yet if he or she breaks one he or she is guilty of breaking them all in the sight of God, as St James says.[40]

In particular, the fourth Commandment, to obey one's parents, provides the writer with an opportunity to make the point that rich and poor, high and low, young and old must observe each other's needs as well as the precepts of scripture for society to be stable; worldly riches do not absolve great ones from the Commandments and do not last. To illustrate care of dependants in general, the author draws on 'The Master of Properties' for the stories of the stork and of the pelican to represent ideal relations of mutual care, dominance and subordination on the text of the Commandment 'thou shalt honour thy father and thy mother'.[41]

The writer goes on to create a further metaphor of society as a structure with interdependent parts, in the image of the tree unshaken by tempest. If each level of the tree holds to its allotted role, the social body will remain firm: the canopy of the tree is like the lords and great men; the tempest is that of pride and sin; the root is the commons, which must hold firm for the tree to survive.[42] The idea of the tree's roots as that which sustains and supports the body of the tree (like the root that nourishes the plant, and the body of a beast which sustains all the limbs and members) was available in the Latin 'Properties' and in the English *Properties*, in Books 17 and 18. Besides the pelican and the tree, the stone called 'crisolite' is another created thing whose properties make it a reminder of the fifth commandment, and again the author refers to the 'Master of Kind's' words on 'crisolite' and its supposed ability to record the passage of time.[43] The author of *Dives and Pauper* offers the reader entry points into an interwoven set of ideas that is also a schema of salvation: pelican, stork, tree, crisolite, ageing, deference to elders and betters, passage of time, arrival at evening. For this complex intellectual purpose the writer invokes a scholarly authority: the Master of Properties, or Master of Kind. But, while this allows us to conclude that Bartholomew had acquired a certain status among scholars, we cannot assume that he was being quoted at first hand.

The second estate had the task of protecting and ruling the realm, and some of those perceived to fail in this have been pinned down for us in caustic verse, under the guise of animals. In the late years of Richard II's reign, the unknown author of the satire *Mum and the Sothsegger* concealed criticism of the court using the bee community as an ideal of industrious citizenship in the garden of England, bothered by pests. The bees forage in a fertile landscape where labourers, beasts and birds can be seen in productive and pleasing array. In a lyrical passage the narrator describes the delights of this domain, where the franklin, 'gardyner of þis garth', keeps all in order, including his beehives. He is busy killing drones as they fly back to the hive — creatures which do not fulfil the natural function of bees but, parasitically, consume the honey. In a polemical passage on 'þe bee-is bisynes' as an example of social equity and order, the speaker cites Bartholomew on 'The bomelyng of þe bees, as Bartholomew vs telleth', in which each bee knows the others' voices, their king rules mercifully, with king and bees supporting each other, while the drones simply 'deceipuen þaym and doon no þing elles'. The franklin assures the narrator that the drones will be discovered and killed, 'As Bartholomew þe Bestiary bablith on his bokes'.[44] This line suggests that the relevant parts of 'Properties' could have the function of a bestiary for people of this time, helping to preserve, with its details and sources, the example of the bee as virtuous, obedient and industrious and of the drone as a mere parasite. Day and Steele consider that the narrator's source is 'ultimately' Bartholomew if not directly, and that he is selective — omitting Bartholomew's description of bees that desert a weak king to join a stronger. This would be in keeping with the poet's wish to present an analogy with strong rule and loyal, industrious subjects.

… and bad behaviour

The estates' mutual dissatisfactions and distrust are recorded by chroniclers, polemicists and satirists during the fourteenth and into the fifteenth centuries — mostly from the point of view of the governing ranks. Voicing the anxieties of those threatened by peasant unrest, John Gower in *Vox Clamantis* — completed in 1381, the year of the Peasants' Revolt — surveys the three estates of Richard's realm and takes to task, at length and in detail, the first and second estates for failing in their duty and allowing the rebellion to occur: ideally 'There are the cleric, the knight, and the peasant, the three carrying on three [different] things. The one teaches, the other fights, and the third tills the fields.'[45] He depicts a nightmare vision of the commons in the form of beasts, over-running the fertile garden of the land, from which emerged the jackdaw 'Wat' [Tyler], and John Ball.[46] In the forefront, rebellious asses 'contrary to nature' were carried away by sudden revolt, and no longer useful: 'They refused to carry sacks to the city any more and were unwilling to bend their backs under a heavy load.' They defied nature, wanting the tails of tigers, the horns of wild beasts, and the trappings of horses. An ox ran amok 'contrary to its rightful duties' and forgetful of 'its own nature'; swine and dogs rebelled, the cat no longer followed 'its natural ways' but joined with the fox in unnatural alliance with the dogs; the ranks of birds exchanged colours, calls and natures in horrible confusion, domestic and wild no longer separated. The scenes epitomise confusion of natural order, as Gower emphasises in the midst of this nightmare.[47]

Gower uses a political rhetoric in which the 'natural' or 'unnatural' properties of animals serve for oblique comment on human behaviour. We know that Bartholomew, in his accounts of the properties of the bee, cow, dog, ass and ox, stresses their natural and useful properties: the ass, for example, is a melancholy, cold and dry animal, naturally heavy, slow and sluggish, stolid and uncomplaining, burden-carrying, long-suffering, used to lowly and scant food.[48] His descriptions of the ideal and 'natural' properties of the workers who were supposed to serve patiently at the bottom of society can help us to appreciate the drama of Gower's vision of the 'unnatural' ass, ox and other beasts, threatening society's very foundations. Conversely, we have better insight into Bartholomew's emphasis on the plight of the superannuated dog and ass if we consider it in the light of early Franciscan involvement with the poorest in society.

'Properties' and a noble English family

For the above writers, 'Properties' was an available work that presented an image of the created world within a divinely ordered cosmos, but that also focused attention upon the physical world in all its immense variety and significance, spiritual and material. It could appeal to both clergy and laity. While the Latin 'Properties' continued to be disseminated among clerics and held safely in abbey libraries, its earliest known associations with England place it in the south-west, at Berkeley Castle in Gloucestershire, in a secular household of local nobility who maintained a strong connection with the work over three centuries.

Thomas Eccleston records that some time after 1240 the Franciscan brothers at the Gloucester house (established by 1230), having parted with some ground at an earlier date, managed to regain it 'with considerable difficulty from Lord Thomas Berkeley only through the wisdom and favour of his lady'.[49] This lady was Joan, wife of Thomas I (1170–1243). As a widow, in about 1250 she 'essentially refounded' the town of Wotton-under-Edge in the neighbourhood of Berkeley Castle, earning the title *domina de Wotton*.[50] There is no evidence that Joan employed a Franciscan chaplain or confessor, but as an interested and influential person who championed the local friars, and whose husband had given them land, she exemplifies the kind of opportunity that existed for friars to become integrated into the upper ranks of English landed society as well as with the poor of the towns — an opportunity for them to introduce their own reading material, attitudes and image of the world.

We lose sight of Joan but there is evidence that the work came into the possession of her daughter-in-law Lady Johanna Berkeley (d.1310), who married Lord Thomas Berkeley II (1245–1326) in 1267, and that it circulated back to a clerical library as a valued commemorative item. This is witnessed in a donation made to the friars before 1310, recorded in a discarded list of donations to the Ipswich Franciscan house (established 1226).[51] One listed donor was *domina Johanna de Berkele*, who also left songs both sacred and secular, stories, saints' lives, glossed books of the Bible, liturgical items and *Hugonem de arca Noe* (which, as we saw in the last chapter, was a text concerning salvation, associated with a form of world map).[52] Bartholomew stands in this list alongside other religious texts, implying high status in the library of a well-read laywoman who considered it worthy of a commemorative function. Her bequest supplements other evidence that 'Properties' may have been circulating in the west country by early in the fourteenth century.[53] It also situates the work within the Berkeley family, members of which continued to be patrons of learning and letters over several generations. According to Smyth, the eighteenth-century Berkeley steward and chronicler, Thomas Berkeley III (d.1361) sponsored 'an hopefull scholler' of the neighbourhood and founded numerous chapels and chantries.[54] It was under Thomas III that John Trevisa started his translation work. Thomas' first wife, Margaret, founded the grammar school at the local town of Wotton-under-Edge. In the 1390s, his son by his second wife, Thomas Berkeley IV (1352–1417), included 'Properties' among the set of prose texts considered worth the effort and expense of translation at the hands of the clerical servant, John Trevisa, whom he inherited from his father.[55] Thomas IV's daughter and heiress, Elizabeth, would continue in her family's footsteps as a patroness of letters and especially of translation.[56]

In 1398 Trevisa, of Cornish birth but a long-time resident and chaplain at Berkeley Castle, completed *On the Properties of Things*, a translation of the 19 Books of 'Properties' into the local dialect of the region.[57] *On the Properties of Things* was not Trevisa's first large literary undertaking for Sir Thomas. In 1387 he had completed his translation of Higden's *The Polychronicon*, another lengthy text.[58] There is no explanatory prologue at the beginning of any of the extant manuscripts of either *The Polychronicon* or *On the Properties of Things*, and it is only at the very end of the latter that Trevisa gives us a glimpse of himself in the act of signing off: 'þise translaciouns i-ended at Berkeleye, the sixte day of

Feuerer ... the ȝeere of my lordes age, Sire Thomas, lord of Berkeley, that made me make this translacioun, seuene and fourty.'[59] To gain some insight into the motivations behind the repeat of such a major undertaking we are obliged to look across the Channel at similar ventures taking place there, and extrapolate from prologues supplied by continental translators of 'Properties' into Italian and French.

'Properties', power and prestige

In 1309, only about 60 years after the original was written, Vivaldo Belcalzer had made an abridged Italian version of 'Properties' in the dialect of Mantua for his patron, Guido Buonalcosi.[60] In 1372, the work had been translated into French for Charles V by his chaplain, Jean Corbechon. At roughly the same time as the English project was under way (before 1391), an anonymous provençal translator produced the *Elucidari de las proprietatz de totas res naturals*, a translation of 'Properties' into the local béarnaise dialect of Toulouse spoken in the northern part of Foix. The recipient was Gaston`Phébus', Comte de Foix (d.1391), a young boy at the time.

Lords of their domains

The prologues and illustrations that accompany these translations reveal a new and secular conception of the work among noble readers and patrons of the fourteenth century. Michel Salvat concludes that Belcalzer's aims, stated in a prefatory dedication to his Italian patron, were both theological and political: the first was to put into the vernacular the writings of saints and philosophers in support of the doctrine of Aristotle, the Platonic doctrine being erroneous and contrary to the faith; his second was to transmit the treasury of wisdom to the rich and powerful who had to govern themselves as well as all their subjects. Jean Corbechon in the prologue to his translation of 'Properties', the *Livre des propriétés des choses* made for Charles V, stresses the notion of wisdom informed by knowledge as a necessary adjunct of government. Like Belcalzer, he states that among all human perfections that the royal heart ought to wish for, the desire for *sapience* ought to hold first place. Like the exemplars Solomon, Ptolemy, Alexander, Julius Caesar, Theodosius and the studious Charles himself, a sovereign must acquire *science et sapience* in order to rule with wisdom and justice. In both Italy and France there had come into existence the concept of a ruler who ought to make himself a `détenteur de la science' to rule his subjects with authority, and that 'Properties' was seen as a means to that end.[61] Donal Byrne concludes from the evidence of illustrations in the béarnais manuscripts that the provençal family of Foix valued knowledge about 'all the matter of nature', and that nature, wisdom and philosophy could form a unified concept for them.[62] The original copy of Charles V's *Propriétés des choses* is lost, but Byrne offers a reconstruction of its frontispiece which, with the textual additions of the translator, reveals, he says, 'a new conception of the meaning and use of the encyclopedia, as well as a concerted attempt to draw this authoritative work into the orbit of royal aims and aspirations'. Byrne suggests that the works translated for Charles formed a systematic program of learning, in which *Propriétés* represented the world of nature, now knowable by Charles as it was by Solomon.[63]

As Maurice Keen notes in his discussion of European chivalric culture, the historical sages referred to in the prologues, such as Solomon, and the Worthies, who included Charlemagne, Arthur, Alexander and Julius Caesar, 'symbolised the significance of a story that was emphatically unconcluded, reminding men at once of the example of the past and that the history of chivalry was still a-making'. Keen adds that in order to understand that story and its immediate implications, an individual needed not only prowess and lineage but also acquaintance with a wide range of associated literature, religious, courtly and historical.[64]

Belcalzer likens his patron to the Nine Worthies, one of whom was Alexander the Great, legendary pupil of Aristotle. This indicates that Bartholomew's inclusion of many references to Alexander and to Aristotle made it a work that could support a materialistic and heroic image of the world as well as a symbolic and moralistic one, for patrons with chivalric interests. A fourteenth-century codex in the British Library, in which 'Properties' Book 15, on peoples and places, is bound together with extracts from the Alexander literature, illustrates such an association. It appears to be a personal and miniaturised compilation of wisdom literature that begins with a copy of Book 15, followed by an extract from Honorius of Autun's *imago mundi*, and extracts from the Alexander literature then available.[65]

The English and the French

The later life and literary achievements of Gaston de Foix may help us to understand this valuation and this concept, and thus to be able to appreciate what 'Properties' could have had to offer him and, by extrapolation, other magnate patrons such as Thomas Berkeley. From what we know of Gaston's life, his recorded devotion to hunting was more than just recreational. The hunting treatise that he wrote consists of two parts, the practical *Livre de chasse* and the devotional *Livre d' oraisons,* which suggests that he found spiritual edification as well as physical satisfaction in his domination of the natural environment of his estates.[66] Reconstructions of extensive pleasure-parks such as the 2000 acres of Hesdin in northern France, created in 1288, suggest that such a domain could have encompassed a wide variety of terrains and habitats, including vineyards, like a mini-creation. The theory and management practices of estates were similar across European chivalric culture. The typical English hunting park averaged about 200 acres, and contained coppiced woodland, dense woodland, open pasture with pollarded trees and vistas, ponds and rivers, all designed to protect but also reveal the many animals enclosed within the banked perimeter.[67] For a nobleman of either country wishing to be seen to possess the full knowledge in practice and also in the form of written authority, 'Properties' would have provided references to ancient authority and covered the necessary ground. Books 17, 18, 13 and 12 treat the flora and fauna likely to be encountered in the lord's domains, including domestic animals and birds, wild game, horses and hounds. Bartholomew includes chapters on the animals and birds of venery included by Gaston in his treatise (for example deer, hare, badger, otter); on the care as well as the physical and moral properties of hounds and horses; on different kinds of hawk and their capabilities; and on timber trees and crop plants. A glance at the *tabula* of 'Properties' would be enough to show a secular lord, even if he had little Latin, that this work held useful facts about the plant and animal life, terrains and waterways over which he aimed to keep his dominion. Nevertheless, the way Bartholomew draws noblemen's secular contacts with the material world into the theological domain could have helped to sanctify for them their everyday lives, environments and status.[68]

In Book 6 of 'Properties', Bartholomew is explicit about the duties and mutual obligations of lords and servants, and the need for lordship to maintain peace, order and good governance.[69] John Trevisa makes these chapters resonate for a fourteenth-century secular lord:

> And þerfore riȝtful lordshchipe is i-ordeyend ... For wiþoute a lord myȝte not þe comyn profit stonde siker neiþir saaf, compenye of men myȝte not be pesible, nothir esy, nothir quyete. For ȝif powere and myȝte of riȝtful lordes were bynome and itake awey, þanne were malis free and godenesse and innocence neuer siker. So seiþ Isidir.

There is much more on this theme, with further citations from Isidore of Seville, St Gregory, St Ambrose and the Bible to support it. Bartholomew asserts, independently of his sources, that obedience to a lord is an ordained means by which people learn to obey God:

> Kende bringiþ forþ alle men iliche in powere and in myȝt, but for diuers worthinesses þe despensacioun of Goddis word settiþ som men tofore oþir þat hy þat drediþ not þe riȝtwisnesse of God may drede þe punyschinge of mannes strengþe.[70]

It does not seem surprising that those who could see in these words authorisation for their own position as 'set before others' would want this book to circulate among their associates. In this same chapter on the good master, Bartholomew also presents a parallel between the situation of people, where God's dispensation sets some before others, and the situation of animals, birds and other creatures such as bees:

> 'Therfore Ambrosius seiþ þat among bestis kende settiþ hem tofore þat beþ most noble and most strong, and makeþ hem kinges, dukes, and leders of oþir, as it farith among bestis and foules and also among been.'[71]

While the clerical or monastic reader could have understood the bees to refer to themselves under their clerical leaders, the secular landowner could have seen in these words a reassuring vision of the ranks of creation over which he or she ruled, bees after all being one of the exploitable creatures on an estate.

We might infer from the cross-Channel examples given by Corbechon and Belcalzer that Berkeley had a similar perception of the writings of the learned and wise as a source of power to be annexed for temporal purposes. Berkeley has been described as the most important baronial castle in the area in the fourteenth century.[72] Removed as they were from London and holding sway over the western port of Bristol, the Berkeley family wielded great power in their domains. Like Gaston de Foix, Thomas Berkeley IV was a great huntsman. According to John Smyth, 'hee and his brothers have kept out four nights and days together with their nets and dogs in hunting of the fox ... and with this delight of hunting this lord began and dyed'.[73] The keeping of hounds, hawks and horses, the buying of land to create new deer parks, and 'sea furnitures in a sumptuous manner' kept for 'delight and recreations' on the river Severn, all indicate both means and leisure. Smyth styled him 'Thomas the Magnificent' in response to his lifestyle and expenditures. Thomas was made Admiral of the Fleet in Bristol, acquiring in effect a private navy. Ralph Hanna notes that his mercantile activities included wool-trading and probable piracy in the Bay of Biscay.[74]

The English and French were at war at the time of the vernacular translations of 'Properties'. Nevertheless they shared a chivalric culture expressed in hunting, heraldry and a body of literature. It is arguable that a highly important function of the English translation was the matching of Charles's achievement, the countering of Corbechon's interpretation, and the reclamation of Bartholomew for England, especially its south-west midlands. Trevisa already knew from Higden's use in the *The Polychronicon* of material from Book 15 of 'Properties' that Bartholomew had presented the English from the comfortable point of view of a compatriot. The compiler had included the story of Britain's Trojan origins and the descent of its kings from Brutus, and of St Gregory's comparison of its children to angels; and the importance to the south-east English of Canterbury, the site of St Augustine's arrival and of the shrine of Thomas Becket. Kent was the only named part of England singled out by Bartholomew, and Trevisa is fluent in rendering the enthusiastically first-hand account of 'þe plenteuouseste corner of þe world, ful ryche a londe þat vnneþe it nedeþ helpe of any londe'.[75] Trevisa's rhythmical alliteration may reflect a clerical reverence:

> Kent is a prouynce in Ynglonde vpon þe Brutisshe occean, þe chief cite þereoffe hatte Canterburye. And þe londe bereþ wele corne and fruyte and haþ many woodes, and is mooste with welles and ryuers and is noblicche yhi3te with hauens of þe see, and ryche of ricchesses and chief in holsomnes of heuene.[76]

Trevisa is fluent, too, in rendering Bartholomew's full and fulsome treatment of the English rose: 'Among alle floures of þe worlde þe flour of þe rose is chief and bereþ þe prys, and þerfore ofte the chief partie of man, þe heed, is crowned with floures of rose, as Plius seith …' For the pious reader these words could evoke the image of the martyrs crowned, or of the Virgin; but also an image of Englishness that would grow in political significance.[77] Trevisa did not need to add or subtract anything in his translation of Bartholomew's accounts of Britain, of Kent, or of the rose. Corbechon, on the other hand, working on the *Livre des propriétés des choses* during the Hundred Years' War, had been obliged to make certain changes. Besides the addition at the end of Bartholomew's chapter on the lily, stating that it was doubly superior to all other flowers, he criticises Bartholomew's biased opinion concerning Brittany and modifies the statement on the German origin of the name of France, to accommodate a Trojan hero for the French genealogy.[78] Trevisa's *Properties* can help us to feel something of the complex dynamics of territorial allegiance at that time. For example, as we read the warmly approving account of Brittany in Book 15, we can imagine its emotive force for people like the Cornishman Trevisa and the people of the Bristol area, who might well feel kinship with Cornwall and Wales and the other Celtic provinces. In Trevisa's words, Bartholomew states that Brittany ('þe lesse Bretayne') is really an offshoot of Britain ('þe more Bretayne') so that the Bretons are in fact Britons of a slightly inferior quality: 'And þei3e þis Bretayne be worþi and noble in many þinges, 3it may nou3t the dou3ter be pere to þe modir.'[79]

The Berkeleys and the king

Hanna notes that Berkeley was expelled from his court post in the conflict between Richard and the Appellants and that this conflict followed him to Gloucestershire.[80] In spite of Richard II's attempts to make an alliance with Charles VI and his second marriage to the French princess Isabel in 1396, hostilities were to be renewed by Henry V in 1415. Richard II's uncle, the Duke of Gloucester, with his military library and deep distrust of the French, was one English nobleman who opposed peace negotiations.[81] Berkeley may well have had similar views reflected in Trevisa's translation of 'Properties'. The record of Thomas IV's troubles with local lawless men in the king's pay shows the effects of the factionalism being generated at this stage of Richard II's reign, and Trevisa's own involvement in support of his lord. Richard II visited Berkeley in 1386 and may have had a particular interest in it as the place where his great-grandfather Edward II had died, but the visit may have been a tense one for both guests and hosts. In the 1380s, as Trevisa was working there as chaplain and translator for the Berkeley family, Richard was enlisting support from the people further north, especially in Cheshire, and favouring the city of York after his quarrel with London.[82] Patronage was a means of giving support to dependents and legitimising aspirations to leadership in society. When Berkeley commissioned from his chaplain translations of Higden's *Polychronicon* and Giles of Rome's *De Principe* he was not only satisfying his own thirst for knowledge; he was also enhancing his reputation at a time when he was being challenged in his domains by the rise of the favourites of King Richard II. To be seen to honour a writer could add greatly to a lord's prestige; it was part and parcel of the process of image-building.[83]

Trevisa's first translation made for Thomas Berkeley IV in 1386, that of the *Polychronicon*, encompassed the history of Britain and the role in it of legendary and recent Worthies. Berkeley too could have sought to project an image of himself as a worthy man of learning, building a library of books to support his wisdom and skill as a military lord. *Properties* arguably had a place as an informational work in Berkeley's library complementary to that of the *Polychronicon*. Ralph Hanna, discussing the question of the 'usefulness' of Trevisa's texts, points to the comprehensive nature of the main items in the Trevisan translation program (Higden's *Polychronicon* 1386, *De regimine principum*, *Properties* 1398):

> Trevisa provided Thomas with a complete analysis of the created world, which placed man among all 'things' (*Properties*); a complete depiction of human activity (in Higden's universal history); and a model for the exercise of control over the world (*De regimine*) … such works offer models for success and failure in the world.[84]

Or, to extrapolate from Elizabeth Salter's discussion of late-medieval poetry, whereas the *Polychronicon* can be said to present a 'typological' account of creation and peoples down the ages, *Properties* presents a 'structural' image of the world predicated upon the doctrine of promise, fulfilment and reward.[85] At the same time, the manuscript Arundel 123 allows us to infer that fourteenth-century readers could associate 'Properties' Book 15, the wisdom of Aristotle, and the Worthies Alexander and Julius Caesar. It suggests that Bartholomew's account of the properties of things could support a quantitative and material, as well as qualitative and moralised, image of the world.

Richard Firth Green suggests that the books that Trevisa (and later John Walton under the patronage of Thomas IV's daughter Elizabeth) translated for the

Berkeley family were the very titles that a nobleman would have needed to instruct him in history, in military practice and chivalric ethos, and in the principles of good government.[86] Sometime between *The Polychronicon* (1386, from the Latin universal history compiled by Ralph Higden c.1350) and *On the Properties of Things* (1398), Trevisa also translated the *Gospel of Nicodemus* (a source of Arthurian matter basic to the chivalric ideal), probably *De Regimine Principum* of Giles of Rome, and Fitzralph's *Defensio Curatorum*. It is instructive to compare this list with the library of the king's uncle, Thomas Woodstock, Duke of Gloucester, which included *The Polychronicon* and *De proprietatibus rerum* in Latin; *De Regimine Principum;* Vegetius' *De Re Militari*; epics, romances and poetry and Mandeville's *Travels* in French.[87] The comparison indicates that the known canon of works translated by Trevisa under the patronage of Berkeley embraced subjects appropriate for a secular nobleman asserting local dominance and promoting a chivalric image of sound learning and lineage.

John Trevisa, a cleric himself, may well have been interested in testing the capabilities of the language for works that combined a devotional with an informational purpose. Waldron sees Trevisa as the introducer of a new genre of faithful prose translation of non-canonical works of historical and scientific information, within a possibly continuous, Alfredian tradition in western England of providing useful learning for nobility.[88] In the 1380s and 1390s, the Cornish-born Trevisa was an innovator, trying out his adopted Gloucestershire vernacular for new purposes, and striving to convey underlying meaning by using the familiar and, at times, colloquial language of his circle.[89]

It seems important to keep in mind, however, that in spite of Trevisa's care to translate the Latin accurately, giving sense for sense, the vernacular must have imposed a late-fourteenth-century interpretation upon the original. His transformation of *natura* into 'kynde', for example, turns the meaning away from that of divine intermediary towards something more mundane, that of breeding or generation. The situation at Berkeley presents a fascinating parallel with that in London, where Chaucer was using the south-eastern dialect to translate Latin literature and present it in the cosmopolitan atmosphere of Richard's court. In Chaucer's work the concept of nature appears as something different again: 'the noble goddess of kind' presiding over the birds in *The Parlement of Foules* is a mythologised and firmly gendered figure far removed both from Trevisa's 'kynde' and Bartholomew's *natura*.[90]

The very provincialism of the Berkeleys suggests a reason for their eagerness for translations and for their appreciation of the Latin 'Properties' as a suitable subject. To Berkeley's desire to exert patronage, and his apparent pride in the English language, could have been added a local inability to take advantage of existing French translations. Trevisa interpolates the comment in *The Polychronicon* that in all the grammar schools of England children are being taught not in French but in English; the disadvantage being that now 'childern of gramerscole conneþ no more Frensch þan can here lift heele ... Also gentil men habbeþ now moche yleft for to teche here childern Frensch.'⁹¹ This suggests a linguistic divide between the south-west (and Trevisa cites schoolmasters with Cornish names) and the Westminster court which, with its French tutors, visitors, books and later queen, was still to some extent bilingual. The French translation made by Corbechon for Charles V in 1372 may have set a precedent for the English translation of 20-odd years later and, according to Michael Seymour, in educated and courtly circles where there was a growing demand for vernacular books, the *Livre des propriétés des choses* was beginning to establish itself.⁹² Nevertheless, a picture emerges of the Berkeley translation project as a regional undertaking, taking a stance on the appropriateness of English prose for serious English writing, within the context of a general and growing demand by laypeople for devotional and utilitarian literature in the vernacular. At this point in the journey of 'Properties' as it lived on in popular and courtly cultures of late-medieval England, we can see patron and chaplain in a regional setting, responding to challenges that were both linguistic and political.

'Properties' in London

Over time, both the French and English translations of 'Properties' became perquisites of the educated and affluent in London as well as the west country. Ralph Hanna and, more recently, Kathryn Kerby-Fulton open up the question of how the translation became better known in the metropolis among literate laity, including merchants and lawyers.⁹³ Hanna surmises that on the accession of Henry IV, Thomas Berkeley resumed his duties at court and his business affairs in London. He argues that Berkeley supplemented his rural living by urban activities in Bristol and London, and that his agent in London (and legatee) was one Robert Knolles, probably related to the alderman and grocer Thomas Knolles in London, and the grocer and merchant William Knolles in Bristol where Berkeley also had shipping interests.⁹⁴ Berkeley's contact with the merchant Robert Knolles shows that his business network extended beyond his own rank. His business activities, contacts and possession of a house in London enabled him to disseminate among other magnates, who met there from time to time on court matters, literary works translated under his patronage. As evidence, Hanna cites an early manuscript of *On the Properties of Things*, now British Library Additional Manuscript 27944, dated to before 1410 and written in a western dialect by three scribes, one of them ('Scribe D') a prolific westerner whose hand has also been identified in copies of works by Gower and Chaucer.⁹⁵ Similar scribal evidence from a manuscript of Trevisa's *Polychronicon* leads Hanna to conclude that a taste for Trevisan translation existed among the circle of magnates who patronised contemporary courtly verse, and who were Berkeley's parliamentary colleagues. Berkeley's activities in London included active publicising of his sponsored works among these colleagues and the book trade, and efforts to promote the commissioning of copies.[96] The active involvement of Scribe D in Berkeley's projects, and the purchase of *On the Properties of Things* by a wealthy lawyer, Thomas Chaworth (1380–1459), supports this view.

Chaworth, of Wyverton, Nottinghamshire, another regional landowner with London connections, commissioned the sumptuous manuscript which is now Columbia University Manuscript Plimpton 263 in about 1440. Chaworth, then, had access to the Berkeley exemplar either personally or through his London agent, the merchant Richard Thorney, and considered it worth the expense of having it copied and embellished. While the record shows that Chaworth inherited his title, was a keen huntsman, the owner of coalmines in Derbyshire, and a Member of Parliament for 40 years, there is nothing in his known library to suggest that he was a scholarly or religious man; rather, that he was a lawyer and man of business. He bequeathed two copies of the *Polychronicon* and some legal works.[97] His copy of *On the Properties of Things* is not mentioned in his will but it evidently stayed in the family, since the Chaworth manuscript passed to Sir Thomas' kinsman and executor Richard Willoughby at the time of his death, and was later used by Wynkyn de Worde as a copy text for the printing of *On the Properties of Things* in Westminster in 1495.[98]

To sum up this chapter: there are some safe conclusions to be drawn from fragmentary and diverse forms of evidence about the role and reception of 'Properties' in England in the thirteenth and fourteenth centuries. Bartholomew's accounts of the properties of things entered the pool of popular preaching and devotional material in England, and began to be diffused in written and in oral form before the end of the thirteenth century. The friars provided a channel for communicating ideas about penance and salvation through their preaching, but how far they used 'Properties' directly cannot well be demonstrated. However, it is arguable that some images and ideas are common to both 'Properties' and some of the sermon and devotional literature of the later Middle Ages, and that preaching was one mechanism for their dissemination through different ranks of society. People from all three estates could have imbibed Bartholomew's imagery with or without a clear idea of its source.

Preserved manuscripts in academic settings and in lay libraries testify that 'Properties' had status as a religious authority in the centuries after it was compiled, among the mendicants and also among scholars of other orders who required a moralised or factual compendium of knowledge. More lavish manuscripts of translations of 'Properties' show that during the fourteenth and fifteenth centuries lay people from the upper layers of society in France, Italy and England, especially, became its owners, patrons and re-writers. In appropriating the compilation they were also taking possession of the authorities within it and, in effect, helping to preserve and pass on the written body of knowledge that encompassed salvation, history and worldly wisdom. It was the economic, social and political patronage of the work as a prestigious possession that propelled 'Properties' and its compiler into the secular sphere and into noblemen's libraries in the later Middle Ages.

While Bartholomew's sub-textual images of pilgrimage, labour and salvation continued to be meaningful for readers, preachers and writers long after his own time, lay noblemen and women continued to find in the work's allegorical depth and moral authority validation for their secular interests and values. As it was commodified by the wealthy and powerful, the conception of 'Properties' expanded and changed to meet the needs of a range of readers scarcely envisaged by Bartholomew. Publicised involvement with the work imbued the nobleman with both the spiritual *gravitas* and the worldly wisdom seen as necessary for good lordship. Moreover, the idea of the universe as a hierarchical system in which everything has its appointed place suggested, for the comfortably-off, a fundamental stability in the *status quo*. A well-made book that endorsed such an image of the world and society was itself a desirable piece of property. It is safe to assume that for patrons such as Thomas Berkeley and Thomas Chaworth, the English word 'property' implied not only a moral or physical attribute but also the family estate, the ships, the coalmines, the London house and the library.[99]

'Properties' reflected and reinforced belief in the right and duty of lords to hold sway over the 'things' of their demesnes, even if in reality they were leasing out those demesnes and losing control over their peasant labour. Reciprocal obligation between the levels of society was an ideal which the powerful could at least acknowledge (if not put into practice) through their patronage of books of wisdom such as 'Properties', in Latin or the vernacular. This compilation's value to noble patrons lay, arguably, in the fact that it was a ready-made compendium of received wisdom on a multitude of 'things', reflecting the diversity of creation itself. But it also presented an image of the world as the centre of an ordered, hierarchical cosmos, validating the ideal of a clearly-differentiated society ruled by those of highest rank.

NOTES

[1] Bartholomew gives us an idea of the remote and fabulous aura surrounding Ireland, an almost mythical island, as hard to reach as Paradise itself: DrP, Bk 15, cap lxxx *De Hybernia*, p.666; cap cxii *De Paradiso*, p.682. It is thought that friars travelled to Ireland from England, establishing houses there in the 1260s: Fitzmaurice, E. B. (OFM), and A. G. Little, eds, *Materials for the History of the Franciscan Province of Ireland*, Vol.9: Manchester University Press, 1920. See Lidaka, 1997, p.395; Moorman, 1968, pp.171–6.

[2] Sherley-Price, pp.1, 15–8. See Cotton, Charles, *The Grey Friars of Canterbury*, Manchester: The University Press, 1924, pp.1–18 for accounts of the arrival of the first friars in England, and documentation of their good relations with clergy and noblewomen in Canterbury.

[3] Sekules, Veronica, "Women's piety and patronage" in *Age of Chivalry*, edited by Nigel Saul, 120–31, London: Collins and Brown, 1992, p.123; see Cotton, p.37, on Queen Isabella's support of the Canterbury Greyfriars.

[4] Sherley-Price, p.36.

[5] The friaries in or near Hereford, Bristol, Gloucester, Leicester, Nottingham, Salisbury and Stamford were all established before 1230, and at Ipswich before 1236: Moorman, pp.171–2.

[6] See Rouse, R. H. and Rouse, M. A., "*Ordinatio* and *Compilatio*" in *Ad Litteram: Authoritative Texts and Their Medieval Readers*, edited by M. Jordan and K. Emery Jnr., 113–34, London: Notre Dame, 1992, pp.287, 300; Lidaka, 1997, pp.398–405.

[7] Corpus Christi College, Cambridge Ms 66, f.67, Rubruck's *Itinerarium terrae Tartarorum*: see Little, 1937, p.66 and Plate 21.

[8] Se Boyar, p.186.

[9] Lidaka, 1997, p.393; Seymour, 1974, "English owners".

[10] Sherley-Price, pp.41–2.

[11] Quoted by Fletcher, Alan J., *Preaching, Politics and Poetry in Late-Medieval England*, Dublin: Four Courts Press, 1998, p.146, from Ms Bodley 95, f.97v.

[12] Keen, Maurice, *English Society in the Later Middle Ages*, London: Allen Lane, 1990, pp.27–47.

[13] The Benedictine Matthew Paris (d.1259), in his *Chronica maiora*, records that two friars sent as envoys by the pope in 1247 came 'concealing the rapacity of the wolf under the wool of the sheep', adopting secular dress, behaviour and occupation, and spurning the Franciscan hospice recently built at St Albans: Vaughan, Richard, *The Illustrated Chronicles of Matthew Paris: Observations of Thirteenth-Century Life*, Stroud: Alan Sutton & Corpus Christi College, Cambridge, 1993, pp.8, 19–24; see Robbins, Rossell Hope, ed, *Historical Poems of the XIVth and XVth Centuries*, New York: Columbia University Press, 1959, for poems expressing hostility to the friars: for example, "On the Minorites" (1382), pp.157–68; Lydgate's "Advice to the several estates" p.232.

[14] Hargreaves, Paul V., "Seignorial reaction and peasant responses: Worcester Priory and its peasants after the Black Death", *Midland History* XXIV (1999): 53–78.

[15] E. B. Fryde, *Peasants and Landlords in Later Medieval England*, New York: St Martin's Press, 1996, pp.248–9.

[16] John Smyth, *The Lives of the Berkeleys* (1883), quoted in Keen, Maurice, *England in the Later Middle Ages*, London: Methuen, 1973, p.194; Saul, Nigel, *Knights and Esquires: The Gloucestershire Gentry in the Fourteenth Century*, Oxford: The Clarendon Press, 1981, pp.19–21, examines this situation in context.

[17] Fryde, pp.191–203.

[18] DrP, Bk 6, cap xi *De ancilla*, p.243; cap xv–xix *De seruo* to *De domino et dominio malo*, pp.249–56; Bk 18, cap xxvi *De aliis proprietatibus canum*, pp.1039–41; cap vii *De asino*, pp.994–8.

[19] Edwards, 1985, p.123.

[20] Van den Abeele, Baudouin, "Bestiaires encyclopédiques moralisés: quelques succédanés de Thomas de Cantimpré et de Barthélemy l'Anglais", *Reinardus: Yearbook of the International Reynard Society* 7 (1994): 209–28. *Stella clericorum* is extant in a set of manuscripts from central Europe dating from the fourteenth to the fifteenth centuries, specifically destined for use by preachers and representing a strain of animal allegory different from that of the bestiary.

[21] Toulmin-Smith, Lucy, "English popular preaching in the fourteenth century", *The English Historical Review* VII (1892): 24–36, pp.27–34: 'Out of the 145 titles or subject sections in the book no less than about eighty-five owe their suggestion to passages or notions drawn from Bartholomew's work.' Hill, Betty, "British Library Manuscript Egerton 613–1", *Notes and Queries* 223 (1978): 394–409, p.407, notes

²² See Chapter 2, note 2.

²³ Toulmin-Smith, pp.33–4.

²⁴ Kratzmann, Gregory, and Elizabeth Gee, *The Dialoges of Creatures Moralysed*, London and New York: E. J. Brill, 1988, pp.5–25.

²⁵ BN Lat. 3332 f.7v: *Incipit liber de moralitatibus corporum celestium, elementorum, avium, piscium, animalium, arborum sive plantarum et lapidum preciosorum qui vel que in veneranda Scriptura vel alias autentice sub signa et eleganti misterio pulcheriformiter continetur.*

²⁶ Friedman, John B., "Peacocks and preachers: analytic technique in Marcus of Orvieto's 'Liber de moralitatibus, Vatican lat. MS 5935'" in Clark and McMunn, eds, 179–96. Philadelphia: University of Pensylvania Press, 1989, p.185.

²⁷ Kratzmann and Gee, pp.48–50. A related line of enquiry would concern the absorption of BA's teaching into early modern printed works that used animals and plants to discuss human morality, such as emblem literature; see Klingender, pp.354, 489–94. See also Van den Abeele, Baudouin, and Christel Meier, eds, *Moraliserte Enzyklopädie im Wandel von Hockmittelalter bis zur frühen Neuzeit*, Munich, 2002, pp.279–304.

²⁸ Owst, G. R., *Preaching in Medieval England*, Cambridge University Press, 1926, p.192, p.65. There is much research still to be done on uses made of 'Properties' in sermons and sermon notes as yet unpublished: Lidaka (personal communication).

²⁹ Seymour, 1974, "English owners"; Seymour, 1974, "French readers".

³⁰ Twomey, 1999, p.331.

³¹ Wenzel, Siegfried, *Fasciculus Morum: a Fourteenth Century Preachers' Handbook*, Pennsylvania State University, 1989, pp.572–5.

³² Barnum, Priscilla Heath, ed, *Dives and Pauper*, Oxford: The Early English Text Society, 1976, p.273: Commandment IX, cap viii.

³³ Goodridge, J. F., ed, *Langland: Piers the Ploughman*, Harmondsworth: Penguin, 1959, p.333 n.4.

³⁴ For example, a carved misericord in St Botolph's church at Boston, a Lincolnshire fishing port, reminds church-goers of the siren and her deadly songs: see Remnant, G. L., *A Catalogue of Misericords in Great Britain*, Oxford: The Clarendon Press, 1969, p.25. The Hereford world map clearly features the siren: see Harvey, 1996, p.8.

³⁵ AV, *Matthew* 20:1–16; Sears, pp.80 foll.

³⁶ See Eldredge, Laurence, "Imagery of roundness in William Woodford's 'De sacramento altaris' and its possible relevance to the Middle English `Pearl'", *Notes and Queries* 223 (1978): 3–5.

³⁷ Barney, 1973; Dolan, 1994: both Barney and Dolan examine the question of why and how the ploughman came to be a heroic figure in some late-thirteenth-century English writings, tracing back the authority of the labourer to the religious symbolism of the preacher as sower, cultivating human society with the ploughshare of the tongue.

³⁸ This sermon demonstrates how 'knights, priests and ploughmen are categories that may blur under the eye of moral interpretation': Fletcher, p.227.

³⁹ Barnum, Commandment V, Chap. iii, p.5.

⁴⁰ Barnum, Commandment V, Chap. xii, p.29.

⁴¹ Barnum, Commandment IV, pp.308–9. Edwards, 1985, p.123, notes a striking similarity to Trevisa's translation of the relevant passages in *Properties* Bk 12, cap ix *De cichonia*, p.619, and cap xxx *De pellicano*, p.636.

⁴² Barnum, Commandment V, Chap. xxvii, pp.357–8.

⁴³ Barnum, Commandment IV, Chap. xxvii, p.358 line 54. On the properties of crisolite Bartholomew simply says, in Trevisa's words, that a type of *crisolitus* called *crisolentus* 'is ycoloured as golde, and is wel faire in sight in þe morwetyde, and þanne as þe day passeþ his colour wexeþ dym (*Properties*, cap xxviii *De crisolito*, p.841). The passage of the day as a constant reminder of the passage of life was one of the key lessons taught by the parable of the vineyard, reinforced by Bartholomew in Bks 6, 9, 13 and 17 and elsewhere, as discussed in Chapter 3 above.

⁴⁴ Day, Mabel, and Robert Steele, eds, *Mum and the Sothsegger*, London: The Early English Text Society, 1936, pp.52–8. *Pace* the editors who state that Bartholomew does not mention the killing of the drones (Introduction p.xxv), he does so in Bk 18, cap xii *De ape* (DrP pp. 1013–9).

[45] Stockton, Eric W., ed, *The Major Latin Works of John Gower: The Voice of One Crying and the Tripartite Chronicle*, Seattle: University of Washington Press, 1962, Bk III, chap. i, p.115 foll. In Books III and IV, Gower reproves the secular clergy, monks, nuns and friars. In Bks V and VI, he deals with men and women of the second estate, and lawyers.

[46] Stockton, Bk I, chaps i-xvi, pp.51-79. That Gower is referring to the events of 1381 is confirmed by the next event in the dream, the appearance of 'a certain Jackdaw' known as a Wat, assuming the rank of command over the mob, and of John Ball, and the murder of the Archbishop of Canterbury; ibid pp.65 foll.

[47] Stockton, Bk I, pp.54–64: 'O what an astonishing thing, when the puny fly tried to surpass the crane in its powers of flight! ... This was the day when everywhere the weak man terrified the strong ... This was the day when the mighty oak suddenly fell, easily uprooted by an ordinary straw.'

[48] DrP, Bk 18, cap vii *De Asino*, pp.994–8.

[49] Sherley-Price, pp.37–8.

[50] Hanna, Ralph III, "Sir Thomas Berkeley and His Patronage", *Speculum* 64 (1989): 878–916, pp.889–901.

[51] Humphreys, K. W., *The Friars' Libraries*, London: The British Academy and the British Library, 1990, p.212. The list survived as the flyleaf for an early fifteenth-century manuscript, now Suffolk Record Office Ms HD 1043/1.

[52] Humphreys gives the entry as follows: *Domina Johanna de Berkele per fratrem J. de Berwam dedit 11 legendas et chori temporale et sanctorum et istorias 13 Matheum cum glosis Alquini mangni[sic] doctoris 14 Passionariam summam(?) que dicitur Ad omne genus hominum 16 Stelle manentes 17 Benedictus 18 Barlam cum vita Kentigarii 19 Hugonem de arca Noe 20 de proprietatibus rerum 21 primam partem Biblie 22 quartum Medie ville et 23 breuiarium.*

[53] Hill, p.409.

[54] Cited by Salter, Elizabeth, *English and International: Studies in the Literature, Art and Patronage of Medieval England*: Cambridge University Press, 1988, p.105, p.311 n.28.

[55] Hanna, 1989, p.890. The fullest and most recent study of Trevisa's life and work is Fowler, D. C., *The Life and Times of John Trevisa Scholar*, University of Washington Press, 1995.

[56] Green, pp.144–55. In 1393 Elizabeth Berkeley married Richard Beauchamp, fifth Earl of Warwick, whose coat of arms adorns a deluxe copy of Trevisa's translated *Polychronicon*, now BL Add. Ms 24194: Waldron, Ronald, "John Trevisa and the use of English", *Proceedings of the British Academy* LXXIV (1988): 171–202, p.178. The signature of a later Richard Beauchamp, bishop of Salisbury (d.1481), occurs in a luxury copy of *Properties*, now Pierpont Morgan Library Ms M875, f.6: Seymour, 1975–88 vol.3, p.23. Genealogical information on the Berkeley family is from Gibbs, Vicary, *The Complete Peerage of England, Scotland, Ireland, Great Britain and the United Kingdom*, Vol.2, London: St Catherine's Press, 1912, pp.123–45.

[57] The absence of Trevisa's known copy-text has led to speculation upon its nature and origins: see Seymour, 1974–88, vol.3, p.1; Lidaka, 1988, p.73.

[58] Fowler, 1995, provides (pp.248–51) a list of mss of the Trevisa canon; Lawler, 1983; Waldron, 1988, "Trevisa"; and Edwards, A. S. G., "John Trevisa" in *Middle English Prose: A Critical Guide to Major Authors and Genres*, edited by A. S. G. Edwards, 133–46, Rutgers University Press, 1984, assess his literary achievement.

[59] *Properties, Complecio tocius operis*, p.1396.

[60] Rhodes, Dennis E., Vivaldo Belcazar and the Mantuan Dialect in the Early 14th Century: A Study of BM Ms Add. 8785 with the edition of Bks I, II and XV, unpublished PhD thesis, University College London, 1956.

[61] Salvat, p.393, defines *sapience* as a mixture of knowledge and wisdom: 'á la fois science et sagesse'.

[62] Byrne, 1981, pp.98–9; see also Byrne, Donal, "The Boucicaut Master and the iconographical tradition of the Livre des Propriétés des Choses", *Gazette des Beaux-Arts* 92 (1978): 149–64, for insights given by ms illustrations into fourteenth–fifteenth-century French interpretations of BA.

[63] Byrne, 1981, pp.97–104, lists the 13 extant illustrated mss of Corbechon's *Livre des propriétés des choses*, from which he deduces an archetypal frontispiece. Each of these mss passed through the libraries of French and Burgundian royalty within the first years of the translation: that is, of Charles V and VI; the House of Orléans; the House of Burgundy; Philip the Bold; and Jean Duc de Berry and his grandson who between them owned four copies of the work in Latin and in French. See Seymour, 1974, "French readers".

[64] Keen, Maurice, *Chivalry*, New Haven and London: Yale University Press, 1984, p.123.

⁶⁵ BL Ms Arundel 123, British Museum, *Catalogue of Manuscripts in the British Museum: Part I The Arundel Manuscripts*, New Series vol.1, 1840, pp.29–30, describes the first item in the codex (ff.1r–23r) as deriving from Isidore of Seville 'and others': *Geographia universalis, ordine alphabetico compilata ex Isidori Hispalensis Originibus, aliisque*. It has a close affinity with DPR, Bk 15 (see Note 83 below). See Appendix A: British Library Manuscript Arundel 123, the contents of the codex.

⁶⁶ Tilander, Gunnar, *Gaston Phébus, Livre de Chasse*, Karlshamn, 1971; on the fifteenth-century English translation of Gaston's work by Edward Duke of York, brother of Henry V, see Gray, Douglas, ed, *The Oxford Book of Late Medieval Verse and Prose*, Oxford University Press, 1985, pp.145–8, 450.

⁶⁷ Landsberg, Sylvia, *The Medieval Garden*, London: The British Museum Press, 1995, pp.22–7: Hesdin 'incorporated villages, and was of the same order of size as the great royal Clarendon and Woodstock Parks in England, already founded by Henry I'; 38 English vineyards are recorded in the Domesday Survey.

⁶⁸ In the later-fifteenth-century context of English enclosures being enforced by lords for sheep-pasture and parkland (see Fryde, pp.185–208), we find Sir John Fastolf, who lists a copy of the French *Propriétés* in his library in 1450, building himself a palace covering five acres: Twomey, 1999, p.358.

⁶⁹ DrP, Bk 6, cap xviii *de bono Domino sive dominio*; cap xix *De malo domino siue dominio*, pp.253–6.

⁷⁰ *Properties*, Bk 6, cap xviii *De bono domino*, pp.317–20.

⁷¹ Loc.cit.

⁷² Saul, 1981, p.258.

⁷³ Salter, 1988, pp.105, 311 nn.28–30.

⁷⁴ Hanna, 1989, pp.906–7.

⁷⁵ DrP, Bk 15, cap xiv, *De Anglia*, pp.631–2.

⁷⁶ DrP, Bk 15, cap xxxv, *De Cancia*, p.642.

⁷⁷ DrP, Bk 17, cap cxxxvi, *De rosa*, pp.913–5.

⁷⁸ Byrne, 1981, pp.100–1; cf. *Properties* Bk 17, *De lilio*, pp.980–2 and Bk 15, *De Francia*, pp.758–9.

⁷⁹ *Properties*, Book 15, cap xxviii, *De Britania* (sic), pp.740–1. Waldron, Ronald, "Trevisa's 'Celtic complex' revisited", *Notes and Queries* xx (1989): 303–7, discusses this aspect of the translation project.

⁸⁰ Hanna, 1989, pp.882–3; 907–8.

⁸¹ M. Keen, 1973, p.289.

⁸² M. Bennett, 1992.

⁸³ Saul, 1981, pp.166, 176–7. See also Fowler, D. C., "New light on John Trevisa", *Traditio* 18 (1963): pp.289–317, on Trevisa's likely involvement in a larger pattern of violence occurring in Gloucestershire during this period.

⁸⁴ Hanna, 1989, p.898, n.50. Higden uses Book 15 of 'Properties' almost verbatim as the first, scene-setting section of the *Polychronicon*; one of his sources is thought to have been the fourteenth-century copy of Book 15 now extant in BL Ms Arundel 123, ff. 5–21r: Taylor, John, *The Universal Chronicle of Ranulph Higden*, Oxford: The Clarendon Press, 1966, pp.53–7, 82–3. Higden rearranges Bartholomew's text so as to begin with the description of Paradise, leading into the four rivers and the provinces of Asia. He also includes an extract from Priscian's *De orbis dimensione* on Julius Caesar's project to measure the world, which an earlier reader had added to that source (see Appendix A below).

⁸⁵ Salter, Elizabeth, "Medieval poetry and the figural view of reality" in *Middle English Literature. British Academy Gollancz Lectures*, edited by J. A. Burrow, 121–40: Oxford University Press, 1989, p.125.

⁸⁶ Green, pp.144–55: `A list of their [Berkeley] translations reads almost like a prospectus of works essential for the formation of a basic aristocratic library.'

⁸⁷ Scattergood, 1983, pp.34–5.

⁸⁸ Waldron, 1988, "Trevisa", pp.176–7; for Trevisa's presentation of translation issues affecting himself and Berkeley, see Waldron, Ronald, "Trevisa's original prefaces on translation: a critical edition" in *Medieval English Studies Presented to George Kane*, edited by E. D. Kennedy, R. Waldron and J. S. Wittig, Woodbridge: D. S. Brewer, 1988. See also Coss, Peter, "Aspects of cultural diffusion in medieval England: The early romances, local society and Robin Hood", *Past and Present* 108 (1985): 35–79), pp.42–3.

⁸⁹ Waldron, 1988, "Trevisa", p.177: `The dialect of the two earliest manuscripts of the *Polychronicon* is assigned to the immediate neighbourhood of Berkeley by the *Linguistic Atlas*'; Seymour, 1975–88

vol.3, pp.38–9: 'Trevisa's spelling habits ... reflect at an exact date (1394–8) the language of a man born c.1340 at Trevisa, Cornwall and living at Berkeley.'

[90] Robinson, F. N., ed, *The Complete Works of Geoffrey Chaucer*, Oxford University Press, 1957, pp.310–8, line 672.

[91] Cottle, Basil, *The Triumph of English*, London: Blandford Press, 1969, p.20.

[92] Seymour, 1975–88, vol.3, p.10.

[93] Hanna, 1989; Kerby-Fulton, Kathryn, "The Medieval Professional Reader and Reception History, 1292–1641" in *The Medieval Professional Reader at Work*, edited by Kathryn Kerby-Fulton and Maidie Hilmo, 7–13, University of Victoria, B. C., 2001.

[94] Hanna, 1989, p.908 and n.73; on a Thomas Knolles (1395–1435) of London involved in book production, see Thrupp, Sylvia, *The Merchant Class of Medieval London (1300–1500)*, University of Chicago Press, 1948, pp.351–2. Coss, 1985, pp.41–2, sees the civil service as a 'major constituent' of the cultural life of London at this time.

[95] Hanna, 1989, p.909 and n.75. See also Kerby-Fulton, 2001, p.12.

[96] Hanna, 1989, p.910 and nn.77, 79; Hanna points out that, since such a large ms would only be copied in response to a purchaser's order, Berkeley could do no more than bring his copy to London, show it to acquaintances and await requests for use of the copy. Plimpton Ms 263 is a lavish workshop-produced ms of *Properties* apparently made for Sir Thomas Chaworth, who also owned a translation of the *Polychronicon*. Lawton, Lesley, "The illustration of late medieval secular texts, with special reference to Lydgate's Troy Book" in Derek Pearsall, ed, *Manuscripts and Readers in Fifteenth-Century England: The Literary Implications of Manuscript Study*, 41–69, Cambridge: D. S. Brewer, 1983, p.xi, deduces from mss illustrations that books were 'one of the recognized ways of holding capital in a portable and negotiable form'.

[97] Holt, J. C. & Anne Wedgewood, *History of Parliament: Biographies of the Members of the Commons House 1439–1509*, London, 1936, pp.175–6.

[98] Mitchner, R. W., "Wynkyn de Worde's use of the Plimpton Manuscript of De Proprietatibus Rerum", *The Library* vi (1951): 7–17. See also Holbrook, Sue Ellen, "The concept of vernacularity in de Worde editions of 1495–96" in *Vernacularity: The Politics of Language and Style*, The University of Western Ontario, Medieval and Renaissance Seminar, 1999, <http://www.uwo.ca/modlang/MedRen/conf99/abstracts/holbrook.html>

[99] The English word 'property' could at this time mean 'The fact of owning a thing (1380+); 'That which one owns' (1300+); 'An attribute or quality belonging to a thing or person ... an essential, special or distinctive quality' (1303+): OED.

Chapter 6. An authoritative source

The last chapter placed the emergence of 'Properties' in England in the context of the church's concern with preaching, the nobility's concern to support with authoritative texts their control of their domains, and social networks of wealthy book owners. In the fifteenth century these concerns and networks combine to uphold the position of 'Properties' as a prestigious and desirable text. We find it commodified as a manuscript or printed book, adapted as an informative manual, and preserved in ecclesiastical and academic libraries. This chapter looks at some examples of how readers and writers made use of Bartholomew's authority in the context of increasing literacy, but also increasing instability and conflict. From the time of Richard II's reign to that of Richard III there is evidence of hostility between England and France, king and subjects, Yorkists and Lancastrians; and between upper and lower ranks as the economic climate changed.

The numbers of prose texts written in English dialects suggest that lay people had better access to the written word, and that the later dissemination and rise in status of 'Properties' occur at a time of increased lay literacy and professional involvement with informative and devotional texts. The wide range in types and quality of manuscripts drawing on our work in Latin and English, from the cramped home-made booklet of recipes and extracts to the beautifully laid-out and decorated workshop manuscript, testifies to the social breadth of writers with access to 'Properties' in whole or part. The record shows that versions in Latin, French and English vernacular were available to both clerical and non-clerical English users.[1]

This chapter will look at some of the evidence that writers and readers responding to the demands of their particular time found a durable source of material and authority 'in Properties' that they could cite or adapt, or commodify as a prestigious piece of personal property. It could be a source of information; a source of moral examples and images; an authority on the properties of specific items; and a valuable commodity for investment, marketing or exchange.

A source of wisdom

Knowledge had been the object of systematising efforts since the twelfth and thirteenth centuries, when the church and the Paris schools required scholastic texts to support the drive to educate an effective body of preachers. As we saw in the prologues by Belcalzer and Corbechon, knowledge could also confer a mantle of wisdom like that of Solomon, which was seen as appropriate to landed lords. For Thomas Berkeley, Trevisa provided volumes in English prose embodying knowledge of the world's history and the world's content.

As we saw in the last chapter, a work such as 'Properties' could be re-created as luxurious copies made from expensive materials, and become solid investments, valuable gifts, and overt declarations of wealth and power. The well-preserved manuscript owned by Chaworth is one example; the badly-damaged fifteenth-century copy of 'Properties' in English now in the Bristol City Library is another.[2] During the fifteenth century, copies of the French and English vernacular versions of the work, made to a high standard of workmanship, became desirable commodities for purchase or commissioning from specialist workshops. In 1482, Edward IV acquired a two-volume copy of the French version made a century earlier for Charles V, superimposing his own coat of arms upon the title-page with its original dedication to Charles. Edward is thought to have commissioned or bought his copy of *Propriétés* from a workshop in Bruges in about 1482, while in exile. The customising of the copy is consistent with a wish, like that of Charles, to assert the legitimacy of his claim to wise kingship. This copy is still part of the English royal library founded by Henry VII.[3] It is not surprising therefore to find 'Properties', either in English or in French, included in an un-headed list of works on chivalry, piety, wisdom and romance, now at Balliol College Library, Oxford:

> Boccachio de casu virorum illustrium/ The siege of Troy/Sanke Royall/ Boicius de consolacione/ de Regimine principum/ Secreta Secretorum/ The Romaunce of Partenope/Rommat de la Ros/Brut e the croniculis/Seynt Kateryne of Seene/ The pylgrymage o the sowle/The tales of Caunterburye/The booke of cheuallerie/The booke of the salutacioun of owre lady/Egidius de Regimine principum/Legenda Aurea/Maister of the game/Pontus/ Maundevile/The booke of the iij kynges of Coleyne/The Revelicioun of Seynt Brigiede/Sydrake/ Bartholomew in tweye bookis of ij volemys.[4]

Whether the list was a catalogue, a record or a wish-list, it shows a fifteenth-century reader including Bartholomew's work among both new and old chivalric and devotional works from England, Italy and France, crossing boundaries of language and genre. The list suggests that these books were for both recreation and edification — they include the *Canterbury Tales* as well as the *Pilgrimage of the Soul*. That 'Properties' was also valued as a religious work that could serve a commemorative purpose and benefit the souls of the deceased is attested to by Sir Thomas Tyrrell of Essex (d.1477), who directed in his will that his copy of 'Properties' be given to his parish church 'theire forth to serve in perpetuite to have my soule and the soule of my wif and of myn Aunte Margarete Rypley'.[5] We find an early Latin manuscript of the work in the careful possession of a west-country vicar in the late fourteenth century. The Reverend John Taylor of Ilminster, Somerset, apparently had the copy re-bound, some old accounts of work in Ilminster church being used in the binding.[6]

Preserving the sources

The global array of authorised knowledge brought together in the compilations became a resource for specialists in separate fields of study, and in the later Middle Ages we can see professionals making customised compendia specific to their fields. 'Properties', with its pull-apart format and comprehensive coverage of worldly matters, evidently lent itself to the making of extracts and adaptation. Users drew excerpts from 'Properties' to compile books for their own use, edification or enjoyment in modernised, functional formats, in Latin — the language of scholars as well as clerics — and in English and French. Braswell's study of utilitarian literature indicates that 'Properties' and other authoritative, informative texts gained repute among the growing numbers of literate professionals in English society who could draw on Latin as well as vernacular versions.[7] In particular, Books 12 to 18 of 'Properties' tended to be copied to make smaller, customised compilations of authorised information. For example, physicians and astrologers made shortened versions and abstracts of 'Properties' with emphasis on harmful, remedial or prognostic properties of animals, stones and plants. Writers on heraldry and history also turned to it as a source on the moral, symbolic and historic properties of those things.

There is plenty of manuscript evidence that people used 'Properties' or material derived from it to put into new writings for their own lives and needs. These needs might be for reliable, authorised information about the physical world such as physicians or alchemists might require in a handy manual format. Others might need the moralised interpretations of things preserved in, for example, the medieval Latin bestiaries as a source for sermons or tracts that they could present in a local vernacular. By contrast, some writers needed accounts of the properties of things that could be interpreted in more than one way for the purposes of irony, satire or emblematic representation. Such writers would include partisan social commentators and representatives, such as propagandists and heralds.

'Properties' was not the only compilation available to late-medieval English readers. Those of Thomas de Cantimpré, Albertus Magnus and Alexander Neckam were available in Latin but were not translated into English. One of the strengths of 'Properties' was that it preserved knowledge laid down by writers of the past and, being organised in clearly defined Books and chapters, could be easily excerpted. Seymour reasonably concludes that Bartholomew's was the most popular of the compilations on the natures and properties of things because it was accessible and adaptable.[8] Adaptations of 'Properties' made in the fourteenth and fifteenth centuries indicate that the Latin 'Properties' in particular was valued as an available repository of useful knowledge carried forward from the past: from the classical writers Aristotle and Plato, Pliny and Solinus via their

Christian mediators, and from the Christian fathers and earlier compilers, Jerome and Gregory, Augustine, Bede and Isidore of Seville.

'Properties' was one available source of information about living things capable of a flexible range of interpretation, and which made ancient knowledge available to readers, regardless of the specialist points of view they brought to the work. We can see in some cases the importance given by writers to acknowledging the sources cited by Bartholomew. For example, in a fourteenth-century volume of Latin extracts from Books 12, 16, 17 and 18 of 'Properties' a reader has underlined the names of authorities as they occur in the text: Pliny, St Gregory, Aristotle, Constantinus, St Basil, St Ambrose, St Denis, the *Book of Job* and Isidore of Seville.[9] In a fourteenth-century codex that includes 'Properties' Book 15, a reader has written: 'Take note of which authors one should put one's trust in' against Bartholomew's reference to Jerome's authority.[10]

Names of sources are included in a home-made collection of remedies and medical notes in Latin, bound with recipes in English, around a core of items from 'Properties' to form what appears to be a personal commonplace book or manual, now in the Bodleian Library, Oxford. The extracts come from Books 16, 17 and 18 of 'Properties' and are introduced by the rubric 'What follows are excerpts from the book entitled De proprietatibus rerum'.[11] In this home-made book the text is taken right up to the margins; no space is wasted and many chapters are omitted, but the writer has squeezed the names of Bartholomew's authorities into the margins. There is no decoration, but red-ink headings and paragraph marks make the whole thing readable as a reference work in spite of the density of text on the page. A comparison with the contents of Trevisa's *Properties,* Book 17, indicates that the plants included tend to be herbs and fruits associated with medicine, food and cooking while the exotic and the generalised are excluded.[12]

As Anthony Edwards has demonstrated, 'Properties' was regarded in the later Middle Ages in England as a source book to be plundered for a diverse range of miscellaneous information, as writers applied its authority to secular, devotional and didactic literature.[13] Sometimes we can see the same manuscript serving as a source for widely different purposes over time, as in the case of British Library Manuscript Add. 27944 which, Ralph Hanna suggests, Thomas Berkeley caused to be made in London to advertise the translation and his own literary patronage.[14] In a very different type of study of the same manuscript, Michael Seymour deduces that it supplied copy-text for a medical practitioner who, in around 1425–50, abstracted material from Book 7 on arthritis, sciatica and gout.[15] The abstract reflects a concern on the part of this reader for segments of the vernacular manuscript with a particular practical, medical application for him or herself, rather than for the work as a whole.

Several such epitomes exist in Latin and in vernacular languages. In another study, Seymour notes that Book 7, in the redaction known as *liber de regimine sanitatis et de virtutibus naturalibus*, had been appointed for use by lecturers at the medical university of Montpellier in 1340. He finds that the content is 'wholly medical', and 'probably reflects the day-to-day concerns of a practising physician ... who wanted an inexpensive summary of contemporary medical opinion'.[16] A more personal, home-made collection of medical extracts occurs in Wellcome Institute Manuscript 335, a narrow octavo notebook convenient for the pocket, containing recipes, prayers and paintings of plants. It comprises a herbal accompanied by extracts from 'Properties' Books 5 and 7 headed 'Excerpts from the book entitled De Proprietatibus rerum (B. Anglici). And firstly, concerning the lung.'[17] This leads into headed excerpts in Latin on the breath, stomach, liver, skin, spleen, gut, kidneys, bladder, urine and dizziness. Prayers to the Virgin and to St Gregory follow, and excerpts from a surgical treatise. Recipes for cures written in French at the start and finish of the codex are further evidence that this collection served a practical need for home remedies, but that these might be accessed in three languages. The Books on birds, stones, plants, animals and substances, and the long chapter on fishes, are barely altered at the level of the chapters; word-by-word examination of the text could reveal whether more detailed cuts have been made.

It may not be clear that a writer had a particular purpose or point of view in making an adapted version of 'Properties'. The unknown maker of British Library Harley Manuscript 512, an abridged Latin 'Properties' entitled 'On the natures and properties of things', included all the Books, shortening them to abridge the whole compendium in a manner *breve et plano* ('brief and to the point'), but with no apparent emphasis on one area of knowledge.[18] Perhaps a reader in a particular locality would pinpoint plant or animal species known or obtainable in the area. Neither do we know exactly how individual readers became familiar with 'Properties' or obtained copy-text. While such processes are hidden from us, the adaptations show that literate people had the means to make copies of parts they wanted for their own use or edification, and to translate, abridge and turn the lengthy and comprehensive work into a manageable text for themselves.

'Bartholomew the bestiary'

Bartholomew's status as an authority on nature tends to be confirmed by re-makers of 'Properties' in Latin and/or English who selected only from Books and chapters concerning birds, plants, stones and animals. For example, a fourteenth-century workshop-produced manuscript with a professional finish and layout, British Library Manuscript Royal 12 E iii, consists of Books 12, 16, 17 and 18 only, in Latin. It is stylishly produced in book-hand, well laid-out, with neatly coloured initials. The focus of the selection is on birds, fishes, stones and minerals, and herbs, with no reference to the elements in which they are found or to the medieval scheme of creation as a whole. The chapters of Book 17 on plants are reduced by the exclusion of the general, the exotic and the processed, while materials from the omitted first chapter on the general properties of trees and plants are made into two short chapters on leaves and flowers. A later hand has added alphabetical tables of the listed birds, stones and animals, as if to further organise the wealth of information.[19] We cannot tell for whom it was made but this selection of Books of 'Properties' again suggests that Bartholomew was regarded as a marketable, acceptable source on the properties of birds, stones, plants and animals.

It does seem arguable that *Properties* in English provided information transmitted in the Latin bestiaries. For the writer of *Mum and the Sothsegger* in the 1390s, 'Bartholomew the bestiary' had been an authority on bees.[20] A manuscript that has been described as a unique late-medieval representative of the bestiary genre in England, now in Cambridge University Library, draws heavily on Bartholomew as an acknowledged source supplemented by readers' annotations in English.[21] It is made in the form of a bestiary, with entries on animals, each with a prominent illustration and with each description of properties followed by a moral *significatio*. Its maker and original purpose are unknown, but the content and marginalia all suggest it could have supplied recreation, instruction and moral edification from bestiary sources. The manuscript indicates that Bartholomew was still seen as an authority and repository of even older authorities on the properties of animals, birds, fishes and plants late in the fifteenth century, but the illustrations suggest that the volume was designed to be diverting as well as instructive.[22] It testifies to a continuity of interest in animals as moral examples along with a more empirical attitude in written texts to animals and birds as local and identifiable objects of interest. In spite of the fact that it does share some features with bestiary manuscripts, we need to ask what function a moralised collection of animal properties could have had in late-medieval England in a non-clerical context.

Moralising properties

Because of the way Bartholomew presented certain creatures as analogous to people interacting with each other, his compilation could later be used in wider contexts as a source for writers of stories where animals might reflect or parody human behaviour. Indeed, Michel Zink argues that medieval literature concerning animals is really to do with people.[23] Writers of devotional texts could invoke readers' knowledge of the symbolism of certain animals and birds, preserved in the bestiary, to teach through allegorical and moralising associations. Bartholomew had defined the properties of things as their 'dispositions, doings and effects'; that is, their characters, behaviours, and relations with each other, and this implied analogies with the relationships and behaviours of people.[24] Although in 'Properties' the things of creation reflect the cosmos in their hierarchical arrangement (as Bartholomew had explained in Books 3 and 4), they also have complementary and opposing properties. In the later Books, the compiler had organised the plethora of things of the world into complementary relationships of alliance or enmity, fertility and infertility, poison and antidote, all under the providence of *natura*. The diversity of living things and their mutual oppositions, purposely ordained by *natura*, forms the theme of Bartholomew's long introduction to Book 18. Even fruit could be described as wild/tame; fair/foul; good/evil.[25] This allowed writers to find, in his chapters and cross-references, analogues for the dynamics of human relationships observable around them.

The writer of the mid-fifteenth-century collection of sermons *Jacob's Well* shows us how 'Properties' could be a vehicle for carrying forward the concept of such mutual tensions through analogy with well-known beasts:

> Bertylmew, de proprietatibus rerum, libro xvijo, he seyth þat an harpe hath strynges of wolfys guttys & of schepys mengyd to hepe, schal neuer be set wele in twene, be-cause þe scheep & þe wolf arn contraraye in kynde.[26]

Since the sheep and the wolf have contrary properties, a harp strung with gut from both of these animals will be discordant. As we saw in Chapter 5, the author of *Dives and Pauper* draws on the same image in the context of his dialogue-sermon on 'Thou shalt not kill'.[27]

In the image of the 10-stringed harp, these two writers rely on their readers' awareness of the predator/prey relationship between wolf and sheep, and the antithetical nature of their properties, to strengthen the point that one failure of Christian observance could vitiate all the rest. They also assume familiarity with the Old Testament story of David, the epistle of James on keeping the whole law, and the parable of the lost sheep.[28]

Bartholomew's account of the wolf combines stories from a number of sources including *Physiologus*, Isidore, 'Cherles', Pliny, Homer, Avicenna, Solinus and Aristotle, that convey the density of fearful myth surrounding the animal, especially its savagery towards sheep; and descriptions of actual wolf behaviour such as fishermen's observations of the way it scavenges for fish offal. He concludes the chapter:

> Also Aristotil seiþ þat al pe kynde of wolues is contrary and aduersary to al þe kynde of schep. And so I haue yradde in a booke þat a strenge ymade of a wolues gutte ydo among harpestrenges ymade of þe guttes of scheep destroyeþ and corrumpeþ hem, as an egle feþer ydo amonge coluere feþeres pilieþ and gnaweþ hem if þey ben ylefte togidres longe in oon place, as he seiþ. Loke tofore *de aquila*.[29]

Bartholomew stresses the contrariness of nature between wolf and sheep, like that between eagle and dove, whereas the later users of this source make explicit the exegetical link to the Ten Commandments and the theme of salvation. We can see how Bartholomew's multiplicity of sources and viewpoints enabled these later writers to use the harp-string anecdote as a basis for sermons with the addition of their own emphasis or interpretation.

The multiple viewpoints and opinions cited by Bartholomew on some matters allowed later writers to recast the properties of things to create ambiguity and double entendre as a basis for social comment. Ambiguity and double entendre offered a useful mode of discourse for those who wished to represent objects of criticism at a safe remove, such as writers of political satire; or who needed to privilege some properties over others in their interpretations of Bartholomew, such as the heralds.

The heralds were allied with lawyers in that their knowledge and records of genealogies could be applied to legal claims of ownership or inheritance in threatening times. Anthony Wagner describes the development of the functions and status of heralds from the earliest mention (c.1170) of their role in tournaments. Their responsibilities and expertise increased during the Hundred Years' War and, by the 1370s, they were compiling rolls of arms and were called to give expert evidence when the right to a coat of arms was disputed. They could also set their hands and seals to certificates or grants of arms, a process tightened under Henry V to control the use of arms by unqualified persons. By the end of the fifteenth century, heraldry was a well-developed system for bestowing and interpreting arms, with its own technical language, rules and body of knowledge. Through the system, they had developed an agreed code of meanings attached to certain animals, birds, plants and colours in use as personal or family emblems. The animal or bird displayed upon the shield, so easily depicted in carved stone and wood, or in the margins of a manuscript, could make an encoded claim interpretable by those who knew about the charges' properties.[30]

The author of the earliest-known heraldic treatise, the Anglo-Norman *De heraudie*, variously dated to between 1280 and 1345, had listed the limited number of natural and fabulous creatures that could be used as charges on the shield — the lion, the leopard, and the griffin; the eagle, the martlet, the popinjay, the crow, the swan and the heron.[31] Although the list of heraldic birds and animals was still quite short, the herald and the armiger were free to draw on puns, or on literary or other sources. Aspiring armigers would have needed the expertise and resources of the heralds to select something suitable.[32]

Bartholomew and the heralds

Like physicians, the heralds were cultivated, professional and pragmatic readers who found an invaluable source of knowledge in 'Properties'.[33] The evident increase in heraldic display in written and graphic forms during the fifteenth century coincides with production of manuscript copies of *Properties*, and of other manuscripts based on 'Properties' or *Properties*, made in workshops and in the home.[34] At the time when Trevisa was working on his prose translations, cognisances and emblems appear in literature and art as weapons in the propaganda wars between Richard II and his critics. Later, during the conflict between Lancastrian and Yorkist factions, 'Properties' could supply or confirm properties of creatures as a basis for some important political image-making.

The *Tractatus de Armis* by Johannes De Bado Aureo, a work contemporary with Trevisa's translation of 'Properties', demonstrates Richard II's participation in heraldry and the part that Bartholomew continued to play in its formal expression, during and after his reign.[35] The writer of this Latin treatise cites Bartholomew on the properties of certain animals and birds depicted in arms.[36] 'Bartholomew of the property of things' is De Bado Aureo's most frequently-cited source, at times referred to by name but often closely though selectively quoted. He notes Bartholomew's agreement with other sources — Aristotle, Isidore, Pliny, and the heralds 'ffranciscus' [de Foveis] and 'dominus Bartholus [di Sasso Ferrato]' — regarding the boar, the horse, the bear, the dragon and the dove.[37] Following technical information on the hierarchy of colours, the *Tractatus* lists the beasts and birds that are, by that time, suitable to be borne as arms (lion, leopard, pard, hart, boar, dog, dragon, horse, bear, eagle, falcon, owl, dove, crow, swan, cock, gryphon, martlet, pike and crab) and explains what character traits or life events a particular emblem might betoken.[38]

De Bado Aureo dedicates his treatise to Richard II's queen, Anne of Bohemia (d.1394). For these patrons it was necessary to present their most prominent emblems, the lion of England and Richard's personal emblem, the white hart, in the best possible light. He had a complex array of properties to draw upon, derived from a range of sources. By the late Middle Ages the bestiary sources on both *leo*, the lion, and *cervus*, the hart or stag, spanned the eras from pre-Christian to contemporary times. We can see from secular literature — fables, secular bestiaries, heraldic treatises, romances and allegories, and moralised hunting treatises — that both the lion and the stag acquired great significance during the thirteenth and fourteenth centuries. The stag accrued a wealth of significance from many different sources, including 'Properties', and became in its various forms one of the most widely adopted personal emblems in the later Middle Ages. For noblemen and women who enjoyed the actuality of the chase, secular and erotic associations were added to the stag's significance as a symbol of Christian endeavour and purity.[39] The lion, bestiary symbol of Christ as all-powerful king, is thought to be the oldest animal symbol used as a European monarch's emblem. The lion's character as a Christian symbol — the Lion of Judah — became further defined through its heraldic association with kingship, and by contrast with its disreputable bestiary relatives, the lioness, the pard and the leopard.[40] Controversy over the emblem shows how the blazon, which could be recorded in an unequivocal verbal format, was a more reliable possession than its variable graphic representations.

Bartholomew had given the scriptural and bestiary accounts of the stag seeking the water brooks, extracting and trampling serpents, helping its companions across water, hiding its hind and her young, and hiding itself while its new antlers grew.[41] But the stag also had some negative connotations of timidity from classical literature, and Bartholomew slips Aristotle's statement that the stag is the friend of the fox into the chapter on *vulpis*; timidity being perhaps an adjunct of guile. In De Bado Aureo's account, the stag's yearly moult and withdrawal while it grows new and bigger antlers, becomes a sign of increasing wisdom, peaceableness and wealth in the bearer of the emblem who was 'poor in first age and substance'. The image would have been appropriate to Richard's long minority under the domination of powerful adults, and compatible with the style of kingship that he adopted.[42] De Bado Aureo's selective account of the properties of the hart shows us how Richard was able to proclaim his kingship to be wise, mature, peaceable and discreet through the heraldic emblem he and his followers displayed.[43]

Bartholomew and the satirist: the hobbling stag

Richard was under great pressure in the last years of his reign. Henry Bolingbroke was exiled in 1397 but returned to effect Richard's deposition and became Henry IV in 1399. At the same time that Richard's followers were displaying his white-hart emblem in the late nineties, some of his opponents were using the same image to undermine his rule. Hassig remarks on the classical notion of the stag's timidity, ignored by the bestiary writers in their emphasis upon its positive scriptural associations. Bartholomew does reveal, however, that the hart or stag, *cervus,* could still be understood as a creature with two sides to its character.[44] We know that the contrary idea of the tainting timidity of the stag was accessible in 'Properties' in the chapter on the fox, and those in possession of this knowledge only had to present the hart in a different light to present the king and his liveried followers as timid and impotent. The author of the alliterative poem *Mum and the Sothsegger,* thought to date from the last years of the reign, uses the negative properties of the stag to attack and mock the king. In Passus II, the writer begins by marvelling at the number of livery badges Richard has granted. He tells Richard that although he has given out so many badges, the harts fail to stand by him because they are afraid of the eagle (an emblem of Bolingbroke). Also, they are dismayed that moulting-time is coming, and so the whole herd runs away to the forest and is scattered. The writer goes on to list the wrongs performed by the harts. They had cumbered the country, stripped the poor, let the king down and spoilt the broth (lines 28–52). For every hart on a badge, Richard lost 10 score of hearts (lines 42–3). In Passus III, the writer makes fun of the stags in old age, hobbling and feeble, searching among the bushes for adders and feeding on venom in an effort to rejuvenate themselves.[45] Whereas De Bado Aureo, writing for Richard's queen, made the stag's property of moulting a token in heraldry of discretion and increasing wisdom, here it is represented as an embarrassment and disgrace.

England's genealogy: the lion and the leopard

A by-product of civil war during the fifteenth century was the demand for more emblems to signal personal qualities and allegiances, as gentry sought to improve their social status, and the rapid development of the ethos and trappings of heraldry to meet this demand. An English translation of the *Tractatus de Armis*, made in the following century in a fine manuscript version, supports this view. This translation, illustrated with the heraldic beasts and blazons it describes, is followed in the codex by an English chronicle of monarchs, starting with the arrival in England of the legendary Brutus, and illustrated with each monarch's retrospectively-created coat of arms.[46] These illustrations suggest that contemporaries saw heraldic properties as a way of confirming and validating the account of England's heroic origins set down in chronicles such as the *Brut*. The maker of the codex includes a discussion of the arms of Brutus, legendary founder of Britain, and his three sons (Locrine, Camber and Albanact, founders of England, Wales and Scotland respectively): a lion rampant with a double head and red lilies on a field of gold.[47] Again we find Bartholomew referred to as confirmation that the lion, as emblem of England, had the necessary supremacy over all other beasts. Nevertheless, like the hart, the lion had potentially conflicting associations.

The two-faced character of the lion derived from its dual function in the Bible as vengeful and merciful.[48] Bartholomew cites *Physiologus* on its Christ-like properties: it is merciful, gentle and of kingly demeanour; nobly-maned and generous in sharing its food; its body has good medicinal virtues.[49] He reserves all the lion's vices, such as cruelty, gluttony, anger, madness and lechery, for his separate chapter on the lioness, citing Pliny and Isidore, Aristotle and Avicenna.[50] Bartholomew provides more information on the leopard, transmitting Isidore's account of it as a very cruel beast engendered in adultery between a lioness and a pard, and adding the opinion of Aristotle that the leopard's method of chasing prey is confused and unnatural. The leopard is one of those unchivalrous creatures which, like the fox and the snake, masters strong ones by craftiness and not by strength. In Trevisa's words: 'And so the lasse beste haþ ofte þe maystrye of the strengere beste by deceipte and gyle ... and dar nouȝt rese on him opentliche in the feelde, as Homerus seiþ.'[51] This was valuable knowledge at the time of the Hundred Years' War, since the leopard was one of the emblems of France.

De Bado Aureo presents the properties of the lion appropriate for the royal emblem of England. The 'nature and kind of the lion', although it could be represented in other ways by this time, is in the translated *Tractatus* unequivocally that which 'the king of England is wont to show' as the 'three lions passing of gold in a field of red', with the kingly attributes implied by the charge and blazon. The author is able to put the French leopard firmly in its place as a derogatory emblem suitable for those born in adultery; or, being like the mule an infertile hybrid, for prelates.[52] We can see, by comparing his selections from Bartholomew on the lion and the hart, how De Bado Aureo presented the properties of these creatures in such a way as to make them accord with the heraldic and personal function they already performed for Richard II, for whose queen he claimed to be writing.

The wild pig and the tame pig

Bartholomew can be of use to the historian in providing a key to coded insult in the long aftermath of civil war in the century after Richard II's deposition. Our knowledge of properties can help us to detect, for example, the force of the satirical attack on Richard by Wyllyam Collyngbourne in 1484, one year before the king's death:

> The Cat, the Rat and Lovel our dog
>
> Rule all England under a hog.[53]

This couplet has often been quoted, but we are made more aware of the verse's potential resonance by the distinction Bartholomew had made between the wild pig, *aper*, and the tame pig, *porcus*:

> The boor hatte *aper* and is a swyn þat lyueþ in woodes or in feelde and is most cruel and nouȝte mylde, as Isidorus seiþ … Alsswyno the boor is so fers a beste and also so cruel þat for his fiersnesse and his cruelnesse he despyseþ and setteþ nouȝt by deþ. And he reseeþ ful spitously aȝeins þe poynt of a spere of þe hontere. And þough it so be þat he be smyten or stiked wiþ a spere þurgh þe body, ȝitte for þe grete yre and cruelte þat he haþ in herte and strengþe to wreke himself of his aduersary wiþ his tuskes. And putteþ himself in perile of deþ wiþ a wonder fersenesse aȝeins þe wepene of his enemy.[54]

This shows how the boar could signify valour and indomitable power in the armiger. The attributes of fierceness, wrath, cruelty, and courage in facing the adversary are appropriate for a military leader fighting for the throne and rallying support among military men. They seem especially appropriate to Richard III in the light of his apparently suicidal courage at Bosworth, and raise the question of how far an armiger might identify with his or her personal emblem.[55]

However, Bartholomew's chapter on the domestic pig, *porcus,* reveals its insulting connotations:

> A swyn hatte *porcus* as it were *sporcus* 'vile and defouled', as Isidorus seiþ *libro xii.* and froteþ and walweþ in drytte and in fenne and dyueþ in slyme and bawdeþ himself þerwiþ and resteþ in stynkyng place. Oracius seiþ þat 'þe sowe is frende to fenne and to pluddes' and þerfore swyn ben accompted foule and vnhoneste.[56]

The English rose

In contrast to the use of hidden properties of animals for social and political comment, we find the Tudors promoting the public display of the national flower as a dynastic symbol with unambiguously positive properties. After the death of the Boar at Bosworth, the new king, Henry VII, in 1485 adopted the rose as emblem of the Tudor dynasty; joined with the white rose of York in his marriage to Edward's daughter, Elizabeth, it became the Tudor rose that would restore the garden of England despoiled by the wallowing swine.[57] Bartholomew had praised the rose as first of all flowers, and Trevisa continues the emphasis on its virtues:

> Among alle floures of þe worlde þe flour of þe rose is chief and bereþ þe prys, and þerfore ofte the chief partie of man, þe heed, is crowned with floures of rose, as Plius seith, and bycause of veirnes and swete smylle and sauour and vertu. For by fayreness þey fedith þe sight, and pleseþ þe smylle by odour, and þe touche by neysshe and softe handelynge, and wiþstondeþ and socoureþ by vertu aʒeins many sicknesses and yueles, as he seiþ, and acordeþ to medicine boþe grene and druye.[58]

In 1486, we find this authoritative view of the rose invoked for an important civic purpose; the pageant for the reception of Henry VII into York, in which the conjoining roses were to play a central part as symbol and emblem of the marriage and new dynasty:

> at the entrie of the Citie and first Bar of the same, shalbe craftely conceyved a place in maner of a heven, of grete joy and anglicall armony; under the heven shalbe a world desolate, full of treys and floures, in the which shall spryng up a roiall rich rede rose convaide by viace, unto the which rose shall appeyre another rich white rose, unto whome so being togedre all other floures shall lowte and evidently yeve suffrantie, shewing the rose to be principall of all floures, as witnesh Barthilmow, and therupon shall come fro a cloud a croune covering the roses.[59]

The entry in the York civic records confirms that there was a sufficiently general awareness of Bartholomew in the upper ranks of York, for his name to lend credence to the emblematic rose as a symbol of flourishing supremacy, one that would turn England from 'a world desolate' beneath the overarching 'heven of grete joy and anglicall armony', into an earthly garden in which the populace rejoice.[60] This glimpse of Bartholomew presented as an authority at the start of Henry VII's reign supplements other evidence that Henry was eulogised in terms of the rose, especially the Tudor rose that united the houses of Lancaster and York and restored the garden of England. To be effective, the eulogy had to be based on a sufficiently general belief in the rose as a symbol of fertility and supremacy, and it is arguable that the currency of 'Properties' helped to establish and develop such a shared understanding, and to make it an effective dynastic emblem. As mentioned earlier, Bartholomew's chapter on the rose combines properties of the flower as religious symbol, medicinal herb and source of confidence in the land that produced it. Thus Bartholomew's text filtered down in fragmentary fashion through successive borrowings and translations.[61] As new social and political situations arose over the fourteenth and fifteenth centuries, writers adapted the stable core of source material available in 'Properties' to meet fresh contingencies.

Because of the multivalent meanings underlying things of the natural world, heraldic emblems, or cognisances, could work both for and against their bearers. An emblem's very allusiveness and multivalence made it possible to make, through personal identification with it, a blatant claim to the loftiest attributes it implied; but also made it possible for others to subvert that claim by treating the same attributes as negative. To be able to participate as non-contemporary observers in this serious play of allusion and counter-allusion, we need access to the layers of potential meaning available to the players. *Properties* can be a starting point in our attempts to understand what people were expressing in their recorded responses to immediate events.

Properties and the press

Bartholomew already had a reputation in Europe as a notable author in his own right. 'Properties' in Latin and in French translation had been in print on the continent since the 1470s; the titles of the printed editions of Corbechon's *Propriétés* indicate a widening function of 'Properties' in France, adding information on elixirs and herbs, remedies against plague and other maladies, and the casting of horoscopes — all 'very useful and profitable for maintaining human health' — and also 'a very useful medicine ... for horses'.[62] These titles suggest that in France the work was seen as a marketable and useful source of information needed by the well-to-do and the professional physician. The printed edition of 'Properties' in England in 1495 implies that in that country there was also a market for the work in an updated and manageable format, in the era of increased book-production and rising literacy.[63]

I have mentioned Seymour's conclusion that the English translation copies were bibliophiles' books. This being so, the implication is that the work would not have been readily marketable on a large scale. In the light of De Worde's business preference during the 1490s for small, saleable items such as schoolbooks, psalters and the like, this printing venture seems anomalously risky. But 'De Worde knew what was "commercial", and the Subsidy Rolls show that he was a fairly rich man'.[64] Anthony Edwards and Carole Meale have explored the marketing considerations in detail and conclude that De Worde emerges as a 'crucial figure' in the consolidation of printing as a commercial structure in London. While the network of printer, merchant and sponsor could indeed be an important factor, it is rarely clear who footed the bill for an edition.[65] We may assume that cost was a major consideration for printers and buyers. Those involved in the first English printed edition of 'Properties' were businessmen well able to calculate risks and returns. Wynkyn de Worde was a Flemish artisan, and William Caxton, his predecessor, master and the founder of his Press, had been an English mercer and merchant venturer active in Bruges before coming to London.

The printing of Trevisa's *Properties* by Wynkyn de Worde at Westminster in 1495 suggests that the work and the compiler had sufficient appeal to warrant such a major undertaking on a speculative basis. The justification for it may have rested on the work's perceived commercial potential and practical value, as well as the prestige of the author. The possibly limited book-buying clientele may well have included other members of the prosperous merchant network: we have a glimpse of a copy of 'Properties' in the inventory of the possessions of Sir John Rudstone (d.1531), a wealthy and eminent member of the Draper's Guild in London, made after his death. 'Item a boke of Bartholome de proprietatibus ijs' is listed among the contents of an expensively furnished chamber that was seemingly used for the display of valuable items.[66] This book, valued at two shillings, could have been either a manuscript or a copy of the 1495 printed edition.

De Worde's verses at the end of his edition suggest that the project may have been made possible by the co-operation of a team of commercially and socially connected patrons, intermediaries and suppliers. De Worde adds 12 stanzas of cumbersome verse, naming in stanzas five and eight those to whom he is indebted:

> By Wyken de Worde whyche thruh his dyligence
> Emprentyd hath at prayer and desyre
> Of Roger Thorney mercer and from thens
> This mocion sprange to sette the hertes on fyre
> Of suche as love to rede in every shire
> Dyvers maters in voydynge ydylnesse
> Lyke as this boke hath shewed to you expresse.

> ...
> And also of your charyte call to remembraunce
> The soule of William Caxton first prynter of this boke
> In laten tonge at Coleyn hymself to avaunce
> That every well disposyd man may theron loke
> And John Tate the yonger Joye mote he broke
> Whiche late hathe in Englonde doo make this paper thynne
> That now in our englyssh this boke is prynted Inne.

These stanzas appear to acknowledge key players in the project, including the supplier of English-made paper. A handwritten note on the back flyleaf of the incunable copy, adjacent to the above printed colophon and dated 1590, states that in 1507 there was a paper mill at Hertford that belonged to John Tate, whose father was Mayor of London. Thus, De Worde would appear to have had the advantages of access to a local manufacturer of paper with powerful civic connections. Sutton and Visser-Fuchs point out that a merchant-adventurer background was the most likely to encourage a man to promote the printed book, not only because of the nature of 'venturing', but also because he could himself import the large quantities of paper required — normally the single most expensive investment of any printing venture.[67]

As in the case of Berkeley's promotion of his manuscript of *Properties* through the good offices of his London agent, Knolles, and Hugh Bryce's use of Caxton to present *The mirour of the world* to his patron, there is some evidence that civic connections were crucial to success as a book producer. When Caxton had printed Trevisa's translation of Higden's *Polychronicon* in 1482, Roger Thorney or Thornye (d.1515) — guildsman, merchant adventurer and book collector — had been involved in the arrangement.[68] Thirteen years later we again find Thorney acting in negotiations with the Chaworth family for the use of their manuscript as a copy-text for the printing of *Properties* by De Worde.[69] Bone describes Thorney as a staunch Yorkist and 'a rich, enlightened mercer, with connexions in Flanders and friends among the humanists'. Evidence for his Yorkist sympathies can be found in his books and verses, and from his active support in the 1480s and '90s for Caxton and his printing ventures under the patronage of Margaret Duchess of Burgundy, sister of Edward IV. He seems to have had a strong bond with John Pickering, Caxton's successor as governor of the English merchants in Bruges.[70] Thorney appears to have used the services first of Caxton and then of De Worde to procure printed versions of the *Polychronicon* and *Properties* for himself or others. The evidence points to a perception of 'Properties' as a viable marketing project, worthy of the combined attention of a diverse group: a wealthy gentry family from the midlands in possession of a fine copy-text, the merchant-venturer fraternity, the manufacturing entrepreneur and the printing house itself.[71] It is reasonable to conclude that the first English edition was a product of a network of interested parties prepared to invest in 'Properties' as a commercially viable title.

Wynkyn de Worde's printed edition of the English *Properties* in 1495 is a fine production, in spite of the doubtful quality of the translation.[72] The woodcuts, one at the start of each Book, indicate further cooperative networking, as there are strong similarities between this edition and those made in France at around the same time and referred to above. Similar or identical blocks appear to have been used in both, and were not necessarily made for *Properties*. A set of wood-blocks can be traced from the printer Verard to the printer Pynson, who either bought or copied them and used them in the *Shepherd's Kalendar*. They then appear in the work of De Worde, and thence amongst the books of the printer Wyer, who for the most part used the cast-off blocks from other offices.[73]

This chapter has examined the passage of 'Properties' from its translation into English to its printed editions. The English translation provided a new route by which 'Properties' could reach yet another cohort of readers. The fact that the translated versions had shed the glosses allowed adaptors to use the factual content at face value. They were freed from the need for a conventional moralising interpretation, but could still exploit its many-sided potential for allegorical treatment. There is much that we do not know about its late-medieval reception, but disparate pieces of manuscript evidence tell us that some fifteenth-century people preserved the work *in toto*. Others took it apart to make new compilations; some at the level of selected detail to incorporate into specialist texts, others at the level of selected Books and chapters.

That things had properties was a fluid concept that could be taken as empirical, remedial, prognostic and moral. We find Bartholomew's work lending itself to not only different genres of writing but also to different modes of production: in the home, in the professional workshop and at the printing press. The extant copies and abstracts of 'Properties' and *Properties*, and the fact that it was printed, testify to the status of 'Properties' as an important prose work that preserved respected authorities from the distant past and made them available in the English language.

The Journey of a Book

Figure 5: Map of the world on the title page of Book 8, *Bartholomeus De Proprietatibus Rerum*. Printed by Wynkyn de Worde, 1495.

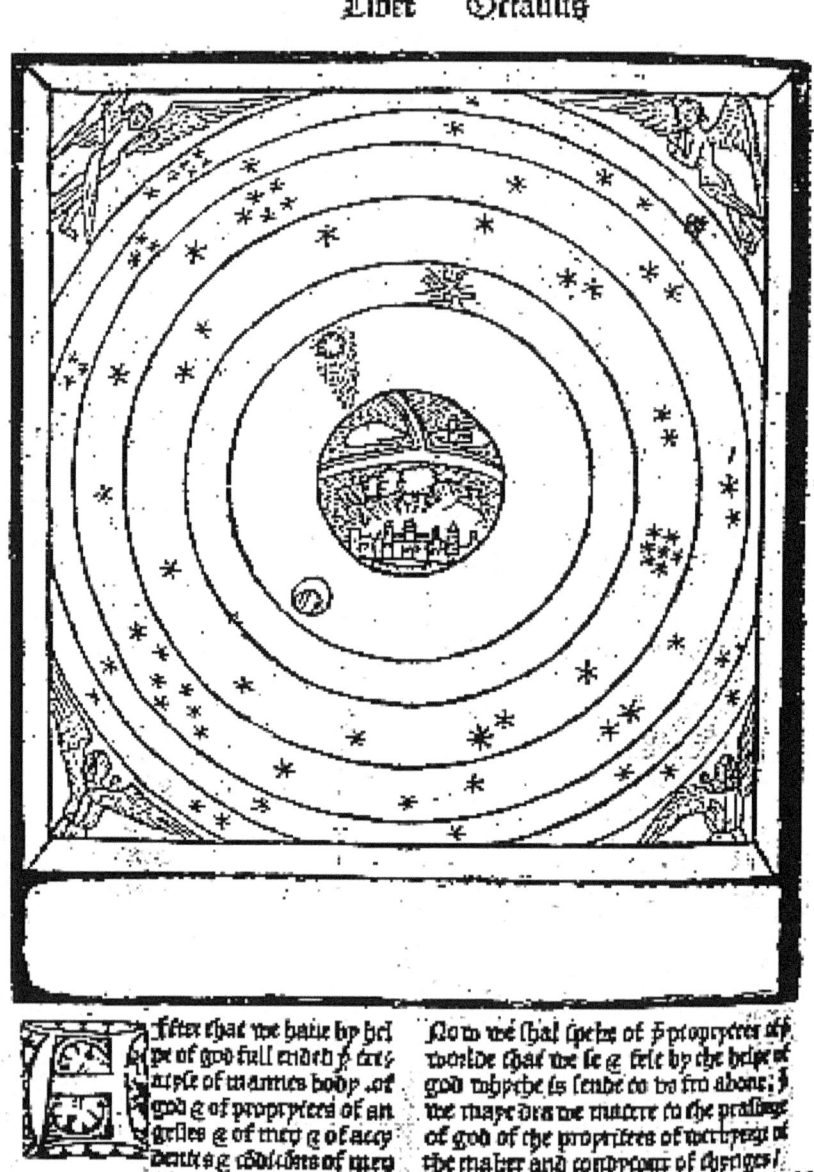

The illustration resembles a medieval T-O map, showing the world in three parts, surrounded by spheres. It is much simplified, however, and lacks the iconography of judgement and salvation associated with earlier maps. Its upside-down orientation, with buildings filling the area occupied by the Mediterranean and Africa, suggests a new importance given to Europe and the notion of urban civilisation.
Used by permission of the British Library.

An authoritative source

Figure 6: Title-page woodcut for Book 19, *Bartholomeus De Proprietatibus Rerum*. Printed by Wynkyn de Worde, 1495.

The illustrations to Books 10, 12 and 13–18 in De Worde's edition show animals, birds, plants and stones still depicted as properties or 'ornaments' of the four elements as Bartholomew had described. On the other hand, the illustration to Book 19 offers a very pragmatic interpretation of Bartholomew's topics: colour as dyestuff or pigment, rather than light; food and drink as cooking ingredients, rather than metaphors for mystical experience; weights and measures as marketplace items, rather than spiritual properties.
Used by permission of the British Library.

NOTES

[1] Parkes discriminates between 'cultivated' and 'pragmatic' readers: Parkes, M. B., "The literacy of the laity" in *The Medieval World*, edited by David Daiches and Anthony Thorlby, 555–77, London: Aldus Books, 1973, p.555. To borrow terms proposed by Kerby-Fulton (2001), some were 'professional readers' in the sense of professional copiers; some can perhaps be categorised as 'dissenting' readers. To venture on a modification, we might add 'discriminating' readers, since some re-writers discard, as well as take from, the broad array of topics and sources in 'Properties'.

[2] Bristol City Library Ms 9.

[3] BL Ms Royal E. 15 ii and iii; see Backhouse, Janet, "Founders of the Royal Library: Edward IV and Henry VII as Collectors of Illuminated Manuscripts" in *England in the Fifteenth Century: Proceedings of the 1986 Harlaxton Symposium*, edited by Daniel Williams, 23–41. Woodbridge, Suffolk: Boydell and Brewer, 1987.

[4] Balliol College Ms 329, f. 172. This un-headed list is in a fifteenth-century northern hand: Mynors, R. A. B., *Catalogue of the Manuscripts of Balliol College, Oxford*, Oxford: The Clarendon Press, 1963, p.339. The ms contains lists of herbs and remedies; *Tractatus de regimine principum*; a verse translation of *Secreta secretorum*; part of Lydgate's *Fall of Princes*. While we cannot conclude that the listed 'Bartholomew in tweye bookis' refers to the two-volume *Propriétés* owned by Edward IV, now BL Ms Royal E 15 ii and iii, William Gray, Bishop of Ely and Treasurer under Edward IV, did leave books to Balliol College: Ross, Charles, *Edward IV*, London: Methuen, 1974, p.268. McFarlane, K. B., *The Nobility of Later Medieval England*: Oxford University Press, 1973, pp.235–42, examines the literary tastes and bequests of noble lay literati in the fifteenth century.

[5] Seymour, "English owners", p.162.

[6] Ker, N., *Medieval Manuscripts in British Libraries*, Oxford: The Clarendon Press, 1969, p.396; Taylor was appointed vicar of Ilminster in 1469, and died in 1515: Moorat, S. A. J., *Catalogue of Western Manuscripts on Medicine and Science in the Wellcome Historical Medical Library, Volume I. Manuscripts written before 1650 AD*, London: Wellcome Institute of the History of Medicine, 1962, p.78.

[7] R. F. Green, pp.140–3; Braswell, Laurel, "Utilitarian and Scientific Prose" in Edwards, 1984, 337–87, enumerates the main genres of utilitarian writings extant in English from the fifteenth century as medical, astrological, mathematical, occult and technical.

[8] Seymour, 1974, "English owners", p.165.

[9] BL Ms Royal 12 E iii.

[10] *Nota quibus auctoribus sunt fides adhibenda*: BL Arundel 123, f.21r.

[11] *H[aec] qui sequuntur excerpta sunt de libro qui intitulatur de proprietatibus rerum*.

[12] See Appendix B, Abridgement of 'Properties' in Bodleian Library Ms Laud Miscellany 682.

[13] Edwards, 1985, p.127.

[14] See Chapter 5, above.

[15] Seymour, M. C., "A literatim Trevisa abstract", *Neuphilologische Mitteilungen* 93 (1992): 185–91, p.185; he describes BL Add. Ms 27944 as: 'written in London or Westminster by three scribes c 1410 in a standardized south-western dialect, with a discernible southern underlay'.

[16] BL Ms Sloane 983 is an epitome in English made from 'Properties' Book 7 (ff.81–94v) and Book 17 (ff.95–102): Seymour, M. C., "A middle English abstract of Bartholomaeus, De Proprietatibus Rerum", *Anglia* 87 (1969): 1–25; Seymour, M. C., "More of a middle English abstract of Bartholomaeus, De Proprietatibus Rerum", *Anglia* 91 (1973): 19–34.

[17] Wellcome Ms 335, f.1r: *Excerpta quedam ex libro qui de proprietatibus rerum intitulatur (B. Anglici). Et primo de pulmone*. Author's paraphrase.

[18] *De naturis et proprietatibus rerum*; BL Ms Harley 512 ff.3r–88v. Other contents of the ms are: ff.1r–2v poems in French; some sayings of Aristotle in French; f.88v an alchemical test (*A cognoistre le vray Basme, si il est Sophistique, ou non*); f.89r prayers (*Tabulae binae, quibus repraesentatur Angelus ante BV Mariam genuflexus*); the codex includes an astrological table (ff.2v–27v).

[19] Later additions are tables of birds, stones and animals, *Tabula Avium* (ff.34r); *Tabula lapidum* (f.35v); *Tabula animalium* (f.169v).

[20] See Chapter 5, p.85.

[21] CUL Ms Gg 6. 5; described in Scott, Kathleen L., *Later Gothic Manuscripts 1390–1490*, London: Harvey Miller, 1996, pp.194–6; Druce, G. C., "An account of the Mermacoleon or Ant-lion", *The Antiquaries Journal* 3, no.4 (1923): 347–64, pp.350–1, 358 n.2.

²² A further line of enquiry concerns the absorption of BA's teaching into early modern printed works that used animals and plants to discuss human morality, such as the *Dialoge of Creatures Moralysed*, and the emblem literature of the sixteenth century: see Kratzmann and Gee; Klingender, pp.354, 489–94.

²³ Houwen, L., "Animal parallelism in medieval literature and the bestiaries: a preliminary investigation", *Neophilologus* 78 (1994), 483–96; Klingender, pp.368–81; Henderson, Arnold Clayton, "Animal fables as vehicles of social protest and satire: twelfth century to Henryson" in Jan Goossens and Timothy Sodmann, eds, *Third Annual Beast Epic, Fable and Fabliau Colloquium, Munster 1979: Proceedings*, 160–73, Cologne: Böhlau Verlag, 1981; Zink, Michel, "Le monde animal et ses représentations dans la littérature française du moyen age" in *Le Monde Animal et ses Représentations au Moyen-Age (XIe–XVe Siecles): Actes du XVème Congrès de la Société des Historiens Médiévistes de l'Enseignement Supérieur Public, Toulouse 1984*, 47–71: University of Toulouse, 1985, p.70: 'ce qui intéresse la littérature médiévale dans l'animal, c'est ce qui touche à l'homme'.

²⁴ See, for example, *Properties* Bk 16, cap lxxxvi *De saphiro*, p.871; Bk 13, *De piscibus*, pp.675–80, Bk 16 *De petra*, p.865, Bk 17, *De arbore*, pp.882–903.

²⁵ *Properties* Bk 18, Cap. Primum, pp.1092–111; Bk 17 cap i *De arbore*, p.887: 'Fulnesse comeþ of þe contrary boþe in trees and in herbes'.

²⁶ Brandeis, Arthur, *Jacob's well*, London: Early English Text Society, 1900, p.90; see Fletcher, pp.257–8 on this collection as an example of the sermon built upon a framework of allegory.

²⁷ See Chapter 5, p. 84.

²⁸ AV, *1 Samuel* 16:23, *2 Samuel* 6:5; *James* 2:10; *Luke* 15:3–6.

²⁹ *Properties*, Bk 18, cap lxxii *De lupo*, p.1224.

³⁰ Wagner, A. R., *Heralds and Heraldry in the Middle Ages*: Oxford University Press, 1956, p.7 foll.

³¹ Woodcock, Thomas, and John Martin Robinson, *The Oxford Guide to Heraldry*: Oxford University Press, 1988, p.51; Dennys, Rodney, *The Heraldic Imagination*, London: Barrie and Jenkins, 1975, pp.59–62: other known treatises are *De Insignia et Armis* of Bartolo di Sasso Ferrato c.1354; *Arbre des Batailles* by Honoré Bonet c.1387; *De Picturis Armorum* by Franciscus de Foveis (known only from citations in other treatises); *Tractatus de Armis* by Johannes de Bado Aureo c.1394; *Le Livre des Faits D'Armes et de Chevalerie* by Christine de Pisan c.1409.

³² We can see in the proliferation of carved shields upon the walls of abbeys and churches, surrounding the tombs of knights and in artefacts, that the late-fourteenth-century heralds provided a way for arms-bearers to advertise prowess, lineage, wealth and patronage: see Dennys, pp.70–3, for illustrated examples, also Binski, Paul, *Westminster Abbey and the Plantagenets: Kingship and the Representation of Power 1200–1400*, New Haven and London: Yale University Press, 1995, p.202.

³³ M. Keen, 1984, pp.83–101,125–42,179.

³⁴ Edwards, 1985, p.126.

³⁵ The identity of 'De Bado Aureo' is unknown but a punning association with Guildford has been suggested: Woodcock and Robinson, p.51.

³⁶ BL Add. 28791 ff.5–38v. The title *TRACTATUS DE ARMIS* occurs on f.1. The evidence of the opening words (f.12r) indicates that the treatise was written for Anne of Bohemia, Richard II's first wife, which dates it to before 1394. De Bado Aureo acknowledges a debt to the writer of another lost treatise, Francis de Foveis.

³⁷ BL Add. 28791 ff.12r–13r.

³⁸ BL Add. 28791 f.5r.

³⁹ Hassig (pp.40–51) analyses portrayals of the stag in bestiary mss; Bath (1979) examines its political and religious significance for Richard II of England and Charles VI of France; see also Bath, M., "The serpent-eating stag in the Renaissance" in *Actes du IVe Colloque de la société Internationale Renardienne, Evreux 1981*, edited by Gabriel Bianciotto and Michel Salvat, 55–70. Paris: Presses Universitaires de France, 1984; and Bath, M., "The stag of justice" in *Atti del V Colloquio della International Beast Epic, Fable and Fabliau Society, Torino-St Vincent, 1983*, edited by Alessandro Vitale-Brovarone e Gianni Mombello, Allessandria, 313–21: Edizioni dell'Orso, 1987, for a sense of the personal and political force of this symbol up to the late Middle Ages.

⁴⁰ Dennys, p.135; Haist, Margaret, "The Lion, Bloodline, and Kingship" in *The Mark of the Beast*, edited by Debra Hassig, 3–21, London and New York: Routledge, 1999; Pastoureau, Michel, "Quel est le roi des animaux?" in *Le Monde Animal*, pp.135–7.

⁴¹ *Properties*, Bk 18, *De cervo*, pp.1175–8.

[42] BL Ms Add. 28791, f.7.

[43] There is much material evidence of Richard II's personal emblem, the white hart, in the form of livery badges, wall-paintings and decorated artefacts made in the later years of his reign when he was trying hard to re-build his image as king: see Binski, p.203. It has been suggested that Richard might, in the first place, have been given this emblem by his mother, and encouraged to identify with it by the pun on 'Richart': Gordon, Dillian, ed, *Making and Meaning: The Wilton Diptych*, London: National Gallery Publications, 1993, pp.49–50.

[44] Hassig, 1995, p.40.

[45] He continues that it is against nature for a hart to attack a horse, a swan or a bear: 'This was aȝeins kynde as clerkis me tolde': Day and Steele, pp.12–3, lines 1–36.

[46] Bodleian Ms Laud Misc. 733.

[47] BL Add. 28791 ff.38v foll: *Portat leonem rampantem cum duplici testu cum floribus gladioli de rubeo contraposite in campo aureo.*

[48] Klingender, p.306.

[49] *Properties*, Bk 18, *De leone*, pp.1214–7.

[50] *Properties*, Bk 18, *De leena*, p.1217–9. In this passage BA was following the lead of the bestiary writers who drew on the church fathers, rather than expressing unusual misogyny.

[51] *Properties*, Bk 18, *De pardo*, p.1235; *De leopardo*, p.1219.

[52] BL Ms Add. 28791, f.6.

[53] Scattergood, V. J., *Politics and Poetry in the Fifteenth Century*, London: Blandford Press, 1971, p.21, comments that the verse was designed to isolate Richard from his supporters, especially Sir William Catesby, Sir Richard Ratcliffe and Viscount Francis Lovell, who are signified by the cat, the rat and the dog. Richard's special cognisant was 'A boar rampant argent, armed and bristled or': Anglo, Sydney, *Images of Tudor Kingship*, London: Seaby, 1992, p.122, stresses the difference between a personal emblem (for example, Richard III's boar, Richard II's white hart) and a dynastic emblem (for example, the Plantagenets' broom-cods, the Tudor rose).

[54] *Properties* Bk 18, cap vii *De apro*, pp.1117–8. We do not know if Richard III owned 'Properties', but Edward IV's French copy of *Propriétés* was already in the royal library.

[55] BL Ms Add. 28791 f.12r. The *Tractatus* author merely states that the wild boar is, according to Bartholomew, a pig of either woods or fields, and can be wild or tame: *Aper ut dicit Barth. de proprietates rerum est porcus silvestris ut agristis.*

[56] *Properties*, Bk 18, cap lxxxvii, *De porco*, p.1237.

[57] Wahlgren-Smith, Lena, "Heraldry in Arcadia: the court eclogue of Johannes Opicius", *Renaissance Studies* 14, no.2 (2000): 210–34. Wahlgren-Smith (pp.225–7) demonstrates that the poets around Henry VII found the heraldic garden a useful motif to celebrate the arrival of the Tudors: in *The Rose of England* (c.1495) the garden is first despoiled by the 'beast men call a bore' who 'rooted this garden upp and downe'; but is then made fair by the return of the exiled branch of the rose and the slaying of the boar; other poets celebrated Elizabeth of York as the white rose joining the red rose in the garden. Anglo, p.35 and Chap.4 'The Rose both Red and White', pp.74–97, examines the iconography of the Tudor rose in court poetry of the early years of the reign and the presentation, through garden imagery, of Henry's kingship as restorative. Robbins, Rossell Hope, ed, *Historical Poems of the XIVth and XVth Centuries*, New York: Columbia University Press, 1959, includes (p.93) the poem 'the Lily-white Rose' of 1486, written in honour of Elizabeth of York.

[58] DrP, cap cxxxvi, *De Rosa*, pp. 913–5; *Properties*, Bk 17, cap cxxxvi, *De rosa*, pp.1029–31.

[59] Scattergood, 1971, p.215: meanwhile Bristol welcomed Henry as the 'delicate Rose of this your Brytaigne'.

[60] The Augustinian convent at York owned two 'Properties' manuscripts in 1372: Seymour, 1974, "English owners", p.162; Humphreys, 1990, pp.145, 172; Robert of Popilton, a citizen of York who became Prior of the Carmelite convent of Hulne in Northumberland, had a copy of 'Properties' in his library in 1368: Friedman, John B., "Cultural conflicts in medieval world maps" in *Implicit Understandings: Observing, Reporting, and Reflecting on the Encounters Between Europeans and Other Peoples in the Early Modern Era*, edited by Stuart B. Schwartz, 64–95: Cambridge University Press, 1994, pp.90–1.

[61] Wagner, pp.72–3, suggests that the heraldic treatise written about 1440 or earlier by Nicholas Upton and dedicated to Humphrey, Duke of Gloucester, is simply a revised version of the treatise by De Bado Aureo, freely incorporated by Upton. Edwards, 1985, p.126, notes that: 'The heraldic utility of

'Properties' was still perceived in the late sixteenth century by John Bossewell in his *Works of Armorie* (1572)' where BA is included among the list of authorities consulted and named in the text.

[62] Corbechon, J., *Histoire universelle* 1476; *Le Proprietaire des choses...*, n.d, 1530; *Le Grand proprietaire de toutes choses...*, 1556 (see Reference List for full titles); Seymour (1992, pp.262–3) summarises the early printed editions made between 1472 and 1609 in Germany, France and England, noting that: 'The printing of eleven editions of the book between 1472 and 1492 is a remarkable witness to its popularity in the later years of the 15th c.'

[63] See Cressy, David, *Literacy and the Social Order: Reading and Writing in Tudor and Stuart England*: Cambridge University Press, 1980, esp. pp.157–70.

[64] Clair, Colin, *A History of Printing in Britain*. London: Cassell, 1965, p.7; see Hodnett, Edward, *English Woodcuts 1480–1535*: Oxford University Press, 1973, for a list of De Worde's known publications; also Bennett H. S., *English Books and Readers 1558–1603*: Cambridge University Press, 1965, pp.242–76.

[65] Edwards, A. S. G. and Meale, Carole M., "The Marketing of Printed Books in Late Medieval England", *The Library*, 6th series, 15 (1993): 95–124.

[66] BL Ms Harley 1231, f. 25v. Thank you to John Tillotson for this information.

[67] Paper for printing was imported from the continent: see Visser-Fuchs, Livia, and Anne F. Sutton, *Richard III's Books: Ideals and Reality in the Life and Library of a Medieval Prince*, Stroud: Sutton Publishing, 1997, p.254; on the Tate family, see Thrupp, p.369.

[68] Plomer, Henry R., *Wynkyn de Worde and His Contemporaries*, London: Dawsons of Pall Mall, 1925, p.54.

[69] Mitchner, pp.7–17: close examination of compositors' marks leads Mitchner to conclude that De Worde used the Chaworth ms (now Columbia University Ms Plimpton 263) plus at least one other as his copy-texts; the ms was probably owned in the 1490s by Sir Henry Willoughby of Wollaton, who was by then head of the Chaworth family.

[70] Bone, Gavin, "Extant manuscripts printed by W. De Worde with notes on the owner, Roger Thorney", *The Library* XII (1932): 284–309, pp.297–302: three mss owned by Thorney contain what are arguably his own Yorkist verses and drawing of a white-rose emblem; evidence for Thorney's wealth comes from his ownership of books and from his bequest of property to Jesus College, Cambridge; evidence for his high social connections can be found in the Jesus College muniments of 1499, where he heads a list of great names including knights, earls, constables, the Lord Deputy of Ireland, aldermen and others. Comparisons of three of Thorney's mss with printed works indicate that he lent several mss to De Worde for use as copy-texts.

[71] Visser-Fuchs and Sutton, p.254: Thorney and Tate 'are a rare indication of how the booktrade was viewed by the more cultivated of English entrepreneurs. Alien and Englishman worked together for profit when opportunity existed, but this could be a temporary alliance.'

[72] Clair (pp.2, 19) considers that *Properties* was one of the best-printed of all De Worde's large books; Mitchner (pp.12–18) details some of the hundreds of modernisations made to Trevisa's language, presumably by De Worde — including many 'careless mistakes' that reversed meanings.

[73] Plomer, p.231; Hodnett, in his Introduction (pp.11–22), analyses the evidence that blocks were shared and copied between De Worde, Pynson, Verard and continental printers, and compares their qualities; see Hodnett, pp.315–7 for detailed descriptions of all 19 woodcuts printed in De Worde's edition of 'Properties'.

Chapter 7. Navigating tides of change: Bartholomew and the English

As we saw in the last chapter, the size and scope of 'Properties' allowed it to become a resource to be mined by specialists of various kinds in the later Middle Ages, but it was still kept and valued as a whole work by religious and scholarly institutions and by book-owning individuals at the highest level of society. This chapter asks how 'Properties' could present an image of the world that was a guide to salvation at a time when faith, not works, was required; as history, that could meet the needs of the Tudors; as library substitute in the age of the printing press; as a guide to the symbolic properties of things when material properties were politically and commercially important.

The printing press aided and reflected the process by which knowledge was being systematised — not only existing knowledge but also new information and ideas. Continental printed works show that a precedent existed for praising Bartholomew as a writer. In 1494 Johannes Tritheim, Abbot of Sponheim (d.1516), had included Bartholomew *natione Anglicus* in his catalogue of notable ecclesiastical writers, describing him as a man extremely devoted to the Scriptures and by no means inferior in learning, who produced works of considerable authority.[1] The title-page of the edition of 'Properties' printed at Nüremburg in 1519 contains a passage praising Bartholomew for his learning, acknowledging his care and labour, commending the work's usefulness as an object of study, noting the demand for it in print, and urging the buyer to go ahead and disregard the cost.[2] The printed editions of 'Properties' in England in 1495, 1535 and 1582 imply that in this country also there was a market for the work in an updated and manageable format, in the era of increased book-production and rising literacy.[3] Yet these dates are associated now with events or developments that seem, in retrospect, to mark major changes in thinking about the world, human society and religious practice. William Harrison in *The Description of England* (1587) describes the population in terms of four, not three, estates — nobility, gentry, yeomen and labourers. He expresses concern at the 'new gentlemen' such as burgesses and merchants, who import expensive wares and disturb the conventional economies.[4] There are indications that people were forming new concepts about the nature of an ideal society or commonwealth based on English Protestant culture rather than a shared European and Catholic culture. In the printed editions of *Properties* we find observable changes in the content to suit an English readership, and circumstantial evidence that influential literary figures appropriated Bartholomaeus Anglicus for England and the English as a symbol of national wisdom and authority.

The Berthelet edition: 'bycause this werke is so profitable'

On the basis of De Worde's 1495 edition of *Properties*, Thomas Berthelet offered readers a much more manageable and orderly text in his new edition of 1535. Berthelet was a successful London printer who produced pamphlets and documents for Henry VIII and was the appointed King's Printer from 1530 to 1547.[5] Contemporary references and his publication record suggest that, as a practical man of business, he fed a growing market for functional, concise editions of legal statutes, health manuals and translations of medical treatises. Together with the printers Pynson, Redman and Grafton, Berthelet was especially active in publishing legal statutes of a few pages only that could be bound together, 'indispensable for those actively engaged in the law'. In 1539, Berthelet issued a volume of legal treatises, reissued in 1544; he also published practical health manuals which sold well, and is recorded as 'talkyng of one boke and of an other' with Thomas Paynell and agreeing on the usefulness of translating the eminently useful medical works *Regimen sanitatis Salerni* (published 1528) and *De morbo gallico* (published 1533).[6]

In his preface to the reader, Berthelet emphasises the educational nature and practical utility of 'This worke intitled Bertholomeus de Proprietatibus Rerum' as a ready reference on material things. He makes much of his referral back to a Latin exemplar, and the accessibility of the revised format:

> newely printed with many places therein amended by the latyne examplare: wherby ye shalle nowe the better understand it, not onely bycause many wordes & sentences that were here & there lefte out, be restored agayne, but also by reson the propre names of men, landes, cites, townes, ryuers, mountaynes, bestes, wodes ... & fishes, be trewely ortografied. And for bycause this werke is so profitable & the manyfold thinges therin conteyned soo nedefull to be knowen and had in a redynes, I have distilleded this table wherby ye shal shortly fynd, what ye liste to rede.[7]

Berthelet omits Trevisa's *prohemium,* and replaces the *tabula* with a detailed list of topics with Book and chapter references but without page numbers, which could have functioned as both a table of contents and as an index (see Figure 7). The content differs little from that of the earlier edition, with Berthelet also diverging from 'the latyne examplare' by omitting all the chapters of Book 1, replacing them with a woodcut illustration of God followed by a passage entitled *De Trinitate,* on the Trinity, condensed from Bartholomew's first two chapters. These changes in the presentation of *Properties* suggest that Berthelet was responding to demands of the market and to competition in the trade, but also to readers who would want interesting informative material, clearly presented and easily accessible.[8]

The climate of the times demanded careful attention to Henry's developing policy on religious observance. Henry's measures against Lutheran infiltration suggest that he was on his guard against this reforming movement in the earlier years of his reign. The *Properties* edition of 1535 was made before controls on Catholicism tightened under Edward VI, but at a time of increasing tension over definitions of heresy. The printing trade was under close scrutiny: in 1525 De Worde had been called on to show cause why he had printed a work by John Gough, a printer and bookseller under suspicion of heresy and sedition; in 1526 Berthelet had been reprimanded for printing translations of three works of Erasmus, having failed to exhibit the works to the Bishop of London's officials.[9] The years 1534 and 1535 saw legislation, including the Act of Supremacy and the Act for the Submission of the Clergy, which affirmed the king's control of the church in England.[10] Indeed, it seems surprising that Berthelet should publish *Properties*, a work of Catholic theology and world-view, at a time of such great religious and political change, and in such close proximity to the centre of government. That Berthelet was able to consider the project at such a time lends support to the view of historians who stress the religious continuities in Henry's reign, and who perceive the break with Rome as a gradual and piecemeal process driven by Henry's immediate political needs and by the sympathies of prelates such as Cranmer and Cromwell. It was not until the reign of Edward VI and then of Elizabeth that the Anglican prayer book, the English Bible and the doctrine of justification by faith alone were firmly instituted. Christopher Haigh presents a range of evidence for the slowness and reluctance of the country as a whole to follow Henry's lead in rejecting Catholic practice.[11] Such gradual change may partially account for Berthelet's ability to market 'Properties' as an acceptable, useful work.

Another reason may lie in the work's continuing status as a repository of wisdom. It has been suggested that Henry's actions were not only driven by expediency and acquisitiveness, but that he identified with Old Testament prophets who purged uncleanness and embodied wisdom. Richard Rex, noting that Henry acted 'as the chif an best of the kings of Israel did, and as all good Christian kings ought to do' in the words of Bishop Cuthbert Tunstall, suggests that Henry saw in himself parallels with the prophet Josiah and with King Solomon: 'The royal supremacy itself, with its power to order the church, could be paralleled from Solomon's establishment of the Temple (2 *Chronicles* 6). And it was as Solomon in judgement that contemporaries saw the white-clothed Henry preside at the trial of Lambert in 1538.'[12]

For Henry, as for Guido Buonolcosi and Charles V nearly 200 years earlier, the learning of the past embodied in Bartholomew's compilation offered a valuable tool for wielding power. *Properties* did not contradict and could support Henry's understanding of universal order and lordly rule. From this point of view, it was permissible to dissolve religious houses and to appropriate their wisdom-conferring libraries.

The evidence suggests that 'Properties' as a printed book survived increasing scrutiny of the press in Henry's time partly because, though a Catholic work, its practical utility answered a need of the times. Moral interpretations implied in the glosses were no longer attached to the text; therefore, the text did not need to be associated only with the preaching of Catholic priests and friars; its scope and content could still cast a flattering mantle of omniscience over those who patronised it. As a financial venture it could succeed through the cooperation of a close network of business backers and associates.

English writers, English history

Bartholomew's supposed Englishness may have been crucial to his official acceptance in early-modern London. To appropriate him as an English national treasure would have helped demonstrate English cultural capital to scholars on both sides of the English Channel. There is evidence to suggest that English historians and antiquarians of the day were promoting Bartholomew as a worthy forefather of English writing, asserting that he was both English and of fairly recent noble birth. In 1533, Henry VIII commissioned the lay antiquarian John Leland to search out and describe England's ancient monuments, and any records of England's ancient history that might be held in monastic and college libraries — a task that took him six years.[13] Fifty years after Berthelet's time, Leland produced his commentaries on British writers, which included a biography of Bartholomew. In this, he describes the compiler as 'Bartholomaeus Glanville descended most nobly (as I understand) from the county of Suffolk'.[14] According to Richard Sharpe, Leland 'picked up the surname 'Glanvile' from the unusual colophon in Cambridge, Peterhouse, MS 67, fol. 203'. Gerald Se Boyar suggests that Leland confused the compiler with a Bartholomaeus de Glanvilla of Suffolk, who died in about 1360.[15] Whatever the reason, Leland was able to claim Bartholomew and his authority for the nation, while implying that the Franciscan commitment was merely an act of Bartholomew's youth before his 'maturer years' of study.[16] Moreover, after mentioning Corbechon's translation (a manuscript of which he claims to have seen at Oxford in Duke Humphrey's library) he implies a lofty English church connection for Bartholomew by stating that an earlier Glanville, called Gilbert, had been Bishop of Rochester and a friend of Thomas Becket.[17] Leland makes no mention of Trevisa or the translation of the work into English, and his readers could have drawn the conclusion that Corbechon translated the work into French from an English original. According to James Carley, some time between 1533 and 1538 Leland had visited the Franciscan library in Oxford, which he found in sad disarray. He also visited the mendicant and monastic houses at Cambridge, listing their contents. He records a copy of 'Properties' in the Dominican library as *Barptolemaeus Anglicus*

Franciscanus de proprietatibus rerum. There is circumstantial evidence that this manuscript could have been among a group sold or sent abroad for safekeeping before 1545 and acquired by Pope Marcellus II, and further testimony to the work's continuing status at this date.[18]

On the basis of Leland's biography of English writers, his friend John Bale (1495–1563) included Bartholomew in his own chronicle of 1548/9.[19] Bale had himself been a Carmelite since the age of 12, but later renounced his vow of celibacy and became a vigorous defender of reformed doctrines under Thomas Cromwell. Bale helped to establish an anti-Catholic discourse that served during later attacks against the Spanish in Elizabeth's reign, and against those perceived as agents of the devil in that of James I.[20] He has been described as 'an impeccable renaissance humanist' who felt a weight of responsibility to expound the apocalyptic meaning of the *Book of Revelation* in terms of the two churches, headed respectively by Christ and by Antichrist. Bale was also among those who, notwithstanding their reforming zeal, were anxious to rescue valuable manuscripts, repositories of knowledge, which were already being pilfered from monastic libraries.[21] Bartholomew and his compilation evidently had a part to play for Bale in his attempt to document, through supposedly English writers, a national past distinguishing the British Isles from the papally dominated countries across the English Channel.

Like Leland, Bale faced the problem of how, in the England of the 1540s and '50s, to claim the writer for England while distancing himself and his subject from the Roman church of which Bartholomew had been a part, and whose doctrine he had expounded. Bale quotes Leland almost verbatim, but he inserts into the second sentence on Bartholomew's mendicancy the crucial phrase *ex nescio qua superstitione* ('from I know not what superstition'), which serves to emphasise that Bale himself is far from condoning membership of the Franciscan order. Like Leland, he accords Bartholomew a noble origin, 'out of the most noble race of the county of Suffolk', and a date, 1360, 'during the reign of Edward the Third', from which it could be inferred that Bartholomew, though unfortunately a Franciscan, was a member of chivalric society. He adds, moreover, that Bartholomew, a good and devout man for his own day and age, worked hard to the end that those coming after him would understand better the Scriptures and their mysteries hidden beneath the figures and properties of natural things. This is close to Bartholomew's own statement of his purpose, and may indeed help to explain Bartholomew's continuing relevance into the Reformation period. The Scriptures were becoming available in the English language, without explanatory glosses, to literate laity. Correct understanding was of paramount importance.

English foundation legends

In the sixteenth century, England's distant history was still cast in the form of national foundation legends; but these were becoming the subject of re-definition and controversy, and Bartholomew has a part to play in this debate. In a recent study, Anke Bernau describes how, in 1534, Polydore Vergil had fuelled the debate by dismissing two well-established legends about Britain's origins: first, Geoffrey of Monmouth's account of Britain's colonisation by Brutus the Trojan; and, second, later accounts of its first discovery by Albina, daughter of the king of Syria and her sisters.[22] Geoffrey's narrative of Brutus had provided Edward II and Edward III with justification of English rights over Scotland and Wales. The Albina story, which appears in the fourteenth century as a preface to the Middle English prose *Brut,* and which John Hardyng included in his Chronicle of 1440–7, came to be used, according to Bernau, as a weapon against the Scots. The Scots had their own female foundation figure, Scota, mythical daughter of a pharaoh of Egypt and foundress of a brave and prosperous race.[23]

A year before Berthelet issued his edition, Polydore Vergil had called into question the veracity of the Albina and Trojan founding myths. However, the legend of the barbarous Albina, her monstrous offspring and their conquest by a civilising 'Bruytane' race, remained popular.[24] In 1542, Henry VIII's *Declaration ... present warre with the Scottis* explicitly cites Brutus's division of Britain to support the claim to English sovereignty, and of London to be the new Troy. As Bernau suggests, this may have been because, just as the giants' savagery justified Brutus's violent colonisation of their land, so allegations of Scottish barbarism could be used to justify English colonisation.

For religious reformers such as Bale it was important to publicise a version of English history that supported the idea of a nation based on political and religious autonomy. We find Bale, writing in 1557, involved in the continuing debate and commenting accordingly on Bartholomew's flattering account of England and the English in his chapter on Britain, *De Brittania*. Bartholomew had recounted part of the legendary material explaining the nation's origins but this did not satisfy Bale. The name of Albion, he says, comes from the giant Albion, son of Neptune, and from the name of the king of Syria's daughter — not from the white cliffs first seen by mariners: 'as brother Bartholomaeus dreamed up in his work De Proprietatibus rerum, along with others who followed his ravings'.[25] As if to emphasise that this is the revision of a common article of belief, Bale's Index includes the item *Bartholomaei de proprietatibus rerum error*, 'Error of Bartholomaeus, On the properties of things'.[26] Another problem for Bale was that Bartholomew, he thought, had omitted the story of Brutus' founding of Britain. *Pace* Bale, who cites the chapter *De Brittania*, Bartholomew does recount the heroic foundation of Britain and its kings in his chapter on England, *De Anglia*.[27] I quote Trevisa's translation which had kept close to the Latin:

> And in passing of tyme lordes and noble men of Troye aftir þat Troye was destroied went þence and gadreden naueye and come to þe clyues of þe forseyde ilond … And þe Troianes fauȝte with geauntes long tyme þat woned þerynne and ouercome þe geauntes boþe with crafte and with strenghþe and conquered þe ilond, and clepid þe londe Breteigne bi þe name of Bruite þat was prince of þat ooste and so þe ilande hatte Bretayn as it were an ilond conquerede of Bruyte þat tyme with armes and with myȝte. Of þis Bruytes ofspring come kynges, and who þat hap likyng to knowne here grete dedes rede he þe storye of þe Bruyte.[28]

Trevisa follows Bartholomew in a further explanation for England's name based on a supposed English foundress:

> Saxones departed þe ilonde amonges hem and ȝaf euery prouynce a name by þe proprete of his owne name and nacioun. And þerfore þey clepid þe ilonde Anglia by þe name of Engelia [þe queen], þe worþiest duke of Saxones douȝter, þat hade þe ilonde in possessioun aftir many batailles.[29]

Bale's insistence on the need for a correct version supports the view that Henry VII had championed the existing Trojan and Arthurian foundation myth for the English crown to emphasise the continuity and validity of the Tudor claim, and that the later Tudors maintained it.[30] There is evidence that during Henry's reign, the king, government and church were keen to build a basis for English autonomy, not only in religion but also in language, history and legend, landscape and cultural achievements. By claiming Bartholomew as a native-born Englishman and writer, antiquaries and churchmen such as John Leland and John Bale were able to construct an identity for him and his work that supported such nationalistic efforts. A prestigious world book that bolstered Henry's image and endorsed the national foundation myth was of obvious value, and Bale goes out of his way to apologise for Bartholomew's apparent shortcoming in this matter.

Stephen Batman 'uppon Bartholome'

The last English edition of *Properties* is an annotated and augmented version entitled '*Batman vppon Bartholome, his booke De proprietatibus rerum*, enlarged and amended by Stephen Bateman'.[31] The Dedication is to Henry Carey, Baron Hunsdon (1526–96), who became Lord Chamberlain to Elizabeth in 1585. He was a nephew of Anne Boleyn and cousin to the Queen. George, the eldest son of this magnate, became Lord Chamberlain in 1596 and the patron of the company of players associated with William Shakespeare, the Lord Chamberlain's Men.[32] Batman, then, was a gentleman scholar serving the established church, and having social connections to the government and court.

In the late 1940s, Elizabeth Brockhurst undertook a detailed but unpublished study of Batman which remains of great value. She found sufficient biographical information from church records to show that Batman, or Bateman, was a married Protestant cleric, a pluralist, and a scholar of gentlemanly rank at the level of archiepiscopal employee.[33] He was a clerical servant of Richard Parker (1504–75), who became Archbishop of Canterbury in 1559 and who, among other achievements, was the author of the *Advertisements* (1566) insisting upon the use of the surplice by parish priests.[34] Batman collected manuscripts for Parker but seems to have been a bibliophile in his own right; his Commonplace Book indicates that he was, in any case, interested in antiquities and had views on the value of historical documents and old authorities. In 1578, Batman wrote:

> He is no wyse men that for the having of spiders scorpions or any other noysom things in his howse will therefore set the whole howse on fier for by that meanes he disfornisheth himself of his howse; and so doo men by rashe borneng of ancient Recordes lose the knowledge of muche learnenge/there by meanes and wayes to presarve the good corne by gathering oute the wedes.[35]

Batman's interest in 'ancient Recordes' was not necessarily casual. Studies of the Parker circle indicate that they turned to Old and Middle English texts for evidence of the antiquity and purity of the English church to provide an historical and ideological basis for the Elizabethan Religious Settlement.[36] Parker's interest in manuscripts is expressed in a letter dated January 24th 1566 to William Cecil, thanking him for the loan of a Latin manuscript of the Old Testament with a 'Saxon' gloss: 'in the riches whereof ... I rejoice as much as they were in mine own. So that they may be preserved within the realm and not sent over by covetous stationers, or spoiled in the poticaries shops.'[37] Batman preserved manuscripts for Parker, who later bequeathed his collection, including a copy of the Anglo-Saxon Chronicle, to Corpus Christi College, Cambridge.[38] According to Jürgen Schäfer, Batman claimed to have collected over 7000 manuscripts for his employer.[39]

Batman may have had personal contact with the group of about 30 antiquaries convened by Archbishop Parker in 1572 and dissolved in 1606 (according to the antiquary Thomas Hearne) on suspicion of heresy and through the machinations of enemies in high places. It numbered among its members William Camden, John Stow, Francis Thynne, William Lombard, Sir William Dethick, Garter King at Arms (who made a Grant of Arms to Batman), Sir Robert Cotton and Lancelot Andrewes.[40] Parker's society met together to read papers, preserved in their records, on antiquarian subjects. In this context, Batman's analogy of separating good corn from weeds can be seen as a form of justification for the eradication of the monasteries but the preservation of their library contents.

Batman's changes

Brockhurst divides Batman's alterations into the following categories: editorial changes; modernising of the language; omissions; and additions of material.[41] The last two consist of expansion of Biblical texts and their more detailed ascription to context; replacements with other material; references to, quotations from or paraphrases of modern authors; and original comments and explanations. These serve as a window into an area of confrontation between old and new knowledge about the world and supply a wealth of ethnographic detail, responses to new discoveries and comments on social or political events.

Batman's re-issuing and updating of 'Properties' confronts us again with the contrast between Bartholomew's Franciscan compilation — with its layers of accrued and hidden meanings awaiting interpretation, written to cater for the specific needs of a controversial new order of mendicant preachers in a frontier area of Christendom — and the urban print culture of late-Elizabethan London. How and why did 'Properties' cross so many barriers separating different cultural attitudes and expectations? Batman's edition is a densely packed source of contemporary comment on Bartholomew, but only some aspects can be looked at in detail here. One is the self-reflexive nature of his comments on Bartholomew; another is the way his responses accord with other evidence for the wish to collect knowledge, possessions and prestige at individual and national levels; a third is the evidence it supplies for the basic continuity of medieval cosmological beliefs well into the early-modern period. David Greetham argues that *Batman uppon Bartholome* allows us to see medieval beliefs persisting far later than one might expect.[42]

In the preliminary pages, Batman identifies himself as a new compiler, acknowledges his patron, and addresses his readers in prologues that emphasise their sophistication in contrast to the archaism of the work. The title page at once points to those features of *Bartholome* that differentiate it from earlier versions of 'Properties': Batman's personal role as author and promoter (a role distinct from that of printer); his personally chosen and composed additions and emendations; his use of an updated range of modern authorities; and his optimistic claim that book-readers might be found among 'all estates'.[43] Batman distances himself and his reader from the earlier work, implying that it is obsolete and incomplete, and emphasising the up-to-date and practical nature of his own version:

> I have ben made able to renew and finish an olde auncient booke, containing the properties of sundrie things, the description of Countries, dispositions of creatures, operation of Elements, effects of simples, and such lyke, no lesse needfull then profitable, as shall appeare, by perusall thereof.[44]

Batman used as his copy-text Berthelet's 1535 edition, but made further changes to the presentation, the language and the content, the appearance and the overall character of the medieval work. In marginal comments, he refers to De Worde's version as 'the olde coppye'.[45]

In his address to the reader, Batman sums up the way he changes *Properties*. Having acknowledged its established reputation, he is going to use the work as a foundation upon which to construct a new account of the properties of things, within a modernised cosmography and geography, from the works of modern writers. His comments and additions demonstrate that his understanding of the physical world was not fundamentally dissimilar to that of Bartholomew, but that his purpose in issuing the work anew was overtly didactic and corrective. They reflect not only his interests and knowledge, but his position as a Protestant clergyman in the difficult later years of Elizabeth's reign, with links, through his patrons, to the centre of government.

An emphasis on English history

Batman's emphasis on 'Bartholomew Glantvyle' at start and finish of the work combines with numerous added references to England and matters English to give the impression that the assumed Englishness and gentility of the original author are important to him, and that he expects his readers to consider them important also. At the end of his printed version of Bartholomew's chapter on Britain, Batman adds a lengthy extract from the *Thesaurus linguae Romae & Britannicae* (1565) by Thomas Cooper, English bishop, lexicographer, physician and writer.[46] He does not say why, but we can assume that Cooper, as part of the pro-Parker network of church reformers and supporters of the Elizabethan Settlement, was for Batman a more reliable proponent of British history than Bartholomew. In this extract Cooper lays out the debate over the nation's origins, first stating that there 'is yet no certain determination' of the naming of the island since 'the olde Britaine bookes (such as were)' had been destroyed by the Saxons; any works by Roman or other writers on the subject 'are utterly perished'. The History of Gildas 'the Briton' cannot be found; Bede can be discounted; even Julius Caesar, while 'an excellent Prince, and also a great learned man', could not discover the origins of the native people. It was, however, called Albion by some, 'that is to saye, more happie or richer'. If there is any writer earlier than Geoffrey of Monmouth or Bede to contest this view, he says, 'to such will I gladlye give place'. Cooper cites John Stowe's description of England on the nation's four peoples — the English, Scots, Welsh and Cornish — saying: 'All they, either in language, condition, or lawes, doe differ among themselves.'

Cooper is not a supporter of the legend of Brutus' foundation of Britain. He states that since the Trojans were treacherous and condoned the adultery of Paris and Helen, the Trojan Brutus is merely 'a vaine Fable': 'Yet this follye is founde almost in all people, which contend to have their Progenitours come first from Troy: which fantasie maye well be laughed at among wise men.' He had always thought it would be more honourable to have received the first name from admixture with 'the most wise and valiant people of Greece, vanquishers and subduers of Troians'. He concedes, however, that England's origins lay with Brutus, and cites the firm opinion of Thomas Lanquet, his contemporary and source, that England was uninhabited when Brutus arrived. After Brutus, his son Locrine ruled England, Camber took Wales and Albanact became king of Scotland. Cooper does not mention the legend of Albina and her giant brood. Batman inserts Cooper's historical account without further comment. However, he does add an account, taken from Lanquet, of the Scots as formerly savage, cruel and cannibalistic, concluding that on the whole they are now 'tractable inough with good governement'.[47] Batman's own interest in pre-Norman English history comes across in comments and additions. To the chapter on Normandy, he adds: 'The people and inhabitants of this Province or countrie were the last that with William Duke of Normandy, subdued England.'[48] On Saxony, he says: 'After the time of Arthur king of Britaine, the Saxons greatly molested the Britons, and helde them in subiection, a long time.'[49] Here he cites Polydore Vergil, perhaps for the sake of a good story:

> Polidorus Virgilius, in his eyght booke of the histories of Englande, maketh mention of Emma, mother of Edwarde, the seconde King of Englande, beeing uniustlye accused by Goodwyn, which after manye attempted iniuryes, ceased not to accuse hir of adulterye, with the Bishop of Winchester ... the Queene in open view cast her selfe into a great fire.[50]

Batman privileges Thomas Cooper, a supporter of Parker and the English Settlement; on the other hand, he makes a point of dismissing a discredited Catholic work on martyrs published in 1526, *Martiloge in englysshe after the use of Salisbury*, a translation from Latin by Richard Whitford, a brother of the Brigittine monastery of Syon. In Book 5, chapter vii on blood, Batman notes with asperity that 'Martiloge, was a booke of all the dedication of saints, and Englished by Richard Whitford, Priest, and brother of Syon, by Richmond, a fond booke'.[51] One might expect to find, but does not, references to churchmen such as Richard Hooker (d.1600) or John Jewel (d.1571) now considered of note.[52] It is hard to believe that Batman did not know of their work but impossible to discern the personal or political nuances that might have caused him to omit them. He does on the other hand refer to a more obscure churchman, William Alley, Bishop of Exeter, to support a lengthy and hostile account of the life of Mahomet which he adds on to Bartholomew's chapter on Greece.[53]

'The fressher writers'

By the last decades of Elizabeth's reign the printing press was a key instrument for the sharing of knowledge.[54] In his new presentation of *Properties* Batman does not obliterate Bartholomew's authorities, but he adds so many others from the many available to him in print that their opinions tend to predominate in certain areas of the work. He tends to direct his readers' attention to present-day rather than antique authors, although he does show a keen knowledge of classical mythology, especially in Books 8, 9 and 15. Batman cites and borrows from many more authors than the ones he names in his preliminary pages, but that list gives us an indication of those he considers most important:

> ... whereunto is added so much as hath bene brought to light by the trauaile of others, as Conradus Gesner of Tygure, Phisition, writing of the nature of beasts, birds, fishes, & Serpents.[55] Fuchsius, Mathiolus, Theophrastus, Paracelsus, and Dodoneus, these wrote of the natures, operations and effects of Hearbs, Plants, Trees, Fruit, Seeds, Metalls and Mineralls.[56] Sebastian Munster, Henry Cornelius Agrippa, and others of Astronomie and Cosmographie.[57] Abraham Ortelius of Antwarpe for maps & discriptions: all which woorkes hath done great good in diuerse and sundrie Common wealths.[58]

Batman's adaptation must be seen, then, in the context of other printed works available at the time from both continental and English contemporary writers. These included the accounts of voyages and new discoveries, catalogues, chronicles, new humanist writings, translations and re-issuings of canonical works, treatises on many subjects, and polemical works from both sides of the religious divide in England. An important authority for Batman is himself; *Batman upon Bartholome* was the last of nine published works which include *The Travayled Pilgrim* (1569), 'an allegorical poem on the subject of man's journey through life'; *A christall glasse of christian reformation wherein the godly maye beholde the coloured abuses used in this our present tyme* (1569); *The Golden Booke* (1577); *The New Arival of the three Gracis into Anglia, Lamenting the abusis of the present Age* (1580); and *The Doome warning all men to the Judgement* (1581).[59] These titles indicate his concern as a churchman to warn and to reform, and suggest that he may have seen 'Properties' as a useful instrument in those causes.

His concerns are also practical and of the moment. He praises modern English writers and notes English translations; for example, 'Hernan Lopes, a Portingall of Castaneda, his discovery of the East Indias, translated into English by Nicholas Lichfield, gentleman, 1582'.[60] He makes approving mention of English scholars, travel writers and translators such as Andrew Boorde (d.1549) and George Turner (d.1610): 'Andrew Bord of Phisicke Doctour, an English man, The Breviary of health, printed Anno. 1547; Dedor Turner Phisition, Anno 1551, one that for his travailes in forren countries, for the onelye benefit of this our realme of England, deserveth perpetuall praise'.[61]

Works by classical writers provided another source of newly printed books, and Batman demonstrates in his comments that he was familiar with many, including modern translations of Ovid and Homer. Batman's evident knowledge of, and interest in, classical mythology is particularly apparent in his marginal comments on Book 8. He stresses the authority of classical writers on India and Asia generally, and he also cites medieval travellers later than Bartholomew's time such as Marco Polo and John Mandeville (with the aside 'but manye Fables are set downe of him').

Many of Batman's comments and additions confirm the view that the experience of things from beyond former horizons, reported and rumoured, generated new stories but amalgamated them with existing fables and moralisations, as well as producing more careful categorisations of natural phenomena.[62] For example, he adds a long extract from Ortelius to Bartholomew's four chapters on elephants (which were compiled from bestiary sources) 'For the better vnderstanding of Elephantes, in what coast they most abound'.[63] His comments demonstrate both a new empiricism and an old adherence to traditional beliefs; thus, into his marginal comment on the monster 'lamia', Batman subsumes the traditional bestiary warning against *sirena*, the monster that seduces and kills sailors. On the other hand, against the chapter on the siren later in the work, he notes pragmatically: 'Sirene, is the swift course of water, that whatsoeuer commeth within the violence of it, is carryed away ... Those [sirens with wings and claws] are Harpie, & both feyned'.

Batman at home

Many of Batman's comments reflect his concerns as a married cleric responsible for a family as well as a parish, in difficult times of war and taxes. Bartholomew had implied in Book 6 that the sacred properties of spiritual birth, nurture and death are manifested in our experience of the times of day, food and drink, processes of growth and nurture, waking, moving, eating, exercising and sleeping. The glosses show that readers could understand the growth of the foetus and nurturing of the infant as the growth of the soul in the womb of the church and its nurturing by the clergy on the milk of the gospel. For the married Protestant minister of the 1580s — struggling to feed his family on an inadequate stipend, with responsibility for the actual upbringing and disposal of children, for care of the parish and control of dissidents, contending with bad harvests and economic exactions — the vision of heavenly peace and plenty and harmonious family life conjured up by Bartholomew in Book 6, *De cena* and *De prandia*, might have seemed ironic rather than consoling.[64] The entries in Batman's *Table of Principall Matters* under the heading 'Liber 6' point to practical rather than allegorical concerns with domestic life and Batman's urge to control and restrain it:

> Of conception
>
> Of chusing wholsome Nurses
>
> Of taking heede of matching with an uncleane Stocke
>
> Against dronkennesse
>
> Of modest Musike
>
> A disquet minde is enemie to digestion

Batman's marginal comments similarly show a practical concern with child rearing, discipline of servants, household economy, diet, health, and clean living: 'A slowe horse must have a quicke spur: & a malepart servaunt meate, drinke, lodging, counsel worke, & stripes.'[65]

How does Batman deal with the sensuous imagery that permeates Books 6, 17 and 19, where Bartholomew conveys the delights of spiritual marriage and of the Lord's *familia* and vineyard? Batman seems to call from the margins for restraint and denial: 'Greedye apetite is hurtfull', he notes in the chapter on the throat and swallowing.[66] At the end of Book 5's chapter on the genital organs, he adds a long passage warning against 'Carnall lust'. This 'tourneth prosperitie into beggerye, health into sicknesse, the soule into sinne: to the bodies covering, the Leprosie, Podegra, the Poxe ... griefe of conscience, and contempt of lyfe'. He goes on to say that 'The love of the world consist in these 3 things, The lust of the flesh, the lust of the eyes, The pride of life'.[67] From Batman's point of view salvation appears to lie not in voluntary poverty or celibacy, but in self-discipline within marriage and family life.

The care of family and parishioners required knowledge of remedies. Batman himself was evidently, from his many marginal comments, an expert in plants and their medicinal uses, noting for example: 'The common elder is hot and dry in the third degree, especially in the bark, the leaves and buddes, the tender crops or buddes sodden in broath: or Potage, doth open the belly, purgeth flegma and cholarike humours'; and 'Garden Parsely is hot in the second degree, and drye in the third, it s good against the cough'.[68] His comments and additions in Book 19 suggest that he chose to ignore the medieval Catholic resonances of useful and familiar items such as, for example, honey — a potent symbol of the 'sweetness' of God for the earlier compilers — in favour of its practical healing properties: 'Hunny is of great quantitie in north regions, as Plinie writeth ... Honnie as well in meate as in drinke, is of incomperable efficacie . . . Sir Tho. Eliot. chap.22 fo.35 in his booke, The Castle of Health.'[69]

One way in which Batman anglicises Bartholomew and his work is to draw topics of particular interest to himself, and his supposed readers, into the domain of the local and immediate. For example, Batman annotates Bartholomew's chapter on the sheep purely from his own experience and opinions. He appears more interested in sheep as a mainstay of the English economy than as a symbol of his pastoral role in the parish:

> Of sheepe, their Wooll is a singular benefit in a common wealth, especially the Cotfell wooll for finenesse. And in Bartholmes time, the Staple for Wooll, was not so well husbanded as it hath bene since. The increase of pasture for sheepe, hath so much decreased the tillage of corne, that untill it be restored againe, there wil grow a poore common wealth.[70]

Batman's many allusions to local points of interest, geography, recent surveys and documentation of the economy and state of the nation accord with the historical evidence we have for such projects during the century. Batman alludes to the work of John Stow (d.1605), whose *Survey of London* was published in 1598, and William Lambert's *Perambulation of Kent*:

> in the booke intituled, The Perambulation of Kent, is sufficiently set downe the fertilitie of the soile, the good disposition of the inhabitants, and their modestie: the onelye platforme and beautie of Englande, whose customes and manners are of greatest antiquitie, libertie, and service: Kent lieng in the Southeast region of this realme, hath on the North the river of Thamise, now called Temmes ... it extendeth in length from Wicombe in the frontiers of Surrey, to Dele, at the sea side, 50 miles.[71]

Batman was not only a scholar, a parish rector, a family man and a herbalist, but also a draughtsman or 'limner'.[72] He makes a significant alteration to Bartholomew's Book 19 by inserting a long passage on 'limning' into the sequence of chapters on colours, altering the focus from the properties of light and its spiritual significance, to the properties of pigments and the techniques of applying them to surfaces. As Batman notes, the old skill was necessary to the new map-makers, including Ortelius, who developed the method of colouring engravings for his *Theatrum Orbis Terrarum*. It was also a technique used by heralds for designing and recording coats of arms. From Batman's addition to Book 19's chapters on colour, one can infer that he saw ignorance about limning as part of the general cultural and moral decline of his country. This is a far cry from the Franciscan's belief in colour and light as signs of divine grace. For Batman, the elements themselves are, for users of colour, salutary reminders of human virtues: 'in studieng for coulours to please the eye, they forget those coulours that beautifie the soule, which are, for fire, love: for aire, faith: for water, hope: for earth, charitie: for voyce, truth: for person, chastitie.'[73]

Batman's complaints

Some of Batman's comments reflect the hostile relations between England and Spain during the 1580s; over competition for New World territory and over the perceived threat from Spain to English autonomy. In this arena, England had suffered some humiliation and economic loss, and the victory over Spain was yet to come in 1588:

> As touching of golde, and silver, Spaine is beholding to the Indies, from whence commeth yearely an infinite masse of treasure: which if slouth and distrust, had not bene Pilates of England in times past, those Indies had served England and not Spaine, for the most part, as more plainly appeareth in the booke tituled, the Decade of the West and East Indies, and Andrew Theuet.[74]

Some additions and comments suggest that topics in *Properties* stimulated Batman to express a desperate level of irritation at the government and its failures. He is enraged by the government's impositions, such as the taxes or 'arerages' imposed on clergy in the late years of the reign:

> The Basiliske or Cockatrice, among creeping wormes is the most pestilent. And among men, the most pestilent minded, are the spoilers of the Clergie with such unconscionable arerages, that many Ministers have bene forced to leave their lyvings, and go a begging … My selfe have bene so plagued, that I speak by experience, and have to shewe by proofe, etc.[75]

This sharp reflection upon the world within his local and personal horizons against Bartholomew's chapter on *basiliscus* ignores the traditional moral associations of the legendary basilisk. Such a self-reflexive attitude is evident in other comments upon the government and economy, such as his diatribe in the margin of Bartholomew's chapter on the rose in Book 17. He starts with direct expository statements based on observation of roses, and concludes with an angry tirade against those whom he sees despoiling the garden of Tudor England. He calls on the Queen, 'rose without thorn', to take note:

> Distilled water of Roses, is necessarie to many uses: the red rose to preserue and to medicine. Dodoneus writeth of ten kinde of roses, among the which, the Eglantine rose, and Muske rose, yeolow and white. There is one rose growing in England, is worth all these, Rosa sine spina; which royall Rose growing in hir proper soyle, is borne up of a well settled stalke, and armed with such thornes, as are apparant to so gentle a kinde, the leaves of lilye hiew, called the orient greene, not withstanding, subiect to flawes of dreadfull blastes, as all our common Roses be to tempesteous windes … May not the buds by the common profites, that are made by dayly pillage of the Cleargie, in abusing the gift of the Maiestie, who are never suffred to be at rest by one extreame assault or

other, the taxe of rerages hath almost beggared, the humble and dutifull subiects. God graunt the view of this note to the royall Rose, that the Cleargie be no more oppressed.[76]

As we saw in the last chapter, when Elizabeth's grandfather came to the throne, Bartholomew's account of the fresh and blooming rose had helped to validate the adoption of the Tudor rose as national emblem. Here, that same account of the rose offers Batman a platform for a scarcely coherent blast against taxation policies under the Queen. Through his comment we can sense something of a commoner's disillusion, a century later, with a somewhat battered and frost-bitten national emblem.

Batman thunders on behalf of the poor as well as the over-taxed clergy. The assertiveness of his comments, and his many references to, and expansions of, biblical texts, also reminds us that he was a popular professional preacher.[77] It has been suggested that medieval people in the differing environments of cathedral school, university and court had each developed a particular form of discourse suited to their immediate context: the Elizabethan scholar was a new kind of professional who was increasingly perceived as someone who could move readily between these different worlds.[78] Batman illustrates this notion as he blends the discourse of natural history with those of bitter political complaint and dogmatic assertion.

Batman and cosmology

At first glance it appears that social and religious changes would form a barrier against the further transmission in England of a scholastic and Catholic text on the factual and moralised properties of things. Nevertheless, representations of the medieval cosmic scheme in printed maps and books demonstrate its continuity from the medieval into the early-modern period; the printed editions of 'Properties' in 1495, 1535 and 1582 are among these representations.

It has been argued that when Christopher Columbus set out on his westward voyage in 1492, his expectations were shaped by biblical, patristic and classical descriptions of geography and world history.[79] He was also impelled by the Christian notion of the individual as *viator* journeying through the time and space of the world, and by a belief in his own destiny as the one destined to find the new heaven and new earth prophesied by St John. At the time when the Americas came to be reached by European travellers, the cosmos could still be conceptualised not only as something spatial surrounding human existence on earth, but also as a temporal process in which the events of world history played a part. Columbus's reading-matter, especially his copy of the *imago mundi* map of Hugo D'Ailly, suggest that beliefs about the form and destiny of the world as expressed in medieval world maps still guided the expectations of travellers in his time.[80] Evidence for the continuation of the medieval conception of the world at the centre of the spheres, bounded by the ring of Ocean, can be seen in fifteenth- and sixteenth-century maps, manuscripts and printed books. In 1481, William Caxton had translated and published *The Mirrour of the World*, a cosmology based on the work of Vincent de Beauvais, Bartholomew's near-contemporary and fellow *compilator*.[81] This conflation of old and new learning based on thirteenth-century authorities and put into the English tongue for the approval of an English lord, shows that for scholars and nobles at the start of the early-modern period the earth still turned at the centre of concentric spheres, subject to motion, to the balance and imbalance of the four sublunar elements and of finite time, and destined for judgement at the end of time. On the face of the earth the peoples created by God inhabited the three regions of Asia, Africa and Europe founded by the sons of Noah after the Flood.

How does Batman respond to Bartholomew's Books and chapters on the cosmic scheme, as he found them in Berthelet's edition? A comparison shows that he makes few major changes to Bartholomew's chapters on the concentric spheres surrounding earth, on the sublunar spheres of the elements, and on the fundamental form of the cosmos described by Bartholomew in Book 8. He gives us glimpses of English travellers venturing abroad for practical purposes but also gives reminders that some places, though more accessible than they had been in the Middle Ages, were still very near the margins of the map, of people's experience and of their mental horizon. For example, of Iceland he mentions the mosquitoes: 'Those that goe thether on fishing, are mervailously troubled with a kinde of Flie like a Gnat, and stinketh foule'; but he also refers the reader to a report of a marvellous property of one of Iceland's mountains:

> mount Hecla, so deepe that no eie canne perceive any bottome, out of the which Abisme, appeareth as it were shapes of men, as though they were drowned, and yet breathing foorth a sound, saieng, that they must depart from thence to mount Hecla: as touching the fearefull noyse of the Ile, Read R. Eden, and R. Wells.[82]

Batman's additions to Books 8, 14 and 15 reveal him as a keen armchair traveller knowledgeable about the current travel literature. He effectively privileges the huge array of 'newe Writers' and 'fresher writers' especially in his additions in Books 14, 15, 16, 17 and 18 on newly discovered places, minerals, plants and creatures. He makes references to many of those who had recorded and shared their findings; for example, Humphrey Gilbert's *A Discourse of a Discoverie for a new Passage to Cataia* (London 1576).[83] He also refers to 'the newe Cards and mappes' as if he expected his readers to have encountered them.[84] By his time, English travellers and the English government were well aware of the New World and had encountered some of its people, although a commentator in the preliminary pages of a copy of Ortelius's *Theatrum orbis terrarum,* in the British Library, considers it wonderful that the map adds to the three parts of the world another two: Magellanica and America.[85] Batman supplements Bartholomew's Book 15 heavily with material from Ortelius, adding the Americas as a fourth to the three major divisions of Asia, Africa and Europe. He adds a lengthy section to the end of Book 15 to rectify the geographical content of the Book in accordance with newly discovered countries and seaways; in particular, with the addition of America.

At the end of the chapter on 'Eiulath', a province of India, Batman quotes Thomas Cooper:

> In the second of Genesis, the river Pison compasseth the whole land of Heuilah, where there is golde, and the gold there is very good, there is Bdelium and the Onix stone. Euilla or Heuilath, a country in the Orient, about the which the riuer Pison, which we call Ganges, that commeth out of Paradise doth runne.

The description reveals that a medieval image of the world as depicted in the Psalter and Hereford *mappaemundi*, in which the four great rivers flow out of Paradise, could still be part of the early-modern scholar's mental furniture. However, it is here combined with a shrewd awareness of the world's material potential for the explorer. In Batman's presentation of the world map we can see a dual focus — that which takes the reader outwards towards the exotic and new, and that which turns inwards towards Batman's national and local concerns. But his comments on the properties of newly discovered or explored places such as America and India show that the two foci are really one; namely, the resources or advantages, or problems, those places might offer the English in the political arena of the time.

Some of his comments do suggest that old certainties were being questioned or transformed: he adds an ambiguous phrase to the heading 'The number of spheres': 'as the truth is, and as Plato and Aristotle describeth them'; and comments in the margin: 'The varietie of opinions concerning the heavens, doe manifest the incertaintie of humane skell: Some of the Mathematicians, omit the burning heaven, and adde the tenth ... The Schoole men omit the seate of God.'[86] What is striking about Batman's cosmological comments is his evident interest in the occult philosophy being expressed by some writers in his own century. In particular, he adds nearly a folio side to the end of Book 8's final chapter 'Of darknesse', saying: 'I have thought good to set before thee, forth of the booke de Occulta Philosophia of Henrie Cornelius Agrippa, his Ladder, wherein is the wonderfull compact of the universall division of the number of 12, beginning with the twelve orders of blessed spirits, omitting the 12 names of God.' There follow lists of 12 'Angells president over the signes', Tribes of Israel, Prophets, Apostles, signs of the zodiac, months, plants, stones, 'principall members' of the body, and 'The 12 pointes of the dampned Divells'. Then come the four seasons and finally 'A briefe note how to understand the Ephimerides'.[87]

Batman follows De Worde and Berthelet in omitting chapters iii to xxi of Book 1 on God and the names of God, but replaces them with an extract on 'the ladder of unity', again from the *De Occulta Philosophia* of 1531, by the contemporary continental magus Henry Cornelius Agrippa. Mystical aspects of Catholic doctrine and worship may have been officially discarded, but Batman shows us that a new mysticism, based on occult interpretations of Pythagoras and Plato, still provided explanations about the cosmos and gave status to those claiming esoteric knowledge of its workings. There is much evidence for the use of astrology at this time — both at the level of popular demand for consultations on day-to-day matters, and as a guiding tool for policy makers.[88] Like the magus Cornelius Agrippa and the popular astrologer Simon Forman, John Dee (1527–1608), an English Cambridge graduate who came within most of the contemporary definitions of 'magus', is another example of the proponents and codifiers of a new form of medieval cosmology more acceptable to Protestant theologians. Dee owned at least two copies of Bartholomew's work, one in Latin and one in English.[89] The manuscripts owned by Dee contain ciphers and notes in the margins, some of which have been identified as being in Dee's hand.[90] By profession he was an astrologer, at one time employed by the Queen but later excluded from the court. His notes and diary record that in 1583 his library in Mortlake was ransacked by angry neighbours who feared him as a conjuror of evil spirits. Some of his property was later returned.[91] The Latin manuscript once owned by Dee and now in the library of Corpus Christi College, Oxford, is missing a folio containing the chapter on the fall of the evil angels, but one can only speculate that it may have been ripped out in such an incident.[92]

In Book 2 of 'Properties', Bartholomew had given a medieval Catholic account of the properties of fallen angels and *spiriti maligni* drawn from scriptural and medieval sources.[93] Batman's response to Bartholomew's accounts of evil spirits tends to confirm that the accepted wisdom on the nature of the cosmos supported the notion of social order based on degree, but also encouraged people at all levels of society to believe in the invisible presence on earth of spirits, both good (personal angels) and bad (the servants and helpers of the Devil). In a long addition to the chapter 'On dreaming' in Book 6, Batman cites, among others, his near-contemporaries Peter Martyr on dreams and Edward Fenton on monstrous births.[94] This Protestant interpretation of Bartholomew's evil angels in terms of human possession by *incubi* is consistent with the social trends documented in the court records of English witchcraft persecutions in the late sixteenth century.[95] The idea of Lucifer and his aides as part of the Protestant vision of the apocalypse still fitted the idea of a cosmos of spheres teeming with celestial and infernal inhabitants. However, Batman adds comments in the margin of Book 1 on the need for faith as the basis for good works; and on the importance of conscience and true contrition, not confession, as the way to forgiveness — comments in tune with the directives of the Protestant church.[96] He does not mention the saints or the Virgin Mary, but a reader in a copy of his work has made an anti-marian note in the margin of Book 1, and later calls her 'an idoll': 'The virgin Mary was not without sin for John acknowledges Christ her saviour Luk. 1.46.'[97]

'Warning all men to the judgement'

A hundred years after Columbus, written sources show a continued sense of the decay of the world and an expectation of its ending. Astronomical events, unusual weather, bad harvests, and national and international conflict seemed to point to the fulfilment of this prophecy.[98] While for Columbus, a Catholic, the apocalyptic vision had been that of the new heaven and the new earth, for English Protestants such as John Bale and Stephen Batman it was the downfall of Antichrist, identifiable with the papacy in the climate of the times.[99] Contemporary works warning of imminent apocalypse include Batman's verse tract of 1581, to which he refers in Book 18 at the end of Bartholomew's chapter about the dragon: 'Of the wonderful greatnesse of Dragons and how manye sortes hath bene, and of the mischiefes they have done, read the Chronicle of the Doome.'[100] In Book 11, he adds a margin note to the column text in the chapter on the rainbow: 'That the rainbowe shall not be seene 40 yeares before the dome.'[101] Such comments indicate that Batman saw his own and others' printed books, especially 'Properties', as tools to use not only for declaring political abuses, but also for saving the souls of his parishioners by reminding them that the end was near.

Bartholomew's chapters on rumoured monsters provide another platform from which Batman inveighs against what he sees as corruption and wickedness, moral and political, in his own country. From his identification of abhorrent and monstrous creatures with the religious sect known as The Family of Love, for example, we can see something of the way the print medium helped to direct establishment hostility towards such non-conformists. In 1578 Batman had likened the founder of the sect, Henry Nicholas, to the monster 'onacratolus', and in 1580 the queen issued a *Proclamation against the Sectaries of the Family of Love*, ordered their books to be burned and members to be imprisoned, but they continued to spread.[102] In Book 5 on the chapter on the head, the column text mentions the fish 'Lamia, that hath as the Glose saith … an head as a maide, and bodie like a grimme beast'. Here Batman adds a long margin note describing the monster:

> Lamie, a kinde of women, by whose sight infants are frighted, & become Elues, they be also those that bee called Ladies of the Fairies, which do allure yong men to company carnaly with them, & after those men are consumed by lechery, they deuour them.[103]

It is arguable that the 'lamia' signified for Batman moral corruption, non-conformist sects and, in particular, the Family of Love. In a copy of *The Doctrine of the Heart*, written in English in an early-fifteenth-century hand, Batman had made a marginal drawing of a scaly bird with a woman's head, wearing a steeple head-dress, and another of a man with a balance; it seems reasonable to speculate on a possible connection between this image of a woman-headed bird and Batman's marginal comment in Book 5.[104] Similarly, in Book 12 against Bartholomew's chapter on *mergus*, the cormorant, he adds: 'Of the doung of these filthie sectes have proceeded a newe Mergus, a cormorant foule, the familie of love.'[105] Batman's shafts aimed at the Family of Love from the margins of *Bartholome* and elsewhere are consistent with the evidence that extreme nonconformist sects were being suppressed during the 1580s.

It is important to note that even though the editions printed by De Worde and by Berthelet, and re-interpreted by Stephen Batman, give *Properties* the appearance of an expository rather than a devotional text, a reader could still find confirmation in them of the belief that the cosmos and the properties of the things within it displayed God's creation of, and purpose for, the world. This was fundamental doctrine for Catholics and Protestants alike. In spite of new discoveries and technologies, at the start of the early modern period Bartholomew's work still supported with its authority a fundamentally medieval conception of the physical world and the larger cosmos, of world history, and of belief in the coming of Judgement Day founded on the Bible's teaching. We can conclude that it was a safe text for readers whatever the prevailing orthodoxy during the reigns of Henry, Edward, Mary and Elizabeth, being an explicitly utilitarian text that could lend itself to a covert devotional purpose.

Collecting knowledge for the nation

At this time, travellers were finding plant and animal life that confirmed, contradicted or confused the received wisdom concerning exotic and fabulous creatures. As a collector of others' work Batman exemplifies a cultural phenomenon that had been gathering pace during the sixteenth century. According to a recent study, a culture of collecting culminated in the seventeenth century in the appropriation by the Royal Society of private collections of exotic natural objects and artefacts, and in the museum movement. However, it had its origins in the intense public interest in the trophies brought back to Europe by the overseas travellers of the later-fifteenth and sixteenth centuries. As Marjorie Swann makes clear, this earlier interest was in objects as novelties and marvels, and did not imply the rationalist methods of enquiry we associate with the Royal Society and the Enlightenment.[106] There is a shift in emphasis here, away from the medieval concept of compilation as the bee-like plundering of morally useful writings of others and towards the meaning for which Swann argues: that of collection, applicable to natural and cultural objects, including works of art and books, and to the knowledge embodied by them.

The known provenance of manuscripts and books as they passed through the hands of collectors in the sixteenth century supports Swann's argument. The dissolution of the monasteries had released many ancient texts into circulation and, in effect, commodified them. We have seen that manuscripts of 'Properties' formerly in religious houses, and of the translation *Properties*, were owned and traded by known collectors including Richard Parker, John Dee, Simon D'Ewes and William Dethick. In the light of Swann's argument, we can consider *Batman uppon Bartholome* as a compilation or collection in which Batman is a declared, named collector of Bartholomew's authorities, but also of modern authorities and the knowledge they embody. His lists and citations of modern and classical writers, and his recounting of classical myths and other stories, confer a kind of authority on Batman himself. At the same time, he is a collector of property in the new material sense: he collects Greek myths; he collects stories about English history and landscape and about exotic customs; he collects facts, through the observation and categorisation of plants and other natural phenomena; and he collects interesting specimens. The following addition to the end of the chapter on the rhinoceros provides a peep-hole on Batman as the possessor of at least one displayable curiosity:

> The Rhinoceros in Aethiopia, a perpetuall enimie to the Elephant, hee is not so high as the Elephant, armed ouer with shells in steed of haire, so that nothing can easily pearce the same: euen so is the little beast, called of the Affricans Tatton, of Gesner Zibet, in fo.20 at the end of his booke of birdes, etc. Which armed case I haue to shew.[107]

Thus, Batman's additions to, and marginal comments in, *Batman uppon Bartholome* constitute a display of his own collections; and of a personal identity that aims to be both authoritative and authorial.[108]

We might also consider the likelihood that Batman, like patrons of 'Properties' in the fourteenth century, was endowing his patron with a flattering mantle of wisdom appropriate for one of England's chief noblemen. Batman expresses the idea of collecting knowledge for the sake of one's country, as well as one's patron, in his preliminary address to the reader. Here, having praised John Bale and other 'famous, and worthy persons, of singular perseuerance and learning', such as 'Gesner, Fuchs, Mathiolus, Paracelsus, Dodoneus, Munster, Agrippa and Ortelius', he aligns his own efforts with theirs:

> I haue therefore as an imitator of the learned, for the good will I bare to my countrie, collected forth of these aforesaid Authors, the like deuises, which they in times past gathered of their elders, and so renuing the

whole booke, as is apparant by additions, is brought home, the Master, the Pilot, and the profit thereto belonging.[109]

In this passage, Batman declares his aim as a collector of others' work, in the sense of both imitator and compiler. Bartholomew had declared a similar aim. Unlike Bartholomew, however, he adds, by means of his maritime metaphor, the connotation of collected wealth from beyond former horizons, like the booty and novelties being brought to English ports from the New World and Asia. Whereas Bartholomew compiled the fruit of others' labours in order to share its moral usefulness widely through an international brotherhood, Batman collects knowledge for the intellectual coffers of England, his patron Carey and himself.

Swann argues further that the development of the culture of collecting during the sixteenth and seventeenth centuries gave a new meaning to the word 'property'.[110] Formerly, the concrete sense of this word had applied to land, but early-modern collectors aimed to fashion an imposing personal identity for themselves through 'property' in the sense of awe-inspiring possessions, collected and displayed. Published catalogues of private collections, descriptions of items and lists of donors were texts symbolic of the collection itself, as well as advertisements of that identity. We can deduce that the concept of the 'property' of a thing lost the connotation of an underlying moral significance or inherent powerfulness that it had carried in the Middle Ages. Rather, things — including ideas — could become the property of a person, or of a nation. Evidence for the wider existence of such an attitude to intellectual property occurs in seventeenth-century verses written on the flyleaf of a manuscript of *Properties* now in the British Library. These verses extol Bartholomew as an Englishman who bestows 'property' on his country, playing on the variable meaning of the word, and as a universal authority:

> On the famouse Bartholomew Glanvill commonly called the English Bartholomew relating to his Booke of the properties of things
>
> Thy country truly, but yet subtly too
> Hath stiled thee the English Barthol'mew.
> Whilst properties of things thou wrotst of, shee
> Makes sure of Getting Property in thee;
> Would from thy name her own new worth Discover,
> And be at once unto all learning Mother.
> But had shee silent been, thy Booke alone
> Had seated thee in a far larger throne:
> This but consulted, none could call thee lesse
> Then Barthol'mew of the great Univers.
> By both these titles be thou euer known,
> One for our glory, tother for thy own.[111]

The verses are followed by a seventeenth-century addition by Julius Glanville of Lincoln's Inn.[112] According to Seymour, Julius Glanville was the son of Sir John Glanville, who 'may have owned the manuscript in the belief that Bartholomaeus, traditionally surnamed Glanville, was an ancestor'.[113] The lofty inscription is consistent with family pride in 'Properties' as a repository of wisdom and a testament to the worth of the owner.

'Shakespeare's encyclopedia'

As Julius Glanville's interest suggests, the story and the journey of 'Properties' does not end with the Tudor era. As far as we know, no editions of the Latin text were printed in England, and there is no evidence that scribes made new manuscript copies of the Latin 'Properties' or of *Properties* in that country after the end of the fifteenth century. For this reason it is usually claimed that Bartholomew disappeared from the English literary scene after 1582. Later evidence shows, however, that the printed edition of 1582 is not followed by the tidy demise that the literature suggests. Manuscripts of *Properties* used and abused by people unknown to us over recent centuries, further published adaptations of the work, and specific references to it by known readers testify to the work's prestige and commodification as a historical curiosity.[114] In the eighteenth century, England's ancient buildings, historical documents and national heroes again came to be valued as an important legacy from the nation's past. Thomas Hearne (1678–1735), one antiquary who expressed concern at the loss of England's medieval manuscripts, pleaded for the re-establishment of an Antiquarian Society of scholars working together to preserve them, such as that founded by Archbishop Parker in 1572.[115] From the seventeenth and into the nineteenth centuries, antiquarians in England and on the continent included Bartholomew among noteworthy authors.[116] English readers continued to make adaptations of it, and claims for it, up to the time of Robert Steele in the 1880s. The belief that Bartholomew was a member of an English aristocratic family may have contributed to the attempts by early Shakespeare scholars — Douce, Anders and Furnivall, followed by Steele, Matrod and Se Boyar — to sustain the view that Bartholomew was a genuine source for Shakespeare, to the extent that the English could not understand Shakespeare without the medieval work as a guide.[117]

Individuals left the mark of their ownership or patronage of 'Properties' on individual copies. One of these is a copy of the 1535 printed edition of *Properties* (see Figure 7). This has the forged signature of Shakespeare at the top right-hand corner of the title page — 'William Shakspeare his Booke 1597' — and the library stamp of Joseph Banks in the centre. The forgery dates from the late eighteenth century; the imprimatur of Joseph Banks from a few decades later. The use of *Properties* as a site for the forgery helps to illumine the role 'Properties' could play in an era when the production of counterfeit medieval texts, such as

Figure 7: Title-page and part of Table of Contents, *Bartholomeus De Proprietatibus Rerum*. Printed by Thomas Berthelet, 1535. Copy BL 456.a.1 formerly owned by Joseph Banks.

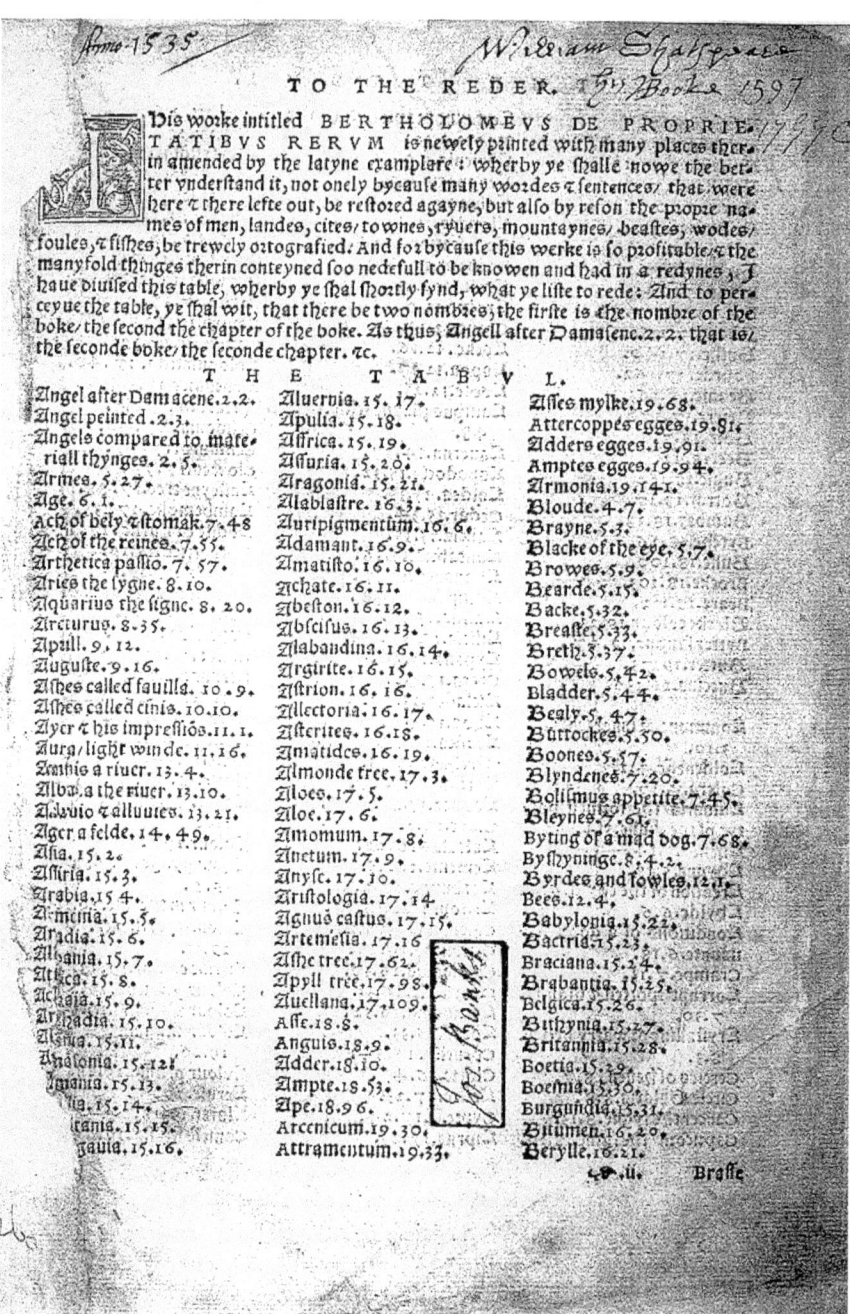

MacPherson's 'Ossian', and Thomas Chatterton's 'Rowley' poems, exploited and reflected a fashion for the medieval gothic.[118] It was also a time of fashionable interest in Shakespeare as a 'primitive' English genius who, it was assumed, must have had access to Batman's edition. As Se Boyar points out, Douce had praised Bartholomew as 'our English Pliny' and used the compilation to elucidate passages in Shakespeare's plays. William-Henry Ireland and his family capitalised on the fashion for Shakespeare by buying up sixteenth-century books and papers to put together a 'library' of works containing the forged signature of Shakespeare.[119] The copy of Berthelet's edition of 'Properties' shown here is among these works.[120]

The title-page illustrated in Figure 7 includes not only the signature of Shakespeare forged by Ireland, but also the genuine stamp of the travelling botanist Joseph Banks (as do the title-pages of other copies of the printed editions in his collection, including that of 1495, bequeathed by him to the library of the British Museum). This emphasises the question of Bartholomew's continuing authority for educated gentry. We do not think of Banks as 'medieval' in his world-view but, rather, as a modern European open to the novelty of the antipodes; yet he had more than one copy of Bartholomaeus in his scientific library. Banks was a voyager and enquirer into the world who lived at a turning point in the way scientific knowledge was conceptualised and systematised — a position comparable to that of Columbus, who knew of Ptolemy but took D'Ailly's *Imago Mundi* on his westward voyage. For Banks, Bartholomew could still be worth owning as 'our English Pliny', the transmitter of knowledge from esteemed scholars of the early and medieval Christian era, and the promulgator of a once-enduring Christian image of the world.

We can conclude that, although Bartholomew's position in the early-modern hall of fame was partly founded on error and prejudice, there are some important continuities in the English reception of 'Properties' that help to explain its passage across daunting cultural barriers. The printed editions of 1495 and 1535, in the current English dialects of the London region, each carried Bartholomew's authority and reputation into another cultural context and readership. As a financial venture, the printing of *Properties* could succeed through the cooperation of a close network of investors and other interested parties. There is evidence that during Henry VIII's reign, the king, government and church were keen to build a basis for English autonomy not only in religion but also in language, history and legend, landscape and cultural achievements. By claiming Bartholomew as a native-born Englishman and writer, antiquaries and churchmen such as John Leland and John Bale were able to construct an identity for him and his work that supported such nationalistic efforts. 'Properties' as a printed book survived increasing scrutiny of the press in Henry VIII's time partly because, though a Catholic work, its practical utility answered a need of the times. Moral interpretations implied in the glosses were no longer attached to the text and thus the text did not need to be associated only with the preaching of Catholic priests and friars; its scope and content could still cast a flattering mantle of omniscience over those who patronised it. Solomonic wisdom was still an ideal connected with nobility, and existing knowledge derived from antiquity underwent a process of accommodation rather than rejection. We might consider the likelihood that Stephen Batman, like patrons of 'Properties' in the fourteenth century, was endowing his patron, Lord Hunsdon, with a flattering mantle of wisdom appropriate for one of England's chief noblemen.

In *Batman uppon Bartholome* we see Bartholomew's representation of the world on the one hand held out to yet another generation of readers as an authoritative text, by a churchman and scholar; and on the other hand partially retracted or modified by him to bring it into line with the new array of printed knowledge circulating in his own day. Batman's additions and marginal comments constitute a display of his own intellectual property — and perspicacity. Whereas Bartholomew had been compiling his work for a growing brotherhood of homeless preachers involved in a new kind of Christian outreach, Stephen Batman's many comments on local objects and topical matters sharply reflect his own domestic life, work and professional interests.

In Batman's as in Bartholomew's day, readers' mental horizons were created by assumptions about the finite nature of the world and its physical extent. Sponsors — whether Pope Alexander IV, King Henry VII or Queen Elizabeth I — sent out travellers for reasons that were political and commercial as well as religious, in both eras. The passion for tangible evidence of other places existing beyond known limits, and the wonder they evoked, suggests an extension of mental boundaries comparable to that of the early Franciscans and Dominicans as they pushed beyond the borders of Christendom.

NOTES

[1] Tritheim, Johannes, *Liber de Scriptoribus Ecclesiasticus*, Basle, 1494, ff.91r–91v. Tritheim (f.91v) lists BA's supposed works in addition to 'Properties': *sermones varios; alia quorum multa scripsisse dicit: sed ad manus nostras minime venerunt* ('various sermons; many other things he is said to have written, but which have not come to hand'): author's paraphrase. It is unknown whether such works ever existed.

[2] *De proprietatibus rerum*, 1519, BL 44Lh4, title page: *Venerandi patris Bartholomei Anglici ordinis Minorum: viri eruditiissimi: opus de rerum proprietatibus inscriptum ... Vale bone lector, eme, necte precii poenitebit.*

[3] See Cressy, pp.157–70.

[4] Rex, Richard, *Henry VIII and the English Reformation*, New York: St Martin's Press, 1993; William Harrison's *The Description of England* (1587), edited by G. Edelen, Cornell University Press, 1968, pp.112–8.

[5] Bennett, H. S., pp.38, 139: Henry had given monopolies to certain printers which 'clearly gave the Crown a useful, continuous control over various kinds of books, particularly ... over service-books and works of elementary religious instruction'; for Henry VIII, Berthelet publicised opinions of the universities in favour of the validity of Henry's marriage to his brother's widow; in 1537/38 he published four books, 'all inveighing against the Pope's proposal to call a General Council'.

[6] Bennett, H. S., pp.42, 81–4, 103; Rex, pp.173–4.

[7] *Bartholomeus De Proprietatibus Rerum. Londini in Aedibus Thomae Bertheleti Regii Impressoris. Cum Privilegio a Rege indulto*, 1535.

[8] Brockhurst, Elizabeth J., The Life and Works of Stephen Batman, unpublished MA thesis, University of London, 1947, p.324: 'De Worde's text badly needed revision, and Berthelet, who was a careful printer, has produced a beautifully clear and correct version; I have compared his Prologue and Bks 1 and II in great detail with the text of De Worde, and in every instance where they differ, Berthelet's text is correct, according to the Latin. Berthelet adds a consistent ending for Bk 1, chapter i, and removes De Worde's extraneous material here. He is, however, modernising the arrangement, and so takes the table of contents out of the text altogether, rearranges it alphabetically, and prefixes it to the Prologue, after the title page. Berthelet also translates De Worde's Latin chapter headings into English.' Brockhurst suggests that Berthelet used a Latin copy text in addition to De Worde's text.

[9] Bennett, H. S., pp.33–4.

[10] Smith, Alan G. R., *The Emergence of a Nation State: The Commonwealth of England 1529–1660*, London: Longman, 1984, pp.4–6. In the decades leading up to Henry's dissolution of the monasteries, the king had been dismantling some traditional roles of church and state in the process of defying papal authority, supported by reforming churchmen such as Thomas Cromwell and Archbishop Cranmer: the singing of masses in chantries, the use of images, candles and incense, prayers to the Virgin Mary and the celebration of saints' days were forbidden. There had been the *praemunire* accusation against the whole clergy in 1530; the 'Submission of the Clergy' in 1532; the Act of Supremacy in 1534; and, in the following year, the visitations and valuations of religious houses were put in train, Fisher and More were executed, and the larger monasteries were surrendered by 1540.

[11] Haigh, Christopher, *The English Reformation Revised*, Cambridge University Press, 1987; Haigh examines (pp.10–1) the question of Henry's 'Anglo-Catholicism' and the personal motivations adduced for his opposition to the papacy and appropriation of monastic possessions.

[12] Rex, pp.173–4.

[13] *The Itinerary of John Leland, Antiquary* was published by Thomas Hearne in 1710: Chandler, John, ed, *John Leland's Itinerary : Travels in Tudor England*, Stroud, 1993.

[14] Leland, 1709, p.336 (see Chapter 1, Introduction, p.1).

[15] Sharpe, Richard A., *A Handlist of the Latin Writers of Great Britain and Ireland before 1540*, Turnhout: Brepols, (1997), 2001, p.69; Se Boyar, pp.169–73.

[16] *Adolscens professionem excolebat Francisconum. Maturior annis factus, Isidis Vadum, Lutetiam atque adeo, si vera conjectura, Romam ipsam celebravit*: Leland, 1709, p.336.

[17] One Gilbert Glanville, Bishop of Rochester 1185–1214, was sent by Becket to the pope shortly before the former's death: Blount, M. N., "Glanville, Gilbert de (d.1214)". ODNB.

[18] Carley, James P., "John Leland on the contents of English pre-Dissolution libraries: The Cambridge friars", *Transactions of the Cambridge Bibliographical Society* 9 (1986), 90–100. The Dominican buildings at Cambridge were being dismantled by 1536/7; shortly before 1545, an unknown person sent as many as 200 Cambridge mss overseas, including *F. Bartolomei Anglis de proprietatibus rerum*. These mss were acquired by Pope Marcellus.

[19] Bale, pp.463–4.

[20] ODCC, p.123; Christianson, pp.13–22, 39.

[21] Wada, Yoko, "Bale to Parker on British Historical Texts in Cambridge College Libraries", *Transactions of the Cambridge Bibliographical Society* 10 (1994), 511–19.

[22] Bernau, Anke, "Myths of origin and the struggle over nationhood in medieval and early modern England" in *Reading the Medieval in Early Modern England*, edited by David Matthews and Gordon McMullan, 106–18, Cambridge University Press, 2007. According to this legend, Albina and her sisters landed on the island, murdered their husbands, and lived off the land in a lawless and lecherous manner. They gave birth to a race of giants. Brutus on his arrival conquered the giants and began to civilise the landscape with cities and farms. He divided the land among his three sons, Locrine, Albanact and Camber, creating England, Scotland and Wales. In 1480, the Albina story had appeared in print in Caxton's *The Chronicles of England*.

[23] Bernau, p.111. On Scota and the Scottish origin myths see Cowan, Edward J., "Myth and identity in early medieval Scotland", *Scottish Historical Review* 63.2 (1984), 111–35.

[24] Readers' annotations and underlinings in manuscripts and printed copies show interest in this theme over time. In the copy of Bale's chronicle of writers perused for this study, a reader has underlined some of Bale's statements indicating a marked response to mentions of the first Britons; readers of

manuscripts of *Properties* have also noted this information with underlinings or marginal notes. To give a single example: in the fifteenth-century ms BL Harley 614, ff.121r and 122v, Bk 15, *De Anglia* and *De Brittania*, a margin note reads 'De Anglia Brutayne'.

[25] Bale, p.23.

[26] Op.cit, Index.

[27] DrP, Bk 15, cap xiv, *De Anglia*, pp.631–2.

[28] *Properties*, Book 15, cap xiiii, *De Anglia*, p.733.

[29] *Properties*, loc.cit.

[30] The myth linking Trojan and Arthurian heroic legend had been given literary form by Geoffrey of Monmouth in his *Historia Regum Brittaniae* (c.1130–40), and embodied in the English verse chronicle *The Brut* (late twelfth century). Updated to 1479, its value to the early Tudors is reflected in the 13 printed editions by 1528: Pope, Peter E., *The Many Landfalls of John Cabot*: University of Toronto Press, 1997, p.130.

[31] Bateman [sic], Stephen, *Batman upon Bartholome*, London, St Paul's Churchyard: Thomas and Lucretia East, 1582, hereafter referred to as BuB. For a most useful discussion of this work, see Schäfer, Jurgen, ed, "Introduction", in Stephen Bateman, *Batman upon Bartholome*, Facsimile edition, Hildesheim: Georg Olms Verlag, 1976. See also Zim, Rivkah, "Batman, Stephan (c.1542–1584)", ODNB, Oxford University Press, 2004. Note: Batman's text is not paginated. East's ms-style foliation is used here for references, but it contains many printing errors.

[32] Brockhurst, 1947, pp.48–50: CCC Cambridge Ms Parker 61, f.150v, contains Batman's signature: 'This is my booke /S.B. geven to me by Mr Cari the xvij Decembre anno 1570'; Brockhurst concludes that the donor may have been Henry Carey's son George (b.1547); he and his siblings were neighbours at Batman's cure in Newington, where Lord Hunsdon owned the manor of Paris Garden in Brixton Hundred.

[33] Brockhurst, 1947, pp.17–29, 46: Batman was rector of Newington in Brixton Hundred from 1569, and also of Merstham in Surrey from 1571; his relations with the See of Canterbury after Parker's death are not known.

[34] Wilson, Alison, "An Elizabethan miniature in the Parker Library, Corpus Christi College, Cambridge", *Transactions of the Cambridge Bibliographical Society* 10 (1994): 461–85; Parker, a pluralist and scholar, was chaplain to Anne Boleyn in 1535, and Archbishop of Canterbury 1559–75: Venn, J. & J. A., *Alumni Cantabrigienses: a biographical list of all known students and holders of office at the University of Cambridge from the earliest times to 1900*, Part I, Vol.3: Cambridge University Press (1922), 1954, p.307. Described as a tolerant conservative, he was involved in publishing the so-called Bishops' Bible in 1563–8 and in 1566 prescribed on ritual matters including the use of the surplice, thus incurring opposition from the Puritan party: ODCC, p.1033. See also Hall, Catherine, "Matthew Parker as Annotator: the Case of Winchester Cathedral MS XXB", *Transactions of the Cambridge Bibliographical Society* 10 (1995): 642–5, p.642.

[35] Trinity College Cambridge Ms B.14.19 f.67v: cited by Brockhurst, 1947, p.1.

[36] McLoughlin, Kate, "Magdalene College MS Pepys 2498 and Stephen Batman's Reading Practices", *Transactions of the Cambridge Bibliographical Society* 10 (1994): 525–34, pp.528–9.

[37] Bruce, John and Thomas Perowne, eds, *Correspondence of Matthew Parker, Archbishop of Canterbury*, Publications of the Parker Society: Cambridge University Press, 1853, Letter 194, p.253. There are many other instances in his correspondence of researches into Anglo-Saxon and other manuscripts and the history of the early church: cited by Brockhurst, 1947, p.428.

[38] James, Montague Rhodes, *A Descriptive Catalogue of the Manuscripts in the Library of Corpus Christi College Cambridge*, Cambridge University Press, 1912.

[39] Schäfer, p.xiii.

[40] Brockhurst 1947, pp.422–4.

[41] Brockhurst, 1947, p.331: without detailed comparative study of his sources against his additions, it is not clear whether he paraphrased borrowed passages or inserted them verbatim, or both, or where some of the longer interpolations merge with his own comments. See Parish, Verna M., "Batman's additions from Elyot and Boorde to his English edition of Bartholomaeus Anglicus" in *Studies in Language, Literature, and Culture of the Middle Ages and Later*, edited by E. B. Atwood and A. A. Hill, 337–46, Austin: University of Texas, 1969, pp.337–8, for a succinct account of Batman's approach as a moderniser.

[42] Greetham, D. C., "On Cultural Translation: From Patristic Repository to Shakespeare's Encyclopedia" in *Voices in Translation: The Authority of "Olde Bookes" in Medieval Literature: Essays in Honor of Helaine*

Newstead, edited by Deborah M. Sinnreich-Levi and Gale Sigal, 69–84, New York: AMS Press, 1992; Schäfer (p.xvi) also makes the point that Batman's changes by no means reflect a break with medieval traditions.

[43] The findings of Cressy (especially pp.157–70), indicate that in Batman's time potential book-buyers could have been found among men (not women) of the first three estates only.

[44] *De Proprietatibus Rerum*, 1535, first page.

[45] Brockhurst, 1947, p.331: 'this "old coppye" is De Worde's edition, but Batman's use of it was probably very occasional; the correspondences with Berthelet are too frequent to be set aside'.

[46] BuB, Bk 15, 'Of Britainia', f.218.

[47] BuB, Bk 15, f.245r.

[48] BuB, Bk 15, chap 108, 'Of Normania', f236r.

[49] BuB, Bk 15, chap 141, 'Of saxonia', f242v.

[50] BuB, Bk 5, chap 7, 'Of bloud', f29v.

[51] BuB, Bk 5, f29v; on the *Martiloge* see H. S. Bennett, 1952, p.163.

[52] Hooker was an Oxford scholar whose *Treatise on the Laws of Ecclesiastical Polity* was not published until 1594–7; Jewel was made Bishop of Salisbury in 1560, had travelled with Peter Martyr (whom Batman does refer to several times) and was a strong supporter of the Anglican settlement, publishing the *Apologia Ecclesiae Anglicanae* in 1562: ODCC, p.738.

[53] 'Of his function ... read the booke tituled, The Poore mans Librarie, set forth by Master William Alley, Bishop of Exceter. 1560'; BuB, Bk 15, chap 68, 'Of Grecia', f.227v.

[54] Rostenberg, Leona, *The Minority Press and the English Crown: A Study in Repression 1558–1625*, New York: De Graaf, 1971; Loades, David, "Books and the English Reformation prior to 1558" in *The Reformation and the Book*, edited by Jean-Francois Gilmont & Karin Maag, 264–91, Aldershot: Ashgate, 1998.

[55] See Ashworth, William B., "Emblematic natural history of the Renaissance" in *Cultures of Natural History*, edited by N. Jardine, J. A. Secord and E. C. Spary, 17–37, Cambridge University Press, 1996, pp.17–36 and passim, on the *Historia animalium* 'the most widely read of all Renaissance natural histories', of Conrad Gesner (1516–65); see H. S. Bennett, p.181, on Gesner's role in the controversy over translations of medical works.

[56] Cunningham, Andrew, "The culture of gardens" in *Cultures of Natural History*, edited by N. Jardine, J. A. Secord and E. C. Spary, 38–56: Cambridge University Press, 1996, pp.50, 64: 'This activity in growing new plants in the garden was reflected in print, and a number of large illustrated books on plants were published during the sixteenth century and found a ready market'; Pietro Andrea Mattioli published *Commentarii* on Dioscorides' *Materia medica* in 1554; Leonard Fuchs published *De historia stirpium* in 1542; Rembert Dodoens published *Cruydeboek* in 1563; Cook, Harold J., "Physicians and natural history" in Jardine et al, eds, 91–105, p.97: 'Because of both their classical education and their daily concerns, then, physicians took the lead among those who worked to identify accurately the simples used in medicines, especially the botanicals. Consequently, it is no surprise that the greatest sixteenth-century herbalists were physicians.'

[57] Theophrastus Paracelsus (1493–1541) was an alchemist who wrote *Liber de nymphis, sylphis, pygmaeis et salamandiis et de caeteris spiritibus*; Sebastian Münster 'was one of the great geographers of sixteenth century Germany; Gesner learned from him what the foxes of Germany and Russia look like': Ashworth, p.28.

[58] On Ortelius, see Nebenzahl, Kenneth, *Atlas of Columbus and the Great Discoveries*, Chicago: Rand McNally, 1990, p.121: Abraham Ortels (1527–98) was a friend and rival of Gerard Mercator. His innovative atlas *Theatrum Orbis Terrarum* was published in several editions from the 1560s to 1590s.

[59] Brockhurst, 1947, pp.52–63.

[60] BuB, Bk 15, 'Of Britainia', f.218v.

[61] BuB, 'List of Authorities'.

[62] See, for example, Ashworth, pp.17–37, on the accommodation of old and new, moral and empirical, in contemporary descriptions of the animal world by Conrad Gesner and others.

[63] BuB, Bk 18, ff.364r–365r.

[64] Batman was possibly married at Bruton, Somerset, in the early 1550s; three daughters were baptised in the years 1554–59. He indicates in his poem *The Travayled Pilgrim* that he favoured the married state. (Brockhurst, 1947, pp.27–9).

65 BuB, Bk 6, f.75.
66 BuB, Bk 5, f.48.
67 BuB, Bk 5, f. 62.
68 BuB, Bk 17, f.319; f.313.
69 BuB, Bk 19, ff.402v–403r. From *The Castel of Helthe* (the popular Latin-English dictionary first produced by Sir Thomas Elyot before 1538, revised by Thomas Cooper in 1548, 1552, and 1559), Batman selected 14 additions to three books: eight to Book 17, 'Of Trees and Herbs'; one to Book 18, 'Of Animals in General; and five to Book 19, 'Of Colors'; BA may have been one of Elyot's sources on, for example, butter: Parish, pp.338–42, p.341; H. S. Bennett, p.90, p.129.
70 BuB, Bk 18, f.376r; see also his added chapter on the rabbit (Bk 18, f.359r); his pragmatic comments on horses (Bk 18, f.362v); on the fox (Bk 18, f.385r); on the domestic pig (Bk 18, f.377v); on honey, milk and cheese (Bk 19, ff.402v–409r); and on plants throughout Book 17.
71 BuB, Bk 15, 'Of Cancia', ff. f.219–21.
72 Brockhurst, 1947, p.398.
73 BuB, Bk 19, ff.390r–v.
74 BuB, Bk 15, f.231r.
75 BuB, Bk 18, f.351r.
76 BuB, Bk 17, f.315v.
77 Ingram, William, "The playhouse at Newington Butts: a new proposal", *Shakespeare Quarterly* 21, no.4 (1970): 385–98, p.394.
78 Findlen, Paula, "Courting Nature" in *Cultures of Natural History*, edited by N. Jardine, J. A. Secord and E. C. Spary, 57–74, Cambridge University Press, 1996, p.58.
79 Nebenzahl, 1990, p.2; Watts, Pauline Moffitt, "Prophecy and Discovery: On the Spiritual Origins of Christopher Columbus' 'Enterprise of the Indies'" in *The European Opportunity*, edited by Felipe Fernández-Armesto, 195–224, Aldershot, U. K. and Brookfield, U. S. A: Variorum, 1995, pp.81–2.
80 Watts, pp.197–201, argues for the importance of contemporary apocalypticism, specifically Franciscan Joachimism, to understanding the mentality of Columbus and his motivations for travel and discovery.
81 Caxton, William, trans, *Vincentius. The Mirrour of the World*, Westminster: Caxton, 1481. A treatise on cosmology by Gossuin de Metz, *L'image du monde* was based on the *Speculum Naturale* of Vincent de Beauvais (c.1250). Caxton states in the preface that he acts on behalf of Hugh Bryce, citizen and alderman of London, who wishes to present it to his patron Lord Hastings.
82 BuB, Bk 15, 'Of Yselondia', f.249v.
83 Contemporary and recent explorers and navigators whom Batman names include 'Abraham Hortelius ... A Dutch man, and Gerardus Mercator the chiefe Geographer of our time'; Richard Eden, Vasco de Gama, Sebastian Munster, Raphael Maffei ('Volteranus'), Pius II, Pierre Gilles, Peter Martyr, Paolo Giovio, Maximilian Transilvanus, Ludovico di Varthema, Laonicus Chalcocondylas, Johannes Macer, Johannes Leo Africanus, Johannes Cuspinianus, Joannes Barreus, Humphrey Gilbert, Guilielmo Gratarolo, Girolamo Fracastoro, Giovanni Battista Ramusio, Gilbert Nazarenus, Georg Rithaymer, Georg Meyer, Frauncis Alvares, Dominic Niger, Cosmas Indopleates, Christopher Columbus, Cherubino di Stella, Battista Agnese, Antoni Tingil, Andrew Thevet, Andrés de Laguna, Ancelm & Christopher Cella, Alvise Cà Da Musto; also 'Ioannes Herbaceus' and 'Christopher Richerius of Sene'. Thanks to Iain McLean for help with identifications.
84 BuB, Bk 15, f.220v; f.221r.
85 Ortelius, Abraham, *Theatrum Orbis Terrarum*, Antwerp, 1575. (BL: no page no.): *Quoque magis mirere, tribus supperaddidit Orbis Partibus hic binas alias.*
86 BuB, Bk 8, f.122r.
87 BuB, Bk 8, ff.140–2.
88 For contemporary evidence of popular consultations see Rouse, A. W., *Simon Forman: Sex and Society in Shakespeare's Age*, London: Wiedenfeld and Nicolson, 1974.
89 Now CCC Oxford Ms 249 and BL Harley Ms 614; James, M. R., "Lists of manuscripts formerly owned by Dr John Dee", *Supplement to the Transactions of the Bibliographical Society* 1 (1921), pp.19, 25; Watson, A.G., "An identification of some manuscripts owned by Dr John Dee and Sir Simonds D'Ewes", *The Library* XIII 5th series (1958): 194–8, p.196; Seymour, 1975–1988 vol.3, pp.24–5.
90 BL Harley Ms 614, for example, f.113r, Bk 13, *De piscibus*: the words 'by signys' and a red hand pointer against the column text 'Also he seith at Delphynus knowen bisynes'; and see James, 1921, p.8

on Dee's identifying signs; on the provenance of the Oxford ms see Clulee, Nicholas H., *John Dee's Natural Philosophy*, London and New York: Routledge, 1988.

[91] James, 1921, p.4.

[92] CCC Oxford Ms 249, f.10, Bk 2, cap xxi *De casu malignorum spirituum*.

[93] DrP, Bk 2, *De proprietatibus Angelorum*, pp.18–45.

[94] BuB, Bk 6, ff.83v–85r.

[95] Sharpe, J. A., *Instruments of Darkness: Witchcraft in England 1550–1750*, University of Pennsylvania Press, 1997, p.41.

[96] BuB, Bk 1, *De Trinitate*, f. 2r.

[97] BuB, BL 456.b.15, f.1, f.2.

[98] Christianson, pp.1–12; Sharpe, J. A., *Early Modern England*, London: Edward Arnold, 1987, pp.106–13; Whitfield, p.70.

[99] Christianson, pp.4–10, 89.

[100] Brockhurst, 1947, p.240, pp.290–2: *The Doome warning all men to the Iudgemente* is an unacknowledged translation of *De Prodigiis et Ostentis* by Conrad Lycosthenes, d.1560; BuB, Bk 18, f.361r.

[101] BuB, Bk 11, f.161r.

[102] Henry Nicholas, a Catholic born in Münster, was much influenced by the Dutch Anabaptist movement and he found many adherents in Holland and in England: ODCC, pp.502, 973. Batman had written prefaces in 1578/79 to John Rogers' book *The Displaying of an horrible secte ... Heretiques and An Answere unto a wicked and infamous Libel*, against The Family of Love. He had also expressed aversion to this sect in *The Golden Booke* of 1577; in *The Doome*, Batman records for the year 1580 a 'blazing stave', seen nightly until the 21st of October, which he interprets as a sign against the Familists: Brockhurst, 1947, p.229.

[103] BuB, Bk 5, f.36v.

[104] Trinity Coll. Ms B 14.15 [301]: Brockhurst, 1947, p.433.

[105] BuB, Bk 12, f.186v.

[106] Swann, Marjorie, *Curiosities and Texts: The Culture of Collecting in Early Modern England*, Philadelphia: The University of Pennsylvania Press, 2001; Schäfer, pp.xviii–xix, similarly notes the importance of the distinction.

[107] BuB, Bk.18, f.378v; on the other hand, he annotates the chapter on the crocodile with a terse comment on the folly of people who pay to go and view crocodile skins (f.359v).

[108] See Tribble, Evelyn B., *Margins and Marginality*, Charlottesville and London: University Press of Virginia, 1993, on the margins of printed texts as a contested area in which some sixteenth-century writers asserted their authorial role by means of glosses.

[109] BuB, 'To the Reader', no foliation.

[110] Swann, p.19.

[111] BL Add. Ms 27944, front fly leaf, recto: "Bartholomew de Ordine; verso: Ecclesiastaicus 44 vers the 1st and the 7th: *Let us now praise famouse men and our ffathers that begate us. All those were honoured in theyr generations and were the glory of theyr times*"; followed by verse. This and the verses are in a seventeenth-century hand.

[112] BL. Add. Ms 27944, f.1v: *Sic subito allusit. Julius Glanvill de Lincolns Inne Echemythus Anno aere christiana 1658*; the ms was made before 1410 and acquired by the British Museum in 1868: British Museum, ed, *Catalogue of Additions to Manuscripts in the British Museum*, 1854–75, p.383.

[113] Seymour, 1975–1988 vol.iii, p.13. Ranulph de Glanville of Suffolk (d.1190) was chronicled in the Middle Ages as a prominent right-hand man of Henry II and a respected writer on law (Hudson, John. "Glanville, Ranulph de (1120s?–1190. ODNB), suggesting that connection to the Suffolk Glanvilles would have been seen as desirable.

[114] For example, in 1607 and 1608 Edmund Topsell adapted the work of Gesner, who had drawn heavily on 'Properties', to produce *The historie of foure footed beastes,* and *The historie of serpents*.

[115] Brockhurst, 1947, p.421.

[116] Wadding, *Annales minorum* (1625) vol.iii, p.238 records 'B.Glainvillus', author of DPR 1367; Wadding, *Scriptores Ordinis minorum* (1650), pp.49–50; Quétif & Echard, *Scriptores Ordinis Predicatorum* (1721) vol.i, pp.49–50; Fabricius, *Bibl. Lat. Mediae et Infimae Aetatis* (1746) vol.i, pp.479–80; Thomas

Hearne, *A Collection of Curious Discourses* (1720); Thomas Warton, *History of English Poetry* (1781) vol.ii, p.128, vol.iii, p.393; J. H. Sbaralea (OFM) *Supplementum ... ad Scriptores Trium Ordinum S. Francisci* (1806), pp.120–1; A. Jourdain, *Recherches Critiques sur l'Age et sur l'Origine des Traductions Latines d'Aristote* (1819), pp.35, 398–400: all these citations are gratefully borrowed from Brockhurst, 1952, p.18.

[117] Douce, Francis, *Illustrations of Shakspeare, and Ancient Manners*, London: Burt Franklin, 1839 (1968); Anders, H. R. D., *Shakespeare's Books*, 1904; Furnivall, R., "On Puck's 'Swifter than the moon's sphere' and Shakspere's astronomy", *New Shakspere Transactions* 1, no.7 (1879): 431–50; Steele, 1893; Matrod, 1912; Se Boyar, 1920; see Chapter 2 above.

[118] Drabble, pp.604, 187–8.

[119] The Ireland family worked together on the project to fabricate a collection of personal papers, library, and amplified canon of plays, allegedly Shakespeare's, for commercial gain. The forgeries were exposed by the Shakespeare scholar Edmond Malone (1741–1812) after an exchange of published statements that included an explanation by Ireland that was also largely fabricated. Ireland does not, it appears, value the works he buys for themselves, but for their usefulness in his project: Ireland, William-Henry, *The Confessions of William-Henry Ireland, containing the Particulars of his Fabrication of the Shakspeare Manuscripts,* London: 1805, pp.99–103; see also Ingleby, C. Marsfield, *The Shakspeare Fabrications*, London: 1859, pp.194–201.

[120] BL shelfmark 456.b.15.

Chapter 8. Conclusion

As a topic for research, 'Properties' is not new or unexplored, but perceptions of it change during our own times just as they evidently did during the Middle Ages. The earlier literature on 'Properties' is an invaluable resource in that so much groundwork has been done as a basis for fresh research into the compiler, the manuscripts, the translations, and the place these occupied in late-medieval English life and letters. Twentieth-century research into the context in which the work appeared, and the excavation of related documents, has brought the compiler more clearly into focus. As a result, this long-lived work, that held value for many different readerships, can indeed help the historian in tracing long continuities in thinking about the world in which we live.

Research into the genre of the thirteenth-century *compilatio* as a tool of the militant Catholic church, and as part of a wider exchange of knowledge between east and west, has improved our understanding of the genre's context and function. The important studies of the English translation, the later-medieval ownership of manuscripts and the literary borrowings from Bartholomew, help to contextualise the work within a widening English readership of the later Middle Ages. However, in the present century important ongoing research is being shared and published in languages other than English. The size and scope of the work has so far prevented the appearance of a detailed reception history, but the present study contributes to such a project by examining, in English, the work's transmission and diffusion in this small but significant area of its medieval and early-modern readership.

In structure, content and purpose, 'Properties' can reasonably be considered as a parallel to the graphic compilations we tend to call *mappaemundi* today. The compilation deserves consideration as a specimen of a particular medieval genre based on a longstanding tradition of *imago mundi* texts that was both verbal and graphic, but essentially didactic in function. The 'world book' might take the form of a written tract or a drawn map, or both, but its function was to teach the world's biblical history, its coming end and God's judgement, and the way for the spiritual pilgrim to reach God. Bartholomew's image of the world, far from being a static account of the properties of things, is potentially dynamic and interactive in its appeal to the reader. It contains descriptions of people and things in action and at rest, in growth and decay, in transit and flux, inviting the reader's involvement through memory and identification of experience. Overall, Bartholomew makes strong contrasting statements about the coldness, instability and trouble of the physical world, set far from the sun, as in the preamble to Book 8; and about the joy and solace to be gained from things put into the world at Creation: light, stars, air, water, land, and the plants and creatures that 'adorn' these elements. His work affirmed the orthodox accounts of Creation derived from *Genesis,* but also accommodated the Neoplatonic literary cosmologies blended into that orthodoxy by intellectuals of the twelfth century, such as Bernard Silvestris.

In setting out an accumulated body of conventional wisdom about matters to do with the material world, Bartholomew was using an up-to-date empirical approach, like earlier writers on nature such as Bernard Silvestris and the Aristotelian translators, and later ones such as Albert the Great.[1] But he was also working in the tradition of monastic instruction, exegesis and consolation for an audience versed in allegorical didactic literature, for whom all nature is 'a book of tropes cleverly arranged by the Creator to teach both logic and morality'.[2] From a small sampling of the work, this study indicates that 'Properties' holds rich reserves of evidence about the ways clerics were taught in the Middle Ages; about the imagery and rhetoric of the Franciscan Order as it was establishing itself throughout Europe; about the models of ideal communal life and social hierarchy that entered the stream of English didactic literature. It also has literary qualities that could relate to the author's need for diplomacy in teaching Franciscan students about their calling. This was a time when the church was alert against heterodoxy; when perceived papal favour towards the mendicants caused some ill-feeling from outside the Order; and when there was growing division within the Order over the definition of poverty. The medieval *compilatio* implies a long-established pastoral metaphor of gathering, as bees gather honey or gleaners gather corn. The way Bartholomew builds upon these familiar analogies leads one to conclude that his readers could engage imaginatively in familiar parables of earthly labour. Fragments from an implied larger narrative — in particular, those of the worker and the traveller, and of the ranks of the *familia* at their occupations indoors and out — invited meditation upon other stories drawn from memory and from the Christian Scriptures. The narrative element in his work suggests that readers, whether clerics or laymen and women, could ruminate upon the fundamental Christian themes of repentance and salvation as they dipped into the work in a spirit of contemplation. In a context of familiarity with the parable of the workers in the vineyard, the ox and oxherd, the bee, the vine, and the good servant all serve as models for material and spiritual labour, reward, fertility and fruition, and thus their recurring presence in the work can be seen as logical and necessary for its didactic purpose. Although this underlying logic in the work is not immediately apparent to us today, we can work towards it with the help of marginal glosses, perpetuated by copyists, reflecting a response by readers relatively close to Bartholomew in time and culture. These readers may not have been those for whom he originally prepared the work and who remain unknowable by us, but the thirteenth-century marginal glosses confirm that later practising preachers could find in 'Properties' a handy guide to help them in their professional work.

We may anticipate that the closer study of the glosses proposed in the forthcoming Latin/French edition will reveal more clearly the ways in which the text was interpretable by clerical readers, and the value of 'Properties' to the church in the context of its preaching crusade.[3]

By the time the Order of Friars Minor was integrated into English society 'Properties' was one of the books long held in the libraries of monasteries, the centres of expertise in salvation, and in the college libraries of Oxford and Cambridge, the centres of learning. It was valuable to scholars in that Bartholomew refers to a range of medieval authorities, including those relevant to practical curricula (such as Aristotle, Galen, Constantinus and Richard Rufus), as well as the Fathers of the church. Comprehensive sources, moral utility and practical applications helped to give the work wide appeal. The presence of 'Properties' in the Trevisa canon of translations made for Lord Thomas Berkeley IV indicates strongly that, in the political and economic upheavals of the late Middle Ages, 'Properties' could be regarded as a component of chivalric literature. However, it was also a source for preachers and a resource for 'pragmatic' readers and re-writers needing factual information. We have seen that the latter drew from it elements they needed to support their own position, to criticise and call to order, and to record knowledge of the material world. The conveniently defined format, flexible array of sources and verbal directness of Bartholomew's text lent itself to such uses and adaptations. Readers could have confidence in what it contained, but could adapt it to make new, authority-based texts that accorded with their needs, tastes and mental horizons. In the fourteenth and fifteenth centuries, Bartholomew was a source which helped people to know 'to which authorities one should give credence', as a reader of BL Ms Arundel 123 notes in the margin close to a mention of St Jerome.[4] But the truths readers could find in 'Properties' were also flexible and complex. They could find scriptural truths — concerning the parable of the vineyard, for example — or the moral significance of the bestiary elephant. They could also perceive truth as in a mirror, reflecting a contemporary ideal: for example, in the normative descriptions of lordship or marriage in Book 6; of the idyll of summer in Book 9; or of the feats of Alexander in Book 15. A third, multivalent or ambiguous kind of truth could emerge from Bartholomew's impartial combinations of source material — as in the case of the bee, the stag, the cock or the lion. As we have seen, readers and writers could exploit the resulting ambiguities within the text to create portraits of living people in the context of the immediate here-and-now, highlighting qualities they wished to advertise or criticise. In the case of heralds and satirical writers, their understanding of the multiple sources feeding into medieval accounts of the created world enabled them to draw on the symbolic as well as observable properties of things, or to build double entendre into the portraits they created.

'Properties' can be a starting point in the historian's attempt to understand, from a historical perspective, what late-medieval people were expressing in their coded responses to immediate events. It was one repository of conventional but multi-stranded knowledge that fed into the exchanges of later-medieval society, particularly in the imagery of the natural world used by writers and artists. To be able to participate as non-contemporary observers in this serious play of allusion and counter-allusion, we need access to the layers of potential meaning available to the players. Our own awareness of the multiple constructions of things and properties available to readers can help us to understand something of the work's function as a source of religious authority, but also of a range of interpretative possibilities for later-medieval readers and writers. It is not possible — or necessary — to claim that readers or writers knew the work directly; but by doing so ourselves we might understand better what was being conveyed in those exchanges.

In the fifteenth century, the making of copies of Trevisa's *Properties*, and of other texts wholly or partially derived from the Latin 'Properties', coincides with evidence for the acceptance of English as a useable and worthy language for prose works. By this time, the compiler himself had gained a reputation as a repository of religious authorities, and as the prime authority on the properties of things. We find the compiler invoked as 'master' of received knowledge about the properties of the created world at a time when much new knowledge was becoming available from classical sources and from direct observation. By this time, the concept of 'property' had broadened to take in commercial and professional senses, but Bartholomew's representation of the divine cosmos, the world and society still supported the beliefs of later-medieval and early-modern Christians. The discoveries of Columbus, Cabot and Amerigo Vespucci in the 1490s posed a great intellectual challenge to the *imago mundi* that described and portrayed a Mediterranean-centred Christendom, based on the people, events and places of sacred history. The printed editions of *Properties* reveal that this image of the world was still meaningful during the period of maritime expansion, and tell us something about the gradual process by which people adjusted their mental horizons to new descriptions of the world's places and peoples.

In spite of its size and bulk, the labour of production and the expense of materials, and possible commercial risk, the translation and the printing of 'Properties' and *Properties* were evidently seen as worthwhile undertakings by those involved. There are many gaps in our knowledge of the dynamics of both the translation project and the later ventures into print, but it does appear that each one was brought about by a team of people making different contributions according to their position and abilities. The historian gains some access to the kind of corporate commercial activity that could centre on a marketable text, at a time when the physical and intellectual expansion of the sixteenth century again presented challenges to accepted images of the world already documented and approved. As the traditional conception of the cosmos was challenged, and Trevisa's 'orisoun' was literally traversed by explorers, 'Properties' could be re-interpreted to support with its underlying authority new models of society and concepts of nature in the late-medieval and early-modern period.

By 1582, 'Properties' had survived changes in readership and conditions of production over three and a half centuries. Scholarly fashions had swung between Aristotelian and Neoplatonic explanations of the universe. Bartholomew's supposed Englishness, combined with his authority as a source of wisdom, would account for the way certain English men of letters promoted the myth of his English birth and respectable status while others saw commercial opportunities in the informative content of the work. We have no firm evidence that Bartholomew had any reason to favour England but passages in 'Properties' and *Properties* could be interpreted as privileging English interests, extolling the character of the English people, and endorsing an acceptable version of English history. In sixteenth-century England, a specific and literal interpretation of *Britannia* and *Anglia* as a fertile land with a genial and vigorous populace was congruent with the nationalism of the time, amid controversy about the English church and its doctrine, social tension over religion, war, famine and royal succession. A thriving print-culture enabled Stephen Batman to bring up to date the cosmology and geography already in 'Properties', since other descriptions (including those of contemporary travellers and magi) were available that he could plunder and incorporate into the work. The greater focus in 'Properties' on scriptural history and eschatology fitted the apocalyptic vision of Batman's own day and his concerns as a preacher. In the later years of the reign of Elizabeth I, Batman claims authorship and possession of the wealth of knowledge in his updated version of 'Properties', but also gives the mantle of wisdom to his patron and the profit of knowledge to his country. His edition can be understood best not as a re-issuing or updating of 'an olde aunciente booke', but as an original contribution to learned debate about the world and about religion that was then being conducted widely with the aid of the printing press. Underlying Batman's commitment to his own country's immediate interests, to his education and political awareness, there is a strong strand of continuity with the past that can be found in his assumption that the created world of place and time was governed by divine providence and will, that people were living in its last age, and would be judged by God. His image of the world differs from that of Bartholomew in culturally specific details, but not in that basic assumption. In a culture where the wisdom of Solomon represented worldly power, patronage of 'Properties' endowed political sanction combined with moral *gravitas*. Its value as a repository of wisdom and knowledge that had both authority and practical usefulness, and sanctioned by its long association with the church and with preaching, enabled 'Properties' to survive the controversies generated by Lollard texts and Protestant reforms. Right up to the time of the gentleman scientists and scholars of the nineteenth century, such as Joseph Banks and Robert Steele, 'Properties' remained the supposed property of the English nation and a symbol of national achievement.

NOTES
[1] Klingender, pp.350–9.
[2] Greetham, 1980, p.671.
[3] See Chapter 1, n.18.
[4] BL Ms Arundel 123, f.21v.

Appendix A. British Library Manuscript Arundel 123, the contents of the codex.[1]

f.5	Geographia universalis, ordine alphabetico compilata ex Isidori Hispalensis Originibus, aliisque, quorum auctoritas saepius allegatur.	Universal description of the world compiled in alphabetical order from original works of Isidore of Spain, and from others whose authority is more often cited.
f. 22v	Quaedam de orbis dimensione ex Prisciano in Cosmographia	Somewhat concerning the dimension of the world out of Priscian in his 'Cosmography'.[a]
f. 24.	Honorii Augustodunensis, sive cuiuscunque sit, Imago mundi	'Image of the world' of Honorius Augustodunensis, or whoever the author may be.
f.33	Apollonii (auctoris spurii) Vita Regis Antiochi	'The Life of the King of Antioch' of Apollonius (a spurious author).
f.43	Liber de vita et morte magni Regis Alexandri Aesopo adscriptus	The book on the life and death of King Alexander the Great ascribed to Aesop.
f.71v	Aristotelis Epistola ad Alexandrum Magnum	Aristotle's Letter to Alexander the Great.
f.73	De Alexandri Magni expeditionibus	On the expeditions of Alexander the Great.
f.74v	De rege Alexandro et ejus origine ex libro Hermeri de dictis philosophorum descripta	On King Alexander and his origin, a description out of the book of Hermes about sayings of the philosophers.
f.80	Dicta Alexandri ex libro ejusdem Hermeri	Sayings of Alexander from that same book by Hermes.
f.81v	Quaedam alia philosophorum dicta licet non omnia in Hermeri libro inventa cum descriptione et progressu originis quorundam eorum ab eodem compilatore addita	Some other sayings of philosophers, not all found in the book of Hermes, together with a description and account of their sources, added by the same compiler.
f.95	Secundi Pythagorei philosophi. Responsa ad quaestiunculas Imp. Hadrianii	After the philosophy of Pythagoras. Answers to the Emperor Hadrian's queries.

[a] The extract from Priscian (f.22v) is added in a second scribal hand. There is a further gloss in a third hand against this addition, stressing the information on quantities of seas, islands, mountains, provinces, rivers and peoples in the world: *quanto maria sunt in mundo nota quanto insula quanto montes quanto provincia quanto flumina et quanto gentes sunt in mundo nota.*

NOTES

[1] British Museum, *Catalogue of Manuscripts in the British Museum: Part I The Arundel Manuscripts.* New Series vol.1, 1840, pp.29–30. Author's paraphrases.

Appendix B. Abridgement of 'Properties' in Bodleian Library Manuscript Laud Miscellany 682.

Books 1 to 15 and Book 19 are omitted wholly.

In Book 16, on rocks, gems and minerals, all chapters are retained.

In Book 17, on plants and trees, only the following chapters are retained:

de amigdalo	On the almond
de aloe	On aloe
de aniso	On anise
de allio	On wild garlic
de absinthio	On wormwood
de apio	On celery
de aristologia	On [an unidentified herb]
de arthemisia	On yarrow, wormwood, tarragon or similar
de beta	On beet
de cynamomo	On cinnamon
de cassia fistula	On laburnum
de cappari	On the caper
de calamento	On calamint
de carduo	On the thistle
de carica	On the rush
de coloquintida	On bitter cucumber or gourd
de croco	On the crocus
de cepa	On the onion
de cepe canino	On the 'biting onion'
de celidonia	On the celandine
de centauria	On centaury
de daphiri	On laurel
de diptanno	On marjoram
de dragancia	On the arum lily
de edria	On ivy
de eleboro	On hellebore
de eruca	On colewort
de enula	On elecampane
de epithimo	On [an unidentified plant]
de ebulo	On the elder tree
de fraxino	On the ash tree
de faba	On the broad bean
de feniculo	On fennel
de iunipero	On juniper
de castanea	On the sweet chestnut
de lactuca	On lettuce
de lappa	On burdock
de moro	On the mulberry

de mandragora	On mandrake
de menta	On mint
de malua	On the apple
de nuce	On the nut
de pruno	On the plum tree
de papavere	On the poppy
de plantagine	On the vine shoot
de petrocilio	On parsley
de pipere	On pepper
de pulegio	On penny-royal
de porro	On the leek
de rosa	On the rose
de rampno	On rampion
de salice	On the willow tree
de sambuco	On the elderflower
de sinapi	On mustard
de tritico	On wheat
de ptisana	On tisane
de vino	On wine
de viola	On the violet
de urtica	On the nettle
de zizania	On broom
de zinzibero	On ginger

In Book 18, on land-animals, only the following chapters are retained:

de agno agniculo	On the lamb
de rana	On the frog
de asino	On the ass
de equa	On the mare
de lepore	On the hare
de mulo	On the mule
de mure	On the mouse
de mustela	On the weasel
de pediculo	On the louse
de pulice	On the flea
de vulpe	On the fox

References

Primary sources

Manuscripts

Balliol College Oxford Ms 329. Un-headed list of books, writer unknown: fifteenth century.

Balliol College Oxford Ms 294. Latin 'Properties': late fourteenth century.

Bibliothèque national de France Ms Lat. 3332. *Liber de moralitatibus corporum celestium, elementorum, avium, piscium, animalium, arborum sive plantarum et lapidum preciosorum*: fourteenth century.

Bibliothèque national de France Ms Lat. 16098. Latin 'Properties': late thirteenth century.

Bodleian Laud Miscellany 733. English translation of BL Ms Add. 28791: fifteenth century.

Bodleian Library Oxford Ms Laud 682. Home-produced abstract of 'Properties': fifteenth century.

Bodleian Library Oxford Ms e Museo 16. English translation of 'Properties', *On the Properties of Things*: late fourteenth century.

Bristol City Library Ms 9. English translation of 'Properties', *On the Properties of Things*: late fifteenth century.

British Library Ms Additional 28791. Latin *Tractatus* on heraldry: late fourteenth century.

British Library Ms Additional 27944. English translation of 'Properties', *On the Properties of Things*: late fourteenth century.

British Library Ms Arundel 123. Collection of extracts from works on world history and 'wisdom' literature: fourteenth century.

British Library Ms Harley 614. English translation of 'Properties', *On the Properties of Things*: early fifteenth century.

British Library Ms Harley 512. Abridged version of Latin 'Properties': fifteenth century.

British Library Ms Royal E 15 ii and iii. Two-volume translation of 'Properties' into French, *Livre des propriétés des choses*: late fifteenth century.

British Library Ms Royal E 12 iii. Workshop-produced collection of extracts from 'Properties': fifteenth century.

Cambridge University Library Ms Gg 6. 5. Home-produced collection of extracts from 'Properties' in the form of a bestiary: late fifteenth century.

Corpus Christi College Oxford Ms 249. Latin 'Properties': fourteenth century.

Wellcome Library Ms 115. Latin 'Properties': late thirteenth century.

Incunables and early printed books

Bale, John, *Illustrium Majoris Brittaniae Scriptorum*, Basle: Johannes Oporinus, 1557.

Bartholomeus Anglicus, *De proprietatibus rerum*, Nüremburg: 1519. BL 44Lh4.

Bartholomeus De Proprietatibus Rerum. Londini in Aedibus Thomae Bertheleti Regii Impressoris. Cum Privilegio a Rege indulto. London: Thomas Berthelet, London,1535. STC 1537.

Bartholomeus De Proprietatibus Rerum, Westminster: Wynkyn de Worde, 1495. STC 1536.

Bateman [sic], Stephen, *Batman uppon Bartholome*. London: Thomas and Lucretia East, 1582.

Caxton, William, trans, *Vincentius. The Mirrour of the World*. Westminster: Caxton, 1481.

Corbechon, Jean, *Histoire universelle*, 1476.

Corbechon, Jean, *Le Proprietaire des choses ... avec aucunes adicions nouvellement adioustees cest assavoir Les Vertus et proprietez des eaues artificielles et des herbes. Les nativitez des hommes et des femmes selon les douze signes. Et plusieurs receptes contre aulcunes maladies. Item ung remede tres utille contre fievre pestilentieuse et aultre maniere depydimie*. P. Lenoir, Paris, n.d.

Corbechon, Jean, *Le proprietaire des choses tres utille ... avecques aulcunes addicions nouvellement adioustees .... Item est adiouste ... une medicine tresutille: appellee la Medicine des chevaulx: et aultres bestes. Le tout reveu et corrige nouvellement*, 1530.

Corbechon, Jean, *Le Grand proprietaire de toutes choses tres utile et profitable pour tenir le corps humain en santé. Contenant plusieurs diverses maladies, et dont ilz procedent, et aussi les remedes preservatifz. Avec les proprietez du Ciel, de la Terre, des Bestes, des Oyseaulx des Pierres, et des Metaulx, et autre matiere ... Additions nouvellement faictes. Les vertus et proprietez des Eaus artificielles, et des Herbes, etc.* Paris: 1556.

Leland, John, *Commentarii de scriptoribus Britannicis, auctore Joanne Lelando Londinate* (1548), vol. 1. Oxford: Antonius Hall, 1709.

Ortelius, Abraham, *Theatrum Orbis Terrarum*, Antwerp: 1575.

Tritheim, Johannes, *Liber de Scriptoribus Ecclesiasticus*, 1494.

Facsimile editions

Angelicus [sic], Bartholomaeus, *De rerum Proprietatibus* (Frankfurt: 1601). Frankfurt: Minerva, 1964.

Bateman [sic], Stephen, *Batman uppon Bartholome* (London: Thomas and Lucretia East, 1582). Hildesheim: Georg Olms Verlag, 1976.

Douce, Francis, *Illustrations of Shakspeare, and Ancient Manners* (London: 1839). New York: Burt Franklin, 1968.

Topsell, Edward, and Konrad Gesner, *The historie of foure footed beastes, describing the true and liuely figure of euery beast, with a discourse of their seuerall names, conditions, kindes, vertues / ... collected out of all the volumes of Conradvs Gesner and all other writers to this present day* (London: 1607). Amsterdam: Theatrum Orbis Terrarum, 1973.

Vincentius, *The Mirrour of the World*, translated by William Caxton (Westminster: Caxton, 1481). Amsterdam: Theatrum Orbis Terrarum, 1979.

Secondary sources

Anders, H. R. D., *Shakespeare's Books*, Berlin: George Reimer, 1904.

Anglo, Sydney, *Images of Tudor Kingship*, London: Seaby, 1992.

Ashworth, William B., "Emblematic natural history of the Renaissance" in *Cultures of Natural History*, edited by N. Jardine, J. A. Secord and E. C. Spary, 17–37. Cambridge University Press, 1996.

Backhouse, Janet, "Founders of the Royal Library: Edward IV and Henry VII as Collectors of Illuminated Manuscripts" in *England in the Fifteenth Century: Proceedings of the 1986 Harlaxton Symposium,* edited by Daniel Williams, 23–41. Woodbridge, Suffolk: Boydell and Brewer, 1987.

Baird, Joseph L., Guiseppe Baglivi and John Robert Kane, eds, *The Chronicle of Salimbene de Adam,* New York: Binghampton, 1986.

Barney, Stephen A., "'The plowshare of the tongue': the progress of a symbol from the Bible to Piers Plowman", *Medieval Studies* 35, no.263 (1973): 261–93.

Barnum, Priscilla Heath, ed, *Dives and Pauper*, Oxford: The Early English Text Society, 1976.

Bath, M., "The stag of justice" in *Atti del V Colloquio della International Beast Epic, Fable and Fabliau Society, Torino-St Vincent, 1983*, edited by Alessandro Vitale-Brovarone e Gianni Mombello, Allessandria, 313–21: Edizioni dell'Orso, 1987.

Bath, M., "The serpent-eating stag in the Renaissance" in *Actes du IVe Colloque de la société Internationale Renardienne, Evreux 1981,* edited by Gabriel Bianciotto and Michel Salvat, 55–70. Paris: Presses Universitaires de France, 1984.

Bath, Michael, "The legend of Caesar's deer", *Medievalia et Humanistica* 9 (1979): 53–66.

Bennett, H. S., *English Books and Readers 1558–1603*, Cambridge University Press, 1965.

Bennett, Michael J., "The court of Richard II and the promotion of literature" in *Chaucer's England: Literature in Historical Context*, edited by Barbara J. Hanawalt, 3–20. Minneapolis: University of Minnesota Press, 1992.

Bernau, Anke, "Myths of origin and the struggle over nationhood in medieval and early modern England" in *Reading the Medieval in Early Modern England*, edited by David Matthews and Gordon McMullan, 106-118, Cambridge University Press, 2007.

Binkley, Peter, ed, *Pre-modern Encyclopaedic Texts. Proceedings of the Second COMERS Congress, Groningen, 1-4 July 1996*, Leiden: Brill, 1997.

Binski, Paul, *Westminster Abbey and the Plantagenets: Kingship and the Representation of Power 1200–1400*, New Haven and London: Yale University Press, 1995.

Blasselle, B. et J. Melet-Sanson, *La Bibliotheque Nationale, Mémoire de l'Avenir*. Paris: Gallimard, 1991.

Blount, M. N. "Glanville, Gilbert de (d.1214)", ODNB, Oxford University Press, 2004.

Boas, George, *St. Bonaventure's Itinerarium Mentis in Deum: The Mind's Road to God*, Indianapolis: Bobbs-Merrill Educational Publishing, 1953.

Bone, Gavin, "Extant manuscripts printed from by W. De Worde with notes on the owner, Roger Thorney", *The Library* XII (1932): 284–309.

Bowie, Fiona and Oliver Davies, eds, *Hildegard of Bingen: An Anthology*, London: Society for the Propagation of Christian Knowledge, 1992.

Brandeis, Arthur, *Jacob's Well,* London: The Early English Text Society, 1900.

Braswell, Laurel, "Utilitarian and Scientific Prose" in *Middle English Prose: A Critical Guide to Major Authors and Genres*, edited by A. S. G. Edwards, 337–87, Rutgers University Press, 1984.

British Museum, *Catalogue of Manuscripts in the British Museum: Part I The Arundel Manuscripts*, New Series, vol.1, 1840.

Brockhurst, Elizabeth J., Bartholomew Anglicus: De Proprietatibus Rerum I–IV, unpublished PhD thesis, University of London, 1952.

Brockhurst, Elizabeth J., The Life and Works of Stephen Batman, unpublished MA thesis, University of London, 1947.

Brooke, Rosalind B. and Christopher Brooke, *Popular Religion in the Middle Ages*, London: Thames and Hudson, 1984.

Brooke, Rosalind B., *The Coming of the Friars*, London: George Allen and Unwin, 1975.

Brooke, Rosalind B, ed, *The Writings of Leo, Rufino and Angelo Companions of St. Francis*, Oxford: The Clarendon Press, 1970.

Bruce, John and Thomas Perowne, eds, *Correspondence of Matthew Parker, Archbishop of Canterbury*, Cambridge University Press, 1853.

Bunt, Gerith H. V., *Alexander the Great in the Literature of Medieval Britain*, Groningen: Egbert Forsten, 1994.

Bynum, Caroline Walker, *Jesus as mother: Studies in the spirituality of the High Middle Ages*, University of California Press, 1982.

Byrne, Donal, "Rex imago Dei: Charles V of France and the Livre des propriétés des choses", *Journal of Medieval History* 7 (1981): 97–113.

Byrne, Donal, "The Boucicaut Master and the iconographical tradition of the Livre des Propriétés des Choses", *Gazette des Beaux-Arts* 92 (1978): 149–64.

Carley, James P., "John Leland on the contents of English pre-Dissolution libraries: The Cambridge friars", *Transactions of the Cambridge Bibliographical Society* 9 (1986): 90–100.

Chandler, John, ed, *John Leland's Itinerary: Travels in Tudor England*, Stroud, 1993.

Chartier, Roger, "Labourers and voyagers: from the text to the reader" in *Readers and Reading*, edited by Andrew Bennett, 132–49, London: Longman, 1995.

Christianson, Paul, *Reformers and Babylon: English Apocalyptic Visions from the Reformation to the Eve of the Civil War*, University of Toronto Press, 1978.

Clair, Colin, *A History of Printing in Britain*, London: Cassell, 1965.

Clark, Willene B. and Meradith T. McMunn, eds, *Birds and Beasts in the Middle Ages: The Bestiary and its Legacy*, Philadelphia: University of Pennsylvania Press, 1989.

Clark, Willene B., "The illustrated medieval aviary and the lay-brotherhood", *Gesta* XXI (1982): 63–74.

Clinton, S. M. M., The Latin Manuscript Tradition in England of the De Proprietatibus Rerum of Bartholomaeus Anglicus. An analysis based on Book 10: unpublished PhD thesis, Northwestern University, 1982.

Clulee, Nicholas H., *John Dee's Natural Philosophy*, London and New York: Routledge, 1988.

Collison, Robert, *Encyclopedias: Their History Throughout the Ages*, New York and London: Hafner, 1966.

Constable, Giles, "The place of the Magdeburg Charter of 1107/08 in the history of eastern Germany and of the crusades" in *Vita Religiosa im Mittelalter: Festschrift für Kaspar Elm zum 70. Geburtstag*, edited by Franz J. Felton and Nikolas Jaspert, 283–99, Berlin: Duncker & Humbolt, 1999.

Cook, Harold J., "Physicians and natural history" in *Cultures of Natural History*, edited by N. Jardine, J. A. Secord and E. C. Spary, 91–105. Cambridge University Press, 1996.

Coss, Peter, "Aspects of cultural diffusion in medieval England: The early romances, local society and Robin Hood", *Past and Present* 108 (1985): 35–79.

Cottle, Basil, *The Triumph of English*, London: Blandford Press, 1969.

Cotton, Charles, *The Grey Friars of Canterbury*, Manchester: The University Press, 1924.

Cowan, Edward J., "Myth and Identity in Early Medieval Scotland", *Scottish Historical Review* 63.2 (1984): 111-135.

Cressy, David, *Literacy and the Social Order: Reading and Writing in Tudor and Stuart England*, Cambridge University Press, 1980.

Cross, F. L., ed, *The Oxford Dictionary of the Christian Church*, London: Oxford University Press, 1974.

Cunningham, Andrew, "The culture of gardens" in *Cultures of Natural History*, edited by N. Jardine, J. A. Secord and E. C. Spary, 38–56. Cambridge University Press, 1996.

Davies, R. T., *The Corpus Christi Play of the English Middle Ages*, London: Faber and Faber, 1972.

Dawson, Christopher, *The Mongol Mission: Narratives and letters of the Franciscan Missionaries in Mongolia and China in the Thirteenth and Fourteenth Centuries*, London: Sheed and Ward, 1955.

Day, Mabel, and Robert Steele, eds, *Mum and the Sothsegger*, London: The Early English Text Society, 1936.

De Boüard, Michel, "Réflexions sur l'encyclopédisme médiéval" in *L'Encyclopédisme. Actes du Colloque de Caen 12–16 janvier 1987*, edited by Annie Becq, 281–90, Paris: Klincksieck, 1991.

Delisle, Léopold, "Traités divers sur les propriétés des choses", *Histoire Littéraire de la Langue Francaise* XXX (1888): 334–88.

Dennys, Rodney, *The Heraldic Imagination*, London: Barrie and Jenkins, 1975.

Déstombes, Marcel, ed, *Mappemondes AD 1200–1500*, Amsterdam: N. Israel, 1964.

Dickens, A. G., *The English Reformation*, London: Batsford, 1968.

Dolan, T. P., "The plowman as hero" in *Heroes and Heroines in Medieval English Literature*, edited by Leo Carruthers, 97–103, Cambridge: D. S. Brewer, 1994.

Drabble, Margaret, ed, *The Oxford Companion to English Literature*, Oxford: The University Press, 1985.

Dronke, Peter, "Bernard Silvestris, Natura, and personification" in *Intellectuals and Poets in Medieval Europe*, edited by Peter Dronke, 41–61, Rome: Edizione de storia e letteratura, 1992.

Dronke, Peter, "Integumenta Virgilii" in *Intellectuals and Poets in Medieval Europe,* edited by Peter Dronke, 63–78, Rome: Edizione de storia e letteratura, 1992.

Druce, G. C., "An account of the Mermacoleon or Ant-lion", *The Antiquaries Journal* 3, no.4 (1923): 347–64.

Duby, Georges and Cynthia Postan (trans), *Rural Economy and Society in the Medieval West*, University of South Carolina Press, 1968.

Edelen, G., ed, *William Harrison, 'The Description of England'*, Cornell University Press, 1968.

Edson, Evelyn, *Mapping Time and Space: How Medieval Mapmakers Viewed Their World*, London: The British Library, 1997.

Edwards, A. S. G., and Meale, Carole M., "The marketing of printed books in late medieval England", *The Library*, 6th series, 15 (1993): 95–124.

Edwards, A. S. G., "Bartholomeus Anglicus, De Proprietatibus Rerum and medieval English literature", *Archiv für das Studium der neueren Sprachen und Literaturen* 222 (1985): 121–8.

Edwards, A. S. G., "John Trevisa" in *Middle English Prose: A Critical Guide to Major Authors and Genres*, edited by A. S. G. Edwards, 133–46, Rutgers University Press, 1984.

Eldredge, Laurence, "Imagery of roundness in William Woodford's 'De sacramento altaris' and its possible relevance to the Middle English 'Pearl'", *Notes and Queries* 223 (1978): 3–5.

Findlen, Paula, "Courting Nature" in *Cultures of Natural History*, edited by N. Jardine, J. A. Secord and E. C. Spary, 57–74. Cambridge University Press, 1996.

Fitzmaurice, E. B. (OFM) and A. G. Little, eds, *Materials for the History of the Franciscan Province of Ireland*, Vol. 9, Manchester University Press, 1920.

Fletcher, Alan J., *Preaching, Politics and Poetry in Late-Medieval England*, Dublin: Four Courts Press, 1998.

Fowler, D. C., *The Life and Times of John Trevisa, Scholar*, University of Washington Press, 1995.

Fowler, D. C., "More about John Trevisa", *Modern Language Quarterly* 32 (1971): 243–51.

Fowler, D. C., "New light on John Trevisa", *Traditio* 18 (1963): 289–317.

Fowler, D. C., "John Trevisa and the English Bible", *Modern Philology* 58 (1960): 81–98.

Freed, John B., *The Friars and German Society in the Thirteenth Century*, Cambridge, Mass: The Medieval Academy of America, 1977.

Freeman, Elizabeth., "Meaning and multi-centeredness in (postmodern) medieval historiography: the foundation history of Fountains Abbey", *Parergon* n.s.16, no.2 (1999): 43–84.

French, Roger and Andrew Cunningham, *Before Science: The Invention of the Friars' Natural Philosophy*, London: Scolar Press, 1996.

Friedman, John B., "Cultural conflicts in medieval world maps" in *Implicit Understandings: Observing, Reporting, and Reflecting on the Encounters Between Europeans and Other Peoples in the Early Modern Era*, edited by Stuart B. Schwartz, 64–95: Cambridge University Press, 1994.

Friedman, John B., "Peacocks and preachers: analytic technique in Marcus of Orvieto's 'Liber de moralitatibus, Vatican lat. MS 5935'" in *Birds and Beasts in the Middle Ages: The Bestiary and its Legacy*, edited by Willene B. Clark and Meradith T. McMunn, 179–96, Philadelphia: University of Pensylvania Press, 1989.

Fryde, E. B., *Peasants and Landlords in Later Medieval England*, New York: St Martin's Press, 1996.

Furnivall, R., "On Puck's 'Swifter than the moon's sphere' and Shakspere's astronomy", *New Shakspere Transactions* 1, no.7 (1879): 431–450.

Goodich, Michael, "Ancilla Dei: the servant as saint in the late Middle Ages" in *Women of the Medieval World*, edited by Julius Kirshner and Suzanne F. Wemple, 119–36, Oxford: Basil Blackwell, 1985.

Goodridge, J. F., ed, *Langland: Piers the Ploughman*, Harmondsworth: Penguin, 1959.

Gordon, Dillian, ed, *Making and Meaning: The Wilton Diptych*, London: National Gallery Publications, 1993.

Grant, E., *Physical Science in the Middle Ages*, New York: John Wiley, 1971.

Gray, Douglas, ed, *The Oxford Book of Late Medieval Verse and Prose*, Oxford University Press, 1985.

Green, Richard Firth, *Poets and Princepleasers: Literature and the English Court in the Late Middle Ages*, University of Toronto Press, 1980.

Green, R. P. H., ed, *Augustine: De Doctrina Christiana*, Oxford: The Clarendon Press, 1995.

Greetham, D. C., "On Cultural Translation: From Patristic Repository to Shakespeare's Encyclopedia" in *Voices in Translation: The Authority of "Olde Bookes" in Medieval Literature: Essays in Honor of Helaine Newstead*, edited by Deborah M. Sinnreich-Levi and Gale Sigal, 69–84, New York: AMS Press, 1992.

Greetham, D. C., "The concept of nature in Bartholomeus Anglicus (floruit 1230)", *Journal of the History of Ideas*, XLI (1980): 663–77.

Haigh, Christopher, *The English Reformation Revised*, Cambridge University Press, 1987.

Haist, Margaret, "The Lion, Bloodline, and Kingship" in *The Mark of the Beast*, edited by Debra Hassig, 3–21, London and New York: Routledge, 1999.

Hall, Catherine, "Matthew Parker as Annotator: the Case of Winchester Cathedral MS XXB", *Transactions of the Cambridge Bibliographical Society* 10 (1995): 642–45.

Hamilton, Ruth Elaine, Of Fire and of Air: Notes and Commentary on Books 10 and 11 of John Trevisa's Translation of Bartholomaeus Anglicus' De Proprietatibus Rerum, unpublished PhD thesis, Northwestern University, 1982.

Hanna, Ralph III, "Sir Thomas Berkeley and His Patronage", *Speculum* 64 (1989): 878–916.

Hargreaves, Paul V., "Seignorial reaction and peasant responses: Worcester Priory and its peasants after the Black Death", *Midland History* XXIV (1999): 53–78.

Harvey, P. D. A., ed, *The Hereford World Map: Medieval World Maps and their Context*, University of Toronto Press, 2006.

Harvey, P. D. A., *Mappa Mundi: The Hereford World Map*, London: Hereford Cathedral and the British Library, 1996.

Hassig, Debra, ed, *The Mark of the Beast*, London and New York: Routledge, 1999.

Hassig, Debra, *Medieval Bestiaries: Text, Image, Ideology*, Cambridge University Press, 1995.

Hathaway, Neil, "Compilatio: from plagiarism to compiling", *Viator* 20 (1989): 19–44.

Henderson, Arnold Clayton, "Animal fables as vehicles of social protest and satire: twelfth century to Henryson" in Jan Goossens and Timothy Sodmann, eds, *Third Annual Beast Epic, Fable and Fabliau Colloquium, Munster 1979: Proceedings,* 160–73. Cologne: Böhlau Verlag, 1981.

Hill, Betty, "British Library Manuscript Egerton 613–1", *Notes and Queries* 223 (1978): 394–409.

Hodnett, Edward, *English Woodcuts 1480–1535*, Oxford University Press, 1973.

Holbrook, Sue Ellen, "The concept of vernacularity in de Worde editions of 1495–96" in *Vernacularity: The Politics of Language and Style,* The University of Western Ontario, Medieval and Renaissance Seminar, 1999: www.uwo.ca/modlang/MedRen/conf99/abstracts/holbrook.html

Holt, J. C., & Anne Wedgewood, *History of Parliament: Biographies of the Members of the Commons House 1439–1509*, London: 1936.

Hoogvliet, Margriet, "Mappae Mundi and Medieval Encyclopaedias: Image versus Text" in *Pre-Modern Encyclopaedic Texts. Proceedings of the Second COMERS Congress, Groningen, 1–4 July 1996,* edited by Peter Binkley, 63–74. Leiden: E. J. Brill, 1997.

Houwen, L., "Animal parallelism in medieval literature and the bestiaries: a preliminary investigation", *Neophilologus* 78 (1994), 483–96.

Hudson, Anne, *Lollards and Their Books*, London: The Hambledon Press, 1985.

Humphreys, K. W., *The Friars' Libraries*, London: The British Academy and the British Library, 1990.

Humphreys, K. W., *The Book Provisions of the Medieval Friars 1215–1400*, Amsterdam: Erasmus, 1964.

Hutchison, Ann McCall, An Edition of Book VI of John Trevisa's English Translation of De Proprietatibus Rerum by Bartholomaeus Anglicus, unpublished PhD thesis, University of Toronto, 1974.

Illich, Ivan, *In the Vineyard of the Text: A Commentary to Hugh's Didascalicon*, University of Chicago Press, 1993.

Ingram, William, "The playhouse at Newington Butts: a new proposal", *Shakespeare Quarterly* 21, no.4 (1970): 385–98.

Ireland, William-Henry, *The Confessions of William-Henry Ireland, containing the Particulars of his Fabrication of the Shakspeare Manuscripts,* London, 1805.

Iser, Wolfgang, "Interaction between text and reader" in *The Reader in the Text: Essays on Audience and Interpretation*, edited by Susan R. Suleiman and Inge Crosman, 109-19, Princeton University Press, 1980.

James, M. R., *The Bestiary*, Oxford University Press, 1928.

James, M. R., "Lists of manuscripts formerly owned by Dr John Dee", *Supplement to the Transactions of the Bibliographical Society* 1 (1921).

James, M. R., *A Descriptive Catalogue of the Manuscripts in the Library of Corpus Christi College Cambridge*, Cambridge University Press, 1912.

Jauss, Hans Robert, "Literary history as a challenge to literary theory" in *New Directions in Literary History*, edited by Ralph Cohen, 11–41. London: Routledge and Kegan Paul, 1974.

Kaske, R. E., Arthur Groos and Michael Twomey eds, *Medieval Christian Imagery: A Guide to Interpretation*, University of Toronto Press, 1988.

Keen, Elizabeth, "Separate or Together? Questioning the relationship between the encyclopedia and bestiary traditions", *Journal of the Australian Early Medieval Association, 2 (*2006):121–39.

Keen, Elizabeth, From Bartholomaeus to Batman: Four hundred years of the Properties of Things, unpublished PhD thesis, Australian National University, 2002.

Keen, Libby, "Under cover of stories: Bartholomew the Englishman and the world of land and sea" in *Our Medieval Heritage*, edited by Linda Rasmussen, Valerie Spear and Dianne Tillotson, 94–108, Cardiff: Merton Priory Press, 2002.

Keen, Maurice, *English Society in the Later Middle Ages*, London: Allen Lane, 1990.

Keen, Maurice, *Chivalry*, New Haven and London: Yale University Press, 1984.

Keen, Maurice, *England in the Later Middle Ages*, London: Methuen, 1973.

Ker, N, *Medieval Manuscripts in British Libraries*, Oxford: The Clarendon Press, 1969.

Kerby-Fulton, Kathryn, "The Medieval Professional Reader and Reception History, 1292–1641" in *The Medieval Professional Reader at Work*, edited by Kathryn Kerby-Fulton and Maidie Hilmo, 7–13, University of Victoria, B. C., 2001.

Kline, Naomi Reed, *Maps of Medieval Thought: The Hereford Paradigm*, Woodbridge: The Boydell Press, 2001.

Klingender, Francis, *Animals in Art and Thought to the End of the Middle Ages*, London: Routledge and Kegan Paul, 1971.

Kratz, Dennis M., *The Romances of Alexander*, New York: Garland Publishing Inc., 1991.

Kratzmann, Gregory, and Elizabeth Gee, *The Dialoges of Creatures Moralysed*, London and New York: E. J. Brill, 1988.

Ladner, Gerhart B, "*Homo viator*: medieval ideas on alienation and order", *Speculum* 42.2 (1967):233–59.

Landini, Lawrence C., *The Causes of the Clericalization of the Order of Friars Minor 1209–1260 in the Light of Early Franciscan Sources*, Chicago: Pontificia Universitas Gregoriana, 1968.

Landsberg, Sylvia, *The Medieval Garden,* London: The British Museum Press, 1995.

Lascelles, Mary, "Alexander and the earthly Paradise in mediaeval English writings", *Medium Aevum* 5 (1936): 31–47; 79–104; 173–88.

Lawler, Traugott, "On the properties of John Trevisa's major translations", *Viator* 14 (1983): 267–88.

Lawton, Lesley, "The illustration of late medieval secular texts, with special reference to Lydgate's Troy Book" in *Manuscripts and Readers in Fifteenth-Century England: The Literary Implications of Manuscript Study: essays from the 1981 conference at the University of York*, edited by Derek Pearsall, 41–69. Cambridge: D. S. Brewer, 1983.

Lidaka, Juris G. "Bartholomaeus Anglicus in the thirteenth century" in *Pre-Modern Encyclopaedic Texts. Proceedings of the Second COMERS Congress, Groningen, 1-4 July 1996,* edited by Peter Binkley, 393-406. Leiden: E. J. Brill, 1997.

Lidaka, Juris, Bartholomaeus Anglicus' De Proprietatibus Rerum, Book XIX, Chapters on Mathematics, Measures, and Music: A Critical Edition of the Latin Text in England, unpublished PhD thesis, Northern Illinois University, 1988.

Lidaka, Juris, "John Trevisa and the English continental traditions of Bartholomaeus Anglicus", *Essays in Medieval Studies* 5 (1988): 71–92.

Lindberg, David, "Medieval Science and its Religious Context", *Osiris* 10 (1995): 61–79.

Little, A. G., *Franciscan History and Legend in English Medieval Art*, Manchester University Press, 1937.

Loades, David, "Books and the English Reformation prior to 1558" in *The Reformation and the Book*, edited by Jean-Francois Gilmont & Karin Maag, 264–91, Aldershot: Ashgate, 1998.

Long, R. James, *On the Properties of Soul and Body: De Proprietatibus Rerum Libri III and IV*, Toronto: Institute of Medieval Studies, 1980.

Louis, Sylvain, "Le projet encyclopédique de Barthélemy l'Anglais" in *L'Encyclopédisme. Actes du Colloque de Caen 12–16 janvier 1987*, edited by Annie Becq, 147–51, Paris: Éditions Aux Amateurs de Livres, 1991.

Matrod, H., "Roger Bacon et Fr. Barthélemy D'Angleterre", *Etudes franciscaines* XXVIII (1912): 468–83.

Matthew, Donald, *Atlas of Medieval Europe*, Oxford: Phaidon, 1983.

McCulloch, Florence, *Medieval Latin and French Bestiaries*, University of North Carolina Press, 1960.

McEvedy, Colin, *The New Penguin Atlas of Medieval History*, London: Penguin Books, 1992.

McFarlane, K. B., *The Nobility of Later Medieval England*, Oxford University Press, 1973.

McLoughlin, Kate, "Magdalene College MS Pepys 2498 and Stephen Batman's Reading Practices", *Transactions of the Cambridge Bibliographical Society* 10 (1994): 525–34.

McVaugh, Michael R., "Johannis Aegidii Zamorensis. *Historia naturalis*. Edited by Avelino Domínguez García and Luis García Ballester. Salamanca: Junta de Castilla y León, 1994", *Isis* 87: 1 (1996), 158.

Meier, Christel, "Organisation of knowledge and encyclopaedic *ordo*: Functions and purposes of a universal literary genre" in *Pre-Modern Encyclopaedic Texts. Proceedings of the Second COMERS Congress, Groningen, 1–4 July 1996*, edited by Peter Binkley, 103–26, Leiden: E. J. Brill, 1997.

Meier, Christel, "Grundzüge der mittelalterlichen Enzyklopädik. Zu Inhalten, Formen und Funktionen einer problematischen Gattung" in *Litteratur und Laienbildung im Spätmittelalter und in der Reformationszeit. Symposium Wolfenbüttel 1981*, edited by Ludger Grenzmann und Karl Stackmann, 467–500, Stuttgart, 1984.

Meyer, Heinz, "Die Enzyclopädie des Bartholomäus Anglicus: Untersuchungen zur Überlieferungs und Rezeptiongeschichte von De proprietatibus rerum", *Münstersche Mittelalter-Shriften* 77 (2000).

Meyer, Heinz, "Zum Verhältnis von Enzyklopädik und Allegorese im Mittelalter", *Frühmittelalterliche Studien* 24 (1990): 290–313.

Meyer, Heinz, "Bartholomäus Anglicus, De proprietatibus rerum: Selbstverständnis und Rezeption", *Zeitschrift für deutsches Altertum und deutsche Literatur* 117 (1988): 237–74.

Michaud-Quantin, Pierre, "Les petites encyclopédies du XIIIe siecle" in *Pensée encyclopédique au Moyen Age*, 105–20. Editions de la Baconniere: Neuchatel, 1966.

Migne, Jacques-Paul, ed, *Patrilogiae cursus completus*, Vol.210, Paris, 1882.

Minnis, A. J., ed, *Late-Medieval Religious Texts and their Transmission: Essays in Honour of A. I. Doyle*, Cambridge: D. S. Brewer, 1994.

Minnis, A. J., A. B. Scott and D. Wallace, *Medieval Literary Theory and Criticism, c.1100–c.1375: the Commentary Tradition*, Oxford University Press, 1988.

Mitchner, R. W., "Wynkyn de Worde's use of the Plimpton Manuscript of De Proprietatibus Rerum", *The Library* VI (1951): 7–17.

Moorat, S. A. J., *Catalogue of Western Manuscripts on Medicine and Science in the Wellcome Historical Medical Library. Volume I. Manuscripts written before 1650AD*, London: Wellcome Institute of the History of Medicine, 1962.

Moorman, John, *A History of the Franciscan Order from Its Origins to the Year 1517*, Oxford: The Clarendon Press, 1968.

Morris, William, Preface, pp.xii–xiii in Steele, Robert, *Medieval Lore from Bartholomeus Anglicus*, London: De la More Press, 1893, reprinted 1905.

Moses, David, untitled, *Notes and Queries* 50:1 (2003), 11–13.

Mynors, R. A. B., *Catalogue of the Manuscripts of Balliol College, Oxford*, Oxford: The Clarendon Press, 1963.

Nebenzahl, Kenneth, *Atlas of Columbus and the Great Discoveries*, Chicago: Rand McNally, 1990.

Owst, G. R., *Preaching in Medieval England*, Cambridge University Press, 1926.

Parish, Verna M., "Batman's additions from Elyot and Boorde to his English edition of Bartholomaeus Anglicus" in *Studies in Language, Literature, and Culture of the Middle Ages and Later*, edited by E. B. Atwood and A. A. Hill, 337–46. Austin: University of Texas, 1969.

Parkes, M. B., "The influence of the concepts of *ordinatio* and *compilatio* on the development of the book" in *Medieval Learning and Literature: Essays Presented to R. W. Hunt*, edited by J. J. G. Alexander and M. T. Gibson, 115–41, Oxford University Press, 1976; reprinted in *Scribes, Scripts, and Readers: Studies in the Communication, Presentation, and Dissemination of Medieval Texts*, edited by M. B. Parkes, 35–69, London: Hambledon Press, 1991.

Parkes, M. B., "The literacy of the laity" in *The Medieval World*, edited by David Daiches and Anthony Thorlby, 555–77, London: Aldus Books, 1973.

Pastoureau, Michel, "Quel est le roi des animaux?" in *Le Monde Animal et ses Représentations au Moyen-Age (XIe-XVe Siecles): Actes du XVème Congrès de la Société des Historiens Médiévistes de l'Enseignement Supérieur Public, Toulouse 1984*, 133–42. University of Toulouse, 1985.

Perdrizet, P., "Barthélemy l'Anglais et son description de l'Angleterre", *Journal des savants* 7 (1909): 170–75.

Phillips, J. R. S., *The Medieval Expansion of Europe*, Oxford University Press, 1988.

Plassmann, T., "Bartholomaeus Anglicus", *Archivum franciscanum historicum* 12 (1919): 68–109.

Plomer, Henry R., *Wynkyn de Worde and His Contemporaries*, London: Dawsons of Pall Mall, 1925.

Pope, Peter E., *The Many Landfalls of John Cabot*, University of Toronto Press, 1997.

Raven, Charles E., *English Naturalists from Neckam to Ray*, Cambridge University Press, 1947.

Reiter, Eric H., "The reader as author of the user-produced manuscript: reading and rewriting popular Latin theology", *Viator* 27 (1996): 151–69.

Remnant, G. L., *A Catalogue of Misericords in Great Britain*, Oxford: The Clarendon Press, 1969.

Rex, Richard, *Henry VIII and the English Reformation*, New York: St Martin's Press, 1993.

Reynolds, Susan, *Kingdoms and Communities in Western Europe, 900–1300*, Oxford: The Clarendon Press, 1984.

Rhodes, Dennis E., Vivaldo Belcazar and the Mantuan Dialect in the Early 14th Century: A Study of BM Ms Add. 8785 with the edition of Bks I, II and XV, unpublished PhD thesis, University College London, 1956.

Ribémont, B., "On the definition of an encyclopaedic genre in the Middle Ages" in *Pre-Modern Encyclopaedic Texts. Proceedings of the Second COMERS Congress, Groningen, 1–4 July 1996,* edited by Peter Binkley, 47–61. Leiden: E. J. Brill, 1997.

Riehle, Wolfgang, *The Middle English Mystics*, London: Routledge & Kegan Paul, 1981.

Robbins, Rossell Hope, ed, *Historical Poems of the XIVth and XVth Centuries,* New York: Columbia University Press, 1959.

Robinson, F. N., ed, *The Complete Works of Geoffrey Chaucer*, Oxford University Press, 1957.

Ross, Charles, *Edward IV*, London: Methuen, 1974.

Rostenberg, Leona, *The Minority Press and the English Crown: A Study in Repression 1558–1625*, New York: De Graaf, 1971.

Rothwell, Harry, ed, *English Historical Documents 1189–1327*, London: Eyre & Spottiswood, 1975.

Rouse, A. W., *Simon Forman: Sex and Society in Shakespeare's Age,* London: Wiedenfeld and Nicolson, 1974.

Rouse, R. H., and M. A. Rouse, "*Ordinatio* and *Compilatio*" in *Ad Litteram: Authoritative Texts and Their Medieval Readers*, edited by M. Jordan and K. Emery Jnr, 113–134. London: University of Notre Dame Press, 1992.

Salter, Elizabeth, "Medieval poetry and the figural view of reality" in *Middle English Literature. British Academy Gollancz Lectures*, edited by J. A. Burrow, 121–40. Oxford University Press, 1989.

Salter, Elizabeth, *English and International: Studies in the Literature, Art and Patronage of Medieval England*, Cambridge University Press, 1988.

Salvat, Michel, "Science et pouvoir á Mantoue et á Paris au XIVe siècle" in *L'Encyclopédisme. Actes du Colloque de Caen 12–16 janvier 1987*, edited by Annie Becq, 389–94, Paris: Éditions Aux Amateurs de Livres, 1991.

Samaran, Charles, "Pierre Bersuire, Prieur de Saint-Eloi de Paris", *Histoire Littéraire de la France* 39 (1962): 259–450.

Saul, Nigel, *Knights and Esquires: The Gloucestershire Gentry in the Fourteenth Century*, Oxford: The Clarendon Press, 1981.

Scattergood, V. J., "Literary culture at the court of Richard II" in *English Court Culture in the Late Middle Ages*, edited by V. J. Scattergood and J. W. Sherborne, 29–43, London: Duckworth, 1983.

Scattergood, V. J., *Politics and Poetry in the Fifteenth Century*, London: Blandford Press, 1971.

Schäfer, Jurgen, ed, "Introduction", in Stephen Bateman, *Batman uppon Bartholome*, Facsimile edition, Hildesheim: Georg Olms Verlag, 1976.

Schönbach, A., "Des Bartholomeus Anglicus Beschreibung Deutschlands gegen 1240", *Mitteilungen des Instituts für Osterreichische Geschichtsforschung* 17 (1906): 56–62.

Scott, Kathleen L., *Later Gothic Manuscripts 1390–1490*, London: Harvey Miller, 1996.

Sears, Elizabeth, *The Ages of Man: Medieval Interpretations of the Life Cycle*, Princeton University Press, 1986.

Se Boyar, G. E. (OFM), "Bartholomeus and his encyclopedia", *The Journal of English and Germanic Philology* XIX (1920): 168–89.

Sekules, Veronica, "Women's piety and patronage" in *Age of Chivalry*, edited by Nigel Saul, 120–31, London: Collins and Brown, 1992.

Seymour, M. C., and Colleagues, *Bartholomeus Anglicus and His Encyclopedia*, London: Variorum, 1992.

Seymour, M. C., "A literatim Trevisa abstract", *Neuphilologische Mitteilungen* 93 (1992): 185–91.

Seymour, M. C., ed, *On the Properties of Things. John Trevisa's Translation of Bartholomeus Anglicus, De Proprietatibus Rerum*, 3 vols, Oxford: The Clarendon Press, 1975–88.

Seymour, M. C., "Some medieval English owners of De Proprietatibus Rerum", *The Bodleian Library Record* IX, no.3 (1974): 156–65.

Seymour, M. C., "Some medieval French readers of De Proprietatibus Rerum", *Scriptorium* XXVII (1974): 100–2.

Seymour, M. C., "More of a middle English abstract of Bartholomaeus, De Proprietatibus Rerum", *Anglia* 91 (1973): 19–34.

Seymour, M. C., "A middle English abstract of Bartholomaeus, De Proprietatibus Rerum", *Anglia* 87 (1969): 1–25.

Sharpe, J. A., *Instruments of Darkness: Witchcraft in England 1550–1750*, University of Pennsylvania Press, 1997.

Sharpe, J. A., *Early Modern England*, London: Edward Arnold, 1987.

Sharpe, Richard A., *A Handlist of the Latin Writers of Great Britain and Ireland before 1540*, Turnhout: Brepols, (1997), 2001.

Sherley-Price, Leo, ed, *Thomas of Eccleston's The Coming of the Friars*, London: A. R. Mowbray, 1964.

Smalley, Beryl, "Ecclesiastical attitudes to novelty c1100–c1250" in *Church, Society and Politics*, edited by Derek Baker, 115–116, Oxford: Basil Blackwell, 1975.

Smith, Alan G. R., *The Emergence of a Nation State: The Commonwealth of England 1529–1660*, London: Longman, 1984.

Smith, Frank, *Understanding Reading: a Psycholinguistic Analysis of Reading and Learning to Read*, Hillsdale, New Jersey: Lawrence Erlbaum Associates, 1986.

Solway, David, *The Properties of Things: The Poems of Bartholomew the Englishman,* Montreal: Véhicule Press, in press.

Southern, R. W., *The Making of the Middle Ages*, London: Hutchinson, 1953.

Steele, Robert, *Medieval Lore from Bartholomeus Anglicus.* London: De la More Press, 1893, reprinted 1905.

Stewart, Aubrey, ed, *Procopius of Caesarea (c560 AD): Of the Buildings of Justinian*, London: Palestine Pilgrims' Text Society, 1896.

Stockton, Eric W., ed, *The Major Latin Works of John Gower: The Voice of One Crying and the Tripartite Chronicle*, Seattle: University of Washington Press, 1962.

Stoneman, Richard, ed, *Legends of Alexander the Great*, London: Everyman, 1994.

Swann, Marjorie, *Curiosities and Texts: The Culture of Collecting in Early Modern England*, Philadelphia: The University of Pennsylvania Press, 2001.

Taylor, John, *The Universal Chronicle of Ranulph Higden*, Oxford: The Clarendon Press, 1966.

Tesnière, M., *Creating French Culture: Treasures from the Bibliotheque Nationale de France*, New Haven and London: Yale University Press, 1995.

Thorndike, Lynn, *Science and Thought in the Fifteenth Century*, Columbia University Press, 1929.

Thrupp, Sylvia, *The Merchant Class of Medieval London (1300–1500)*, University of Chicago Press, 1948.

Tilander, Gunnar, ed, *Gaston Phébus, Livre de Chasse*, Karlshamn: E. G. Johansson, 1976.

Toulmin-Smith, Lucy, "English popular preaching in the fourteenth century", *The English Historical Review* VII (1892): 24–36.

Tribble, Evelyn B., *Margins and Marginality*, Charlottesville and London: University Press of Virginia, 1993.

Twomey, Michael W., "Towards a reception history of western mediaeval encyclopaedias in England before 1500" in *Pre-Modern Encyclopaedic Texts. Proceedings of the Second COMERS Congress, Groningen, 1–4 July 1996*, edited by Peter Binkley, 329–62, Leiden: E. J. Brill, 1997.

Twomey, Michael W., "Appendix: Medieval Encyclopedias" in *Medieval Christian Imagery: A Guide to Interpretation*, edited by R. E. Kaske, Arthur Groos and Michael Twomey, 182–215. University of Toronto Press, 1988.

Van den Abeele, Baudouin, H. Meyer & B. Ribémont, "Editer l'encyclopédie de Barthélemy l'Anglais: Vers une édition bilangue du De Proprietatibus Rerum", *Cahiers de Recherches Médiévales (13m–15m s)* 6 (1999): 7–18.

Van den Abeele, Baudouin, " Moralisierte Enzyklopädien in der Nachfolge von Bartholomäus Anglicus: das 'Multifarium' in Wolfenbüttel und der 'Liber de exemplis et similitudinibus rerum' des Johannes de Sancto Geminiano" in *Die Enzyklopädie im Wandel vom Hochmittelalter bis zur frühen Neuzeit*, edited by Christel Meier, 279–304. Munich, 2002.

Van den Abeele, Baudouin, "Bestiaires encyclopédiques moralisés: quelques succédanés de Thomas de Cantimpré et de Barthélemy l'Anglais", *Reinardus: Yearbook of the International Reynard Society* 7 (1994): 209–28.

Varty, Kenneth, *Reynard the Fox; a Study of the Fox in Medieval English Art*, Leicester University Press, 1967.

Vaughan, Richard, *The Illustrated Chronicles of Matthew Paris: Observations of Thirteenth-Century Life*, Stroud: Alan Sutton & Corpus Christi College, Cambridge, 1993.

Venn, J. & J. A., *Alumni Cantabrigienses: a biographical list of all known students and holders of office at the University of Cambridge from the earliest times to 1900*. Part I, Vol.3, Cambridge University Press (1922), 1954.

Visser-Fuchs, Livia, and Anne F. Sutton, *Richard III's Books: Ideals and Reality in the Life and Library of a Medieval Prince*, Stroud: Sutton Publishing, 1997.

Voigt, Edmund, "Bartholomaeus Anglicus, De proprietatibus rerum: Litterarhistorisches und bibliographisches", *Englische Studien* 41 (1910): 337–59.

Wada, Yoko, "Bale to Parker on British Historical Texts in Cambridge College Libraries", *Transactions of the Cambridge Bibliographical Society* 10 (1994): 511–19.

Wagner, A. R., *Heralds and Heraldry in the Middle Ages*, Oxford University Press, 1956.

Wahlgren-Smith, Lena, "Heraldry in Arcadia: the court eclogue of Johannes Opicius", *Renaissance Studies* 14, no.2 (2000): 210–34.

Waldron, Ronald, "Trevisa's 'Celtic complex' revisited", *Notes and Queries* 20 (1989): 303–7.

Waldron, Ronald, "Trevisa's original prefaces on translation: a critical edition" in *Medieval English Studies Presented to George Kane*, edited by E. D. Kennedy, R. Waldron and J. S. Wittig, Woodbridge: D. S. Brewer, 1988.

Waldron, Ronald, "John Trevisa and the use of English", *Proceedings of the British Academy* LXXIV (1988): 171–202.

Wallis, F., Structure and Philosophy in Mediaeval Encyclopaedias, unpublished M.A. thesis; McGill University, Montreal, 1974.

Watson, A.G., "An identification of some manuscripts owned by Dr John Dee and Sir Simonds D'Ewes", *The Library* XIII 5th series (1958): 194–8.

Watts, Pauline Moffitt, "Prophecy and Discovery: On the Spiritual Origins of Christopher Columbus's 'Enterprise of the Indies'" in *The European Opportunity*, edited by Felipe Fernández-Armesto, 195–224. Aldershot, U.K. and Brookfield, U.S.A: Variorum, 1995.

Wells, James M., *The Circle of Knowledge: Encyclopedias Past and Present,* Chicago: The Newberry Library, 1968.

Wenzel, Siegfried, *Fasciculus Morum: a Fourteenth Century Preachers' Handbook*, Pennsylvania State University, 1989.

Wessley, Stephen, "Female imagery: a clue to the role of Joachim's Order of Fiore" in *Women of the Medieval World*, edited by J. Kirchner and S. Wemple, 161–78. Oxford: Basil Blackwell, 1985.

Westrem, Scott D., *The Hereford Map*, Turnhout: Brepols, 2001.

Whitfield, Peter, *The Image of the World: 20 Centuries of World Maps*, London: The British Library, 1994.

Williams, David, *Deformed Discourse: The Function of the Monster in Mediaeval Thought and Literature*, University of Exeter Press, 1996.

Williams, Jane Welch, *Bread, Wine & Money: The Windows of the Trades at Chartres Cathedral*, The University of Chicago Press, 1990.

Wilson, Alison, "An Elizabethan miniature in the Parker Library, Corpus Christi College, Cambridge", *Transactions of the Cambridge Bibliographical Society* 10 (1994): 461–85.

Woodcock, Thomas, and John Martin Robinson, *The Oxford Guide to Heraldry*, Oxford University Press, 1988.

Woodward, David, "Medieval mappaemundi" in *Cartography in Prehistoric, Ancient and Medieval Europe and the Mediterranean*, edited by J. B. Harley and David Woodward, 286–370. Chicago and London: The University of Chicago Press, 1987.

Woodward, David, "Reality, Symbolism, Time, and Space in Medieval World Maps", *Annals of the Association of American Geographers* 75 (1985): 10–21.

Woolgar, C. M., *The Great Household in Late Medieval England*, Yale University Press, 1999.

Yapp, W. B., "Medieval knowledge of birds as shown in bestiaries", *Archives of Natural History* 14, no.2 (1987): 175–210.

Yapp, W. B., "A new look at English bestiaries", *Medium Aevum* 54, no.1 (1985): 1–19.

Zacher, Christian K., *Curiosity and Pilgrimage: the Literature of Discovery in Fourteenth Century England*, Johns Hopkins University Press, 1976.

Zim, Rivkah, "Batman, Stephan (c.1542—1584)", *Oxford Dictionary of National Biography*, Oxford University Press, 2004.

Zink, Michel, "Le monde animal et ses représentations dans la littérature française du moyen age" in *Le Monde Animal et ses Représentations au Moyen-Age (XIe–XVe Siecles): Actes du XVème Congrès de la Société des Historiens Médiévistes de l'Enseignement Supérieur Public, Toulouse 1984*, 47–71. University of Toulouse, 1985.

Websites

www.cyclopes.fltr.ucl.ac.be/index.htm, *Encyclopédies comme images du monde et comme vecteurs d'échanges intellectuels dans l'Islam et l'Occident au Moyen Age*, Projet F. S. R. de l'Université catholique de Louvain, Belgium, 2006. Last accessed 02/04/07.

www.bl.uk/onlinegallery/themes/mapsandviews/psaltermap.html, last accessed 02/04/07.

www.danforthreview.com/features/interviews/solway/david_solway.htm, last accessed 02/04/07.

www.uwo.ca/modlang/MedRen/conf99/abstracts/holbrook.html, last accessed 02/04/07.

Index

Achilles, 62
Act of Submission of the Clergy, 129
Act of Supremacy, 129
Advertisements, 134
Ahasuerus, feast of, 41
Albanact, 113, 137
Albert the Great (Albertus Magnus), 3, 105, 162
Albina, 132, 137
Albion, 132, 136
Albumazar, 36
Alexander the Great, 62, 63, 70, 71, 89, 93, 163
    as unifier of physical world, 64
Alexander IV, Pope, 154
Algazel, 36
Alley William, Bishop of Exeter, 137
'Amazonia', 62–3
America, 145
angels
    fallen (*spiriti maligni*), 146
    Protestant interpretation of, 146
    properties of, 36
Anglicus, Johannes, 2
animals
    symbolism of, 108–10
    mutual oppositions, 109
Anne of Bohemia, 111
Antichrist, 60, 131, 147
Aquinas, Thomas, 48
Aristotle, 1, 3, 20, 21, 32, 34, 36, 43, 49, 59, 60, 88, 89, 105, 113, 145, 163
Arnoldus Saxo, 19
Arthur, 137
Arundel 123, 93, 101, 163, 167
Asia, Africa and Europe, 144
Augustodunensis, Honorius (see also 'Honorius of Autun'), 19
Avicenna, 32, 113

Babylon, destruction of, 70
Bacon, Roger, 16, 21
Bale, John, 131, 132, 147, 149, 153
Banks, Joseph, 151, 153, 166

Bartholomaeus Anglicus, 2, 15, 127
Bartholomaeus Glanville, 1, 15, 130, 151
Bartholomaeus de Glanvilla of Suffolk, 130
Bartholomew of Cremona, 59
Bartholomew the Englishman (*natione Anglicus*), 1, 127
    and the heralds, 110–12
    and the English, **127–60**
    as English national treasure, 130–31, 165
    and the sea, 59–61
    as 'Master of Kind', 83, 85
    as 'Master of Properties', 84, 85
    as source for Shakespeare, 151–4
    '…the bestiary', 107–8
'Bartholomew Glantvyle', 136
Bartholomew of Prague, 2
basilisk, the, 142
Batman (Bateman), Stephen, 5, 9, 133, 138, 147, 154, 165
    Batman uppon Bartholome…, 133–51
    The Chronicle of the Doome, 147
    The Doctrine of the Heart, 148
Beaufort, Margaret, 79
Becket, Thomas, 91, 130
Bede, 19, 106, 136
bee, image of, 30, 44, 46, 85, 91, 162
bees, properties of, **32–5**, 50
Belcalzar, Vivaldo, 5, 88, 91, 103
Benedict XI, Pope, 5
Benedictine Order, 57
Berkeley
    Elizabeth, 87, 93
    Lord Thomas I, 86
        Lady Joan (wife of), 86, 87
    Lord Thomas II, 87
        Lady Johanna (wife of), 87
    Lord Thomas III
        Lady Margaret (first wife of), 87
    Lord Thomas IV, 5, 87, 91, 92, 93, 95, 97, 103, 118, 163
Berkeley Castle, 86
Berkeley family, 79, 86, 91, 94
    and the king, 92–5
Bernard of Clairvaux, 31, 42, 48
Bernard of Salisbury, 64
Bersuire, Pierre, 5, 21

Berthelet, Thomas, 5, 16, 128, 146
bestiaries, 23, 38, 105, 107, 112
bestiary iconography, 23, 163
bestiary literature, 24, 30
Black Death, the, 77, 79
Boar, the, 115
Bonaventure, 36, 81
Book of Revelation, 59, 73, 131
Bosworth, battle of, 114, 115
Bozon, Nicolas, 80
Britain, Trojan origins of, 91
Brockhurst, Elizabeth, 16, 29, 134
Bromyard, John, 81
Brunetto Latini, 19
Brut, 113, 132
Brutus (the Trojan), 91, 113, 132, 136
Bryce, Hugh, 118
Buonalcosi, Guido, 5, 88, 129
Byrne, Donal, 88, 89

Cabot, 164
Calcidius, 36
Camber, 113, 137
Cambridge, 1
canicula, 60
Canterbury Tales, 10, 104
Cantimpré, Thomas de, 3, 19, 80, 105
Carey, Henry, Baron Hunsdon, 133, 150, 154
Cathar heresy, 20, 21
Catholic church, 20, 77, 131, 161
Catholic culture, 127
Catholic doctrine, 23, 146
Caxton, William, 117, 118, 144
Cecil, William, 134
celibacy, 42–3
Charles V of France, 88, 95, 104
Charles VI of France, 78, 92
Chartres, 1, 2,
 School of, 36, 64
Charybdis, 59, 62, 82
Chaucer, Geoffrey, 3, 10, 94, 95
Chaworth family, 118
Chaworth, Thomas, 96, 97, 104
Christ, 131
 as unifier of spiritual world, 64

Cistercian Order, 57
clerical life, 41–2
Collyngbourne, Wyllyam, 114
Columbus, Christopher, 143, 147, 153, 164
compilatio (see also 'mediaeval compilations'), 3, 5, 6, 21, **22-4**, 32, 50, 161, 162
Constantine, 33
Constantinus, 106, 163
Contes Moralisés, 80
Cooper, Thomas, 136, 137
Corbechon, Jean, 88, 91, 92, 95, 103
cormorant (*mergus*), 148
Cornelius Agrippa, Henry, 146
crane, image of, 44
Creation, 23, 162
Cromwell, Thomas, 129, 131
Crusades, the, 57

D'Ailly, Hugo, *imago mundi* map of, 143, 153
Damascene, John, 36, 41
da Pisa, Uguccione, 19
De Arca Noe Mystica, 61
De Bado Aureo, Johannes, 111, 112, 113, 114
de Balbis, Johannes, 19
de Beauvais, Vincent, 3, 4, 19, 22, 144
De Boüard, M.
De Callataÿ, Godefroid, 23
Dee, John, 146, 149
D'Ewes, Simon, 149
de Foix, Gaston ('Phébus'), 88, 89–92
De heraudie, 110
Delisle, Léopold, 1, 15, 29
De natura rerum, 3, 80
De naturis rerum, 3, 19
De ordine creaturarum, 19
De proprietatibus rerum (see also 'Properties'), 1, 4, 15
 The 19 Books of, 7
 Latin manuscripts of, 8
De rerum naturis, 19
Dethick, William, 149
De Worde, Wynkyn, 5, 18, 96, **117-21**, 129, 146

Dialogus creaturatum moralizatus, 81
Didascalicon, 30
Dionysius (St Denis), 41
discipline, submitting to, 37–8
Dives and Pauper, 82, 83, 84, 109
Dominic, 58
Dominicans, 21, 78
dove, 109
Dronke, Peter, 35, 64

eagle, 109
Eccleston, Thomas (of Eccleston), 2, 77, 79, 86
Edward I, 78
Edward II, 92, 132
Edward III, 132
Edward IV, 104, 118
Edward VI, 129
Edwards, A.S.G. (Anthony), 18, 80, 117
elements and humours, 66
Elias (Franciscan Minister General), 3
Elizabeth's reign, 138, 165
Elizabethan Religious Settlement, 134
Encyclopaedia Britannica, 18
encyclopaedias, mediaeval, 18, 19, 22, 30–1
encyclopaedic texts, 23, 38, 39, 186, 192, 194, 195, 197, 200
English church, 165
English foundation legends, 132–3
    Arthurian myth, 133
English Psalter Map, 65, 66, 67, 68, 71, 145
English Reformation, the, 6
Etymologiae, 3, 19
exempla, 34, 77, 78, 80, 81
Exiit qui seminat (papal Bull), 3

familia, the, 40–2, 50, 80, 140, 162
Family of Love, The, 147, 148
Fasciculus Morum, 82
Fenton, Edward, 146
fertility, metaphors of, 31
Forman, Simon, 146
Fountains Abbey, 31
Fourth Lateran Council, 58

Fowler, David, 17
fox, the bestiary, 38, 112
Francis of Assisi (see also 'St Francis'), 32, 58
Franciscan
    early writers, 2
    homeless mendicancy, 57
    ideal of worship, 32
    library, Oxford, 130
    Order, 3, 5, 7, 8, 15, 82, 162
    way of life/beliefs, 1, 21, 34, 43
Friars Minor (see also 'Minorites'), 3, 31, 77, 163
    in England, 77–9
Friars Preachers (see also 'Order of Preachers'), 31
Fryde, E.B., 79

Galen, 163
Geoffrey of Monmouth, 132, 136
Gleaners/gleaning, 30–2, 50
Gilbert, Humphrey, 144
Giles of Rome, 93, 94
Giordano of Giano, 2, 59
Glanville, Sir John, 151
Glanville, Julius, 150
God
    properties and names of, 41, 45
    reconciliation with, 46, 48–51
Gough, John, 129
Gower, John, 83, 85, 86, 95
Greek myths, 149
Greetham, David, 21, 35, 135
Gregory IX, Pope, 31

Haigh, Christopher, 129
Hanna, Ralph, 92, 95
Hardyng, John, 132
Harrison, William, 127
Hassig, Debra, 30, 112
Hathaway, Neil, 31
Haymo of Faversham, 2
Hearne, Thomas, 134, 151
Henry III, 78
Henry IV (Bolingbroke), 95, 112
Henry V, 92, 110

Henry VII, 115, 116, 154
Henry VIII, 128–30, 153
Henry of Mainz, 65
Henry of Sandwich, Sir, 78
Hercules, 62
heretics, 58
Hermes Trismegistos, 49
Higden, Ranulph, 3
    The Polychronicon, 3, 87, 91, 93, 94, 118
Hildegard of Bingen, 19, 38
Historia Mongolorum, 59
Homer, 139
Homeric legend, 61
Hoogvliet, Margriet, 24, 65
Hooker, Richard, 137
House of Lancaster, 116
House of York, 116
Hugh of Kirkstall, 31, 32
    Cistercian chronicle, 34
Hugh of St Victor, 30, 48, 61
Hugonem de arca Noe, 87
Humphries, K.W., 18
Hundred Years' War, 92, 110, 113

Imago Mundi, 65
Imago mundi, 3
imago mundi, 22, 65, 71, 89, 143, 164
incunables, 5, 15, 17, **172**
Illich, Ivan, 30
Ireland, William-Henry, 154, 160
Iser, Wolfgang, 9, 10
    theory of reading, 9
Isodore of Seville, 3, 19, 22, 32, 90, 106, 113

Jacobs Well, 81, 109
Jerusalem, 58
Jewel, John, 137
John of Plano Carpini, 58, 59
John XXII, Pope, 5
Julius Caesar, 88, 89, 93, 136

Kaske, R., 18
Keen, Maurice, 79, 89
Kerby-Fulton, Kathryn, 95
Knolles, Robert, 95, 118

Knolles, Thomas, 95
Knolles, William, 95
Kratzmann, Gregory, 81
'kynde' (see also '*natura*'), 94

labour (see also 'rest and reward'), 37, 97
    as metaphor for Christian life, 80
labouring and voyaging, 82–3
Lambert of St Omer, 19, 64
Lambert, William, 142
'lamia', 139, 147
Lancastrians, 103, 111
Langland, William, 83
Lanquet, Thomas, 137
Lawrence of Portugal, 59
Leland, John, 1, 15, 130, 131, 133, 153
Le Livre des Propriétés des Choses (see also *Propriétés*), 37, 88, 92, 100, 104
leopard as symbol, 110, 111, 112, 114
Liber moralizatae (see also '*Proprietates rerum moralizatae*'), 21, 80
Liber de natura rerum, 19
Liber rerum moralizatae, 44
light, 36, 41, 46
Lidaka, Juris, 15, 17, 22
Lindberg, David, 20
lion as Christian symbol, 111, 113
Locrine, 113, 137
Lollards, 17, 25, 83, 165
London Greyfriars, 78
Lords and servants, obligations of, 90
Loretta, Countess, 78
Louis IX, Pope, 59
Louis, Sylvain, 19, 49
Lucidarius, 19
Lucifer, 41, 146

Magdeburg, 2, 10, 16
Magellanica, 145
Mahomet, life of, 137
mappamundi/mappaemundi, 23, 57, 65, 69, 161
    Hereford/Ebstorf, 65, 145
    spiritual meaning of, 65, 161
map-makers, 45, 141
Marcellus II, Pope, 131
Marco Polo, 139

Margaret, Duchess of Burgundy, 118
Martiloge in englysshe after the use of Salisbury, 137
Martyr, Peter, 146
Matrod, H, 16, 151
Maurus, Rabanus, 19
mediaeval compilations (see also '*compilatio*'), 3, 15, 18, 20, 21, 23, 57, 65, 105, 161
Meier, Christel, 21, 22, 23, 49
Meyer, Heinz, 21, 22
Michael of Northgate, 80
Michaud-Quantin, Pierre, 17
Minorites, 57, 58
Mongol empire, 58
Monte Verna, 36, 44, 58
Morris, William, 16
Moslems, 58
Mount Ararat, 70
Mount Olivet, 44
Mum and the Sothsegger, 85, 107, 112

natio anglicana, 2
natura, 33, 34, 38, 49, 64, 94, 109
    Franciscan vs. Dominican uses, 36
and remedies, 35–37
Neckham, Alexander, 3, 19, 105
Neoplatonic universe, 36, 162, 165
New Testament, 41
Nicholas III, Pope, 3
Nicholas, Henry, 147
Noah, 61, 69, 71, 144

Odysseus (Ulysses), 59, 62, 71
Odyssey, 62
Old Testament, 41, 83
On the Properties of Things (see also *Properties*), 4, 15
Order of Preachers, 58
Ortelius, 139, 141
    Theatrum Orbis Terrarum, 141, 144
Ovid, 139
Oxford, 1, 2

'pagan follies', 64
Paradise, 70
Paris, 1, 2, 16

Bibliothèque nationale, 15, 16
pecia system, 78
Paris, Matthew, 64
Paris and Helen, 136
Parker, Richard, Archbishop of Canterbury, 134, 149
group of antiquaries, 134, 151
Paynell, Thomas, 128
Pearl, 82
Peasants' Revolt, 85
Perdrizet, P, 16
peregrinus, 62, 65
physical things/spiritual meanings, 38
Physiologus, 32, 109, 113
Pickering, John, 118
Pig as symbol, 114–5
pilgrimage, 58–9, 82, 97
Pilgrimage of the Soul, 104
Plassmann, T, 16
Plato, 1, 34, 105, 145, 146
Pliny, 1, 32, 38, 63, 105, 113
Polydore Vergil, 132, 137
primary sources, 171–2
printing press, 127, 138
Proclamation against the Sectaries of the Family of Love, 147
'Properties', 5, 7, 10, 23, 94, 106, 111, 119, 130, 149, 163, 164
and the English noble family, 86–8
and the French, 89–92
as authoritative source, **103–25**
as guide to salvation, **29–56**, 127
as 'world book', 45
Batman's changes to, 135–7, 148
Berthelet's edition, 5, 16, 128–130, 136, 148
De Worde's edition, 117–121, 136, 148
in London, 95–7
in print, **116–21**, 127, 143, 164
salvation and social order, **77–102**
Properties (see also '*On the Properties of Things*'), 84, 92, 111, 119, 142, 149, 150
Berthelet's edition, 128–30, 151, 153
printed editions, 127, 153, 164
Proprietates rerum moralizatae (see also '*Liber moralizate*'), 15, 81

Propriétés (see also '*Le Livre des Propriétés des Choses*'), 104, 116
Protestant church
Protestant culture, 127, 165
Pseodo-Dionysius, 36
Pseudo-Hugh of St Victor, 19
Ps-Isidore, 19
Pythagoras, 146

Raven, Charles, 20
Reductorium morale, 5
repentance, 50
rest and reward, 39–40, 41, 46, 49, 82
Rex, Richard, 129
Richard II, 83, 85, 103, 114
Richard III, 103, 114
Roman de Renard, 39
Rome, 58
rose, 142
    the English, 92, 115–6
    the Tudor rose, 115, 143
    the white rose of York, 115
Royal Society, The, 148
Rudstone, Sir John, 117
Rufus, Richard, 163

Salimbene of Parma
Salvat, Michel, 88
salvation, 40, 50, 97, 110
    works on, 81
Saxonia, 2
Schäfer, Jürgen, 134
Schönbach, Anton, 16
Scota, 132
Scots, the, 132
'Scribe D', 95, 96
Scylla, 59, 62, 82
Se Boyar, Gerald, 16, 130, 151
Second COMERS Congress, Groningen, July 1996, 11, 26, 174, 180, 182, 183, 185, 188
servant
    celibate, 42–3
    good/bad, 39–42, 50, 53, 80, 81, 90, 141, 146, 162
Seymour, Michael, 17, 18, 36, 81, 105, 106, 117

Shakespeare, William, 16, 133,
    supposed influence of Bartholomew on, 151–4
    forgeries of signature, 153, 154, 160
    scholars, 151, 153
Sharpe, Richard, 131
sheep, 109, 141
Shepherd's Kalendar, 119
Silvestris, Bernard, 35, 162
Simon of Langton, 78
sirena, 139
sirtes, 60
Smyth, John, 79, 87, 91
Solinus, 105, 109
Solomon, the wisdom of, 88, 89, 103, 129, 154, 165
Speculum maius, 3, 19
speculum mundi, 22
Speculum naturale, 3
St Ambrose, 32, 33, 36, 44, 90, 106
stag as symbol, 39, 53, 63, 111, 112
St Augustine, 34, 36, 61, 106
St Basil, 36, 106
St Bernard, 41
St Croce, library of, 18
St Denys, Order of, 2
St Francis, 3, 8, 32, 44, 50
St Gregory, 36, 90, 91, 106
St Jerome, 31, 106, 163
St Paul, 44, 50
Steele, Robert, 16, 151, 166
Stowe (Stow), John, 136, 141
Subsidy Rolls, 117
Swann, Marjorie, 148, 149

Tate, John, 118
Taylor, Reverend John, 104
Ten Commandments, 83, 84, 110
The Book of Wisdom, 47
The Description of England, 127
The mirour of the world, 118, 144
Thesaurus linguae Romae & Britannicae, 136
'things'
    diversity of, 49
    inner substance, 48
    outer appearance, 48

spiritual and liturgical associations, 47–8
Thorndike, Lynn, 20
Thorney, Richard, 96
Thorney (Thornye), Roger, 118
Toulmin-Smith, Lucy, 80
Tower of Babel, 70
Tractatus de Armis, 111, 113, 114
travel, as part of religious life, 58
traveller, the, 46, 48, **61–5**, 70
    archetypal, 61
travelling through the world, 43–7
travelling toward God, 66–71
tree, image of, 84
Trevisa, John, 4, 5, 17, 87, 91, 92, 93, 94, 103, 111, 113, 163
    On the Properties of Things (see also *Properties*), 4, 5, 9, 10, 16, 17, 83, 90, 106, 111, 117, 128, 132, 164
    Polychronicon, 95
Tritheim, Johannes, 127
Trojans, 136
Tunstall, Bishop Cuthbert, 129
Tudor England, 142
Tudors, the, 9, 115, 116, 127, 133
Twomey, Michael, 19, 30
Tyrrell, Sir Thomas, 104

utilitas, 22-3, 30

Van den Abeele, Baudouin, 23, 80
Vespucci, Amerigo, 164
vine/vineyard, the, image of , 37, 40, 50, 82, 140, 162
Virgil, 32
Virgin Mary 30, 64, 65, 147
Vision of Piers the Plowman, 83
Voigt, Edmund, 16
Vox Clamantis, 83, 85

Waldeby, John, 81
Walton, John, 93
Whitford, Richard, 137
William, Duke of Normandy, 137
William of Conches, 62
William of Rubruck, 59, 78
Willoughby, Richard, 96

Wimbledon, Thomas, 81
wolf, 109
Worcester Priory, 79
Woodstock, Thomas, 94
world, the
    divine framework, 70
    journey through, **57–76**
    separation from, 57
world book
    Batholomew's, 77
    tradition of, 20–1, 49
Worthies, the, 89, 93
Wotton-under-Edge, 86

Yorkists, 103, 111

www.ingramcontent.com/pod-product-compliance
Lightning Source LLC
Chambersburg PA
CBHW060930170426
43192CB00031B/2885